THE GRAND MOGUL

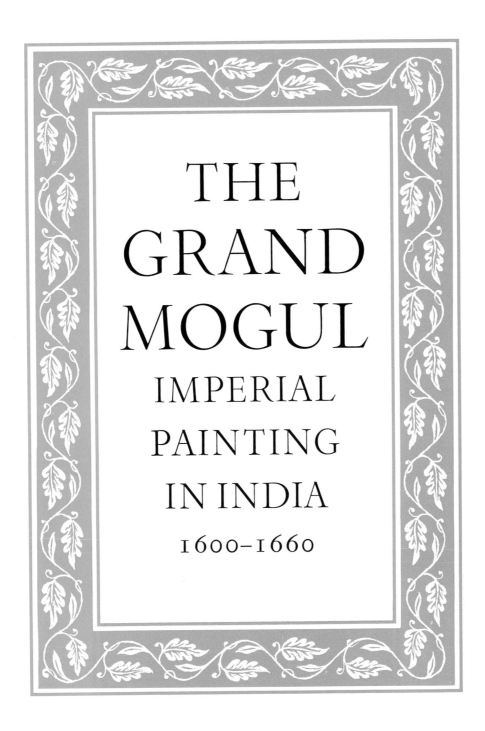

THE GRAND MOGUL

IMPERIAL PAINTING IN INDIA

1600–1660

By Milo Cleveland Beach

WITH CONTRIBUTIONS BY
STUART CARY WELCH AND GLENN D. LOWRY

Sterling and Francine Clark Art Institute · Williamstown, Massachusetts

This catalogue accompanies an exhibition held at the
Sterling and Francine Clark Art Institute, Williamstown, Massachusetts
between September 25 and November 5, 1978
at the Walters Art Gallery, Baltimore, Maryland
between November 20, 1978 and January 10, 1979
at the Museum of Fine Arts, Boston, Massachusetts
between February 2 and March 25, 1979
and at the Asia House Gallery, New York City
between April 19 and June 10, 1979.

The exhibition and catalogue were substantially aided
by a generous grant from the
National Endowment for the Arts, a federal agency.

COVER:
Shamsa, probably from an Album of Shah Jahan
circa 1640–50, detail of *no. 21* in this catalogue.

TABLE OF CONTENTS

LENDERS TO THE EXHIBITION

The Art Institute of Chicago

Ralph Benkaim, Beverly Hills

Edwin Binney 3rd, San Diego

The Cleveland Museum of Art

Fogg Art Museum, Harvard University, Cambridge, Massachusetts

Free Library of Philadelphia

Mr. and Mrs. John Gilmore Ford

Los Angeles County Museum of Art

Metropolitan Museum of Art, New York

Pierpont Morgan Library, New York

Museum of Fine Arts, Boston

Museum of Fine Arts, Springfield, Massachusetts

Nelson Gallery—Atkins Museum, Kansas City, Missouri

Axel Röhm, New York

St. Louis Art Museum

The Walters Art Gallery, Baltimore

Williams College Museum of Art, Williamstown

Two Anonymous Private Collectors

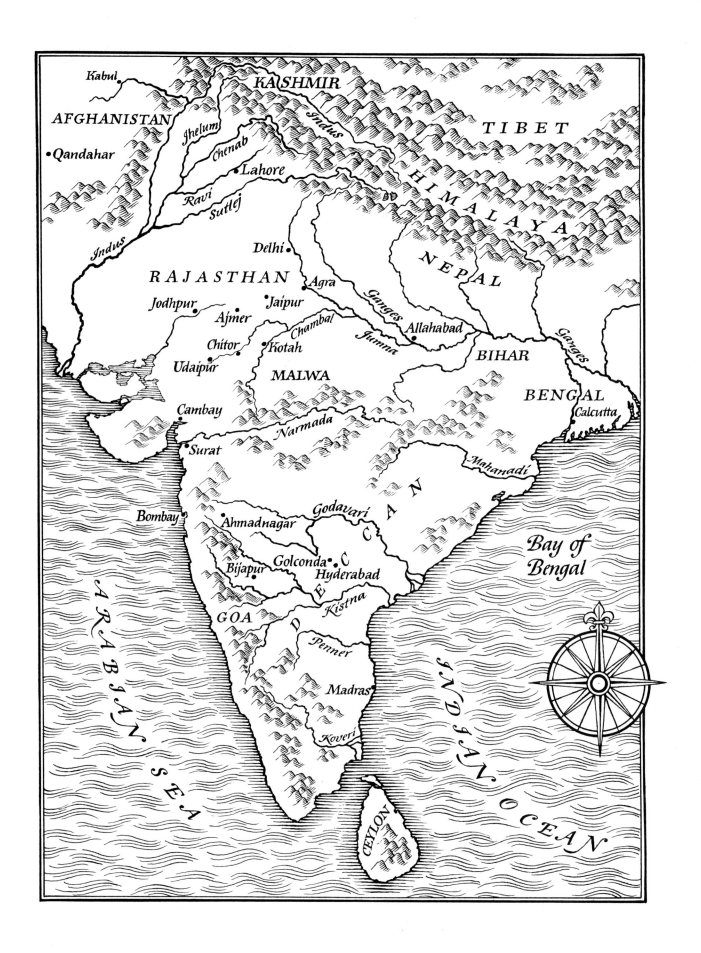

FOREWORD

THIS EXHIBITION focuses on the central achievement of the Mughal school, the exploration of naturalism in the early seventeenth century. In so doing it departs somewhat from earlier and broader exhibitions. Moreover, it is drawn entirely from sources in this country, and it should be noted that American museums and collectors have been especially active in this area in recent years; many of the paintings included here have not been published or exhibited previously.

The creation of this exhibition and catalogue has been shared by several people, and began partly in the form of discussions with students at Williams College. We are especially grateful to Milo C. Beach for providing such a splendid and perceptive witness to the flowering of Mughal art, and to Stuart Cary Welch for his sensitive and evocative essay. The exhibition will be shared with three institutions which have all had special associations with the field of Indian art. The Walters Art Gallery, co-organizer of the exhibition, has a superb small collection which is too little known. In the past two decades, Asia House Gallery has held a series of extraordinary surveys of Indian painting which have done much to stimulate modern interest and activity in this area. And finally, it was the earlier collecting and writings of Ananda K. Coomaraswamy, Keeper of the Indian Collections at the Museum of Fine Arts, Boston, that really sparked twentieth century concern with Indian painting and sculpture.

Without the generous support of the lenders and the aid of the National Endowment for the Arts, neither exhibition nor catalogue could have been realized. We are also very grateful to Jan Fontein and Joyce Paulson at the Museum of Fine Arts, Boston; to Lilian M. C. Randall at the Walters Art Gallery; and to Allen Wardwell at Asia House Gallery for their help and cooperation. And we would like to pay special tribute to George Heard Hamilton who, as former director of the Sterling and Francine Clark Art Institute, gave enthusiastic support to the exhibition at its inception.

David S. Brooke, *Director*
Sterling and Francine Clark
Art Institute

Richard H. Randall, Jr., *Director*
Walters Art Gallery

PREFACE AND ACKNOWLEDGMENTS

THERE MAY BE initial confusion, for the title of this exhibition uses the archaic—and rather more evocative—spelling *Mogul* for a term elsewhere found in the catalogue as *Mughal*. Both seem to be traditional adaptations of *Mongol*, for Genghiz Khān was a direct ancestor of the Mughal Emperors of India.

Mughal painting has been known and appreciated in Europe since the early seventeenth century. Sir Thomas Roe, the English ambassador to the Mughal Court between 1615 and 1618, brought paintings back to England, and in 1639 a Mughal album was presented to the Bodleian Library at Oxford University by Archbishop Laud. Moreover, Rembrandt's copies (made in the 1650s) of Mughal portraits are generally familiar. Exhibitions of Indian painting have appeared in both England and the United States recently with considerable frequency. These have usually been either broad surveys and comparisons of the many types of painting done throughout the subcontinent, or else investigations of the entire Mughal tradition from the mid-sixteenth to the nineteenth centuries. In being severely limited to just six decades, however, and to one school, this exhibition demands far more of the viewer, for the range of artistic intention is very restricted. The extremes of style and taste which so enliven the wide-ranging survey are replaced by the exploration of one small—but absolutely central—phase of the Mughal tradition: the achievement of what is usually termed "Mughal naturalism."

No effort of this sort could—or should—be the product of a single individual. I am especially indebted to George Heard Hamilton, former director of the Sterling and Francine Clark Art Institute, for accepting instantly and enthusiastically the initial proposal for the exhibition; without his support it would not have existed. I am grateful, as well, to the Trustees of the Institute, and to David S. Brooke, its present director, for endorsing a project in which they had no formal reason whatsoever to be interested. Whitney S. Stoddard, former chairman of the Art Department, Williams College, has been consistently encouraging.

Martha Asher, Registrar of the Clark Art Institute, and Edith Howard, who typed the manuscript, have provided indispensable and superbly efficient help. Elise K. Kenney copy-edited the text with necessary thoroughness, and Klaus Gemming has provided advice and aid far beyond his official role as designer of the catalogue; the successful presentation of a rather complex text is due entirely to their skill and sensitivity.

I am grateful, also, to The JDR 3rd Fund and its director, Richard Lanier, for a grant to examine paintings in London and Tehran. The generosity of the lending museums and private collectors must also be acknowledged. American collections have become extraordinarily rich in Mughal paintings, and—with one exception—every institution approached immediately and willingly consented to lend any work that was physically in condition to withstand travel.

The compilation of information in the catalogue was possible only because of work done by many scholars—so many, in fact, that they must unfortunately be identified by references in the Bibliography. In particular, however, I am once again indebted to Stuart Cary Welch who has always dispensed information and visual judgment with generosity and extreme perceptiveness. Robert Skelton, Keeper of the Indian Collections, Victoria and Albert Museum, London, Zirka Filipczak, Williams College, and Ellen Smart have been helpful with specific information; B. N. Goswamy, Panjab University, Chandigarh, and M. Wheeler Thackston, Harvard University, provided substantial help in reading inscriptions. Glenn D. Lowry, also of Harvard, served as a supporting force for the exhibition during undergraduate years at Williams College; as well, he wrote the section on the painter Manōhar, and helped to form the Bibliography and Genealogy. Other students who have enrolled in courses on Indian painting at Williams over the years have provided uninhibited and challenging criticism of the ideas and approaches found here. To them a very basic debt is due.

Finally, the catalogue could not have been accomplished without the support of my wife, Robin, and of our children, Olga, Toby, and Sophie.

Milo Cleveland Beach

Williams College
Williamstown, Massachusetts

INTRODUCTION

THE PATRONS

THE ostentatious wealth of the Indian subcontinent in the early sixteenth century, together with the fragmented and chaotic political situation, made the area a perfect
target for quick raids by an adventurer and petty chieftain from just beyond the barriers of
the northwest, the mountains known as the Hindu Kush. Zahir-ud-dīn Muhammad Bābur
had become ruler of the eastern Iranian territory of Ferghana in 1494 at the age of eleven, and
he immediately set out to increase his territories by the capture of Samarkand, about two
hundred miles to the west. That fabled city had been the capital of his patrilineal ancestor
Tīmūr (Christopher Marlowe's Tamerlane), and thus it was the focus of Bābur's early
ambitions. Three times he gained and lost the city, and eventually he was ousted from
Ferghana as well. He descended to Kabul (in present-day Afghanistan), from which he made
treasure-seeking expeditions farther south, to northern India. This, too, he considered his
rightful patrimony; it also had once come under Tīmūr's control. By 1525, Bābur more
seriously considered the establishment of a large power base there, and the following year
he defeated the Sultān of Delhi, Ibrāhīm Lodī, becoming the first of the Mughal emperors.

Bābur did not like India, and what he wrote about it rehearses an attitude we meet as well,
over and over again, during the British raj:

> Hindustan [India] is a country of few charms. Its people have no good looks; of social intercourse,
> paying and receiving visits there is none; of genius and capacity none; of manners none; of handi-
> craft and work there is no form or symmetry, method or quality; there are no good horses, no
> good dogs, no grapes, muskmelons or first-rate fruits, no ice or cold water, no good bread or
> cooked food in the *bāzārs*, no Hot-baths.[1]

This antagonism is made more powerful because Bābur's memoirs (the *Bābur-nāma*), from
which we quoted, are among the most perceptive and sensitive of reminiscences. He remarked on the beauty of flowers, and described them carefully and scientifically in detail;
he noted curious animals; he discussed the character of men around him; and he revealed
quite extraordinary facets of his own personality. He did not react negatively to India, it
seems, because he was insensitive, as we might have suspected, but because he was super-
sensitive. He elsewhere bemoaned the lack of "charm, air, regularity, and symmetry" in
Indian residences, and he did not like the absence of free human interaction. In the expecta-
tions and standards thus put forth, therefore, Bābur established a value for life that set the
Mughals apart from their contemporaries in India and the Muslim world; it was based on a
recognition that the elements of the physical world are unique, individually distinctive, and
worthy of prolonged investigation.

There is no solid evidence that painters accompanied Bābur on his final descent into India
in 1526. Nor is there any reason to think that his rather provincial base of power in Ferghana
had allowed him to patronize the arts there to any major degree. The court of the Safavid
Shāhs at Tabriz, fantastically rich and intensely involved in the arts, attracted large numbers
of artists, and this made subimperial patronage difficult, while at the same time increasing
the desire for such activity among the nobles. Bābur, a littérateur and poet, would have found
painting a sympathetic form of expression, however. His memoirs show extraordinary visual
alertness, as in the following passage:

> When within two miles of the Āb-i-istāda, we saw a wonderful thing,—something as red as the
> rose of the dawn kept shewing and vanishing between the sky and the water. It kept coming and

*Zahir-ud-dīn
Muhammad
Bābur*

Bābur-nāma

going. When we got quite close we learned that what seemed the cause were flocks of geese, not 10,000, not 20,000 in a flock, but geese innumerable which, when the mass of birds flapped their wings in flight, sometimes shewed red feathers, sometimes not.[2]

At other times, we are told of his interest in books, but, for the present, suggestions about works which he might have commissioned from painters in India, are highly tentative.[3]

Nāsir-ud-dīn Muhammad Humāyūn Bābur died in 1530, and he was succeeded by his eldest son, Nāsir-ud-dīn Muhammad Humāyūn, who was about twenty-two. Much less is known of Humāyūn than of his father, but he emerges as a less interesting figure. Bābur, at one point, noted in the *Bābur-nāma*: ". . . much rain was falling; parties were frequent; even Humayun was present at them and, abhorrent though it was to him, sinned [i.e., drank alcohol] every few days. . . ."[4] And the prince, abstemious in his youth, became increasingly dependent on alcohol and opium, which—together with the delights of the harem, three prime Mughal pastimes—were to contribute to his eventual downfall. Humāyūn, the second Mughal emperor, was defeated by Sher Shāh, an Afghan, and was chased from India in 1543. This event, which tells us of the early frailty of Mughal control on the subcontinent, is of the greatest importance for the arts. Humāyūn spent part of his exile at the court of his cousin, the Iranian Shāh Tahmāsp Safavī, from whom he received troops to aid his return to India. He was also able to hire several of the greatest Iranian painters—notably Mīr Sayyid ʿAlī and ʿAbd-as-Samad (see *no. 5 recto*)—for Tahmāsp had recently become more orthodox and therefore less active as a patron. (To the strictly orthodox Muslim, image making was, and still is, blasphemous, for it usurps the life-giving functions which God alone can exercise.) The transfer of these painters to Humāyūn's entourage has been well studied, as has their role in the establishment of the royal workshops under Humāyūn's son, ʿAbd al-Fath Jalāl-ud-dīn Akbar.[5]

ʿAbd al-Fath Jalāl-ud-dīn Akbar Akbar succeeded his father in 1556, the year after Humāyūn regained India, and he is the most dynamic and endlessly intriguing of all the Mughal emperors. Born in the deserts of Sind as his father was fleeing the subcontinent, he came to power at the age of twelve, and instantly began to consolidate his control. He almost immediately put painters and architects to work as well, for buildings and even well-stocked libraries were tangible and necessary proofs of power in the Islamic world.

Akbar inherited Humāyūn's throne and painters, but he was more akin to Bābur in temperament. He, however, found the world of India full of information, challenge, and delight. In the early years of his reign, he surrounded himself with Hindus (and married Hindu princesses), invited Zoroastrians and Jains to explain their rituals, and asked Jesuit priests to bring him a Bible. Insatiably curious in his youth—and one finds reflections of both momentary and long-term interests in the style and subject of the paintings he commissioned—his taste in the arts, nonetheless, slowly withdrew from receptivity to Hindu ideals. In the 1590s, his biographer Abūʾl Fazl, when praising the development which painting underwent during the reign, noted that: "Most excellent painters are now to be found, and masterpieces, worthy of a Bihzad [a great Iranian painter], may be placed by the side of the wonderful works of the European painters who have attained worldwide fame."[6] Europe and Iran were thereby set up as the artistic ideals of the mature Mughal regime; there is no mention of Hindu India. Abūʾl Fazl also remarked on an album of portraits that the emperor commissioned, saying: "Those that have passed away have received a new life, and those who are still alive have immortality promised them."[7] And this refers to the most radical of Akbar's artistic innovations, the interest in actual portraiture; for particularities of physiognomy and attempts to probe character were not part of either pre-Mughal Indian or Islamic traditions. Akbar's absorption in the physical world and his energy, parallelled Bābur's, but he was a far more complex personality. His initial interest in non-Muslim doctrine, itself scandalous to the orthodox, was a result of genuine, rational, intellectual probing. But he was also subject to intuitive insights and even visions. The most important occurred in 1578, and soon afterwards he established the *Dīn-i-Ilāhī* ("Divine Faith"), a new religion that sought to reconcile whatever was personally acceptable among the various faiths Akbar had studied.

A detailed study of Akbar's rule is not our purpose here. However, his interest in physical reality and the natural world, his intellectual curiosity and experimentalism, his religious unorthodoxy, his intense involvement in the arts, and his dominant and overpowering personality and political strength, must all be taken into account when examining the reigns of Jahāngīr and Shāh Jahān. Nūr-ud-dīn Muhammad Jahāngīr, first known as Prince (or *Sultān*) Salīm, Akbar's eldest son, was born in 1569, and acceded to the throne at the age of *Sultān Salīm* thirty-six. He had grown up amidst unassailable political power and stability, and pervasive physical opulence; so completely opposite is this to the background which Akbar brought to the throne that it is not surprising to find in Jahāngīr a very different personality.

Even before his accession, Salīm was an enthusiastic patron of the arts. By 1588–89, when the prince was not yet twenty, the recently arrived Iranian painter Āqā Rizā was already in his employ; and it is clear that by the time of Salīm's rebellion and move to Allahabad in 1600, his ménage included architects, builders, and all the apparatus of the arts of the book.

This rebellion was inspired simply by the son's impatience to take over the power to which his father so tenaciously, and rightfully, clung; and it is a pattern repeated by Shāh Jahān, in turn, and then by Aurangzēb. Salīm moved his establishment to Allahabad, and proclaimed himself *shāh*, or king. Eventually, and unlike his successors, he returned to court for a recon- *Nūr-ud-dīn* ciliation; there were no other sons remaining to the elderly and ailing Akbar. And upon *Muhammad* officially acceding to the throne in 1605, Salīm chose as his title the name by which we know *Jahāngīr* him best, Jahāngīr ("The World Seizer"). Since the Mughal territories were stable and well administered, Jahāngīr could spend much of his time indulging in the aesthetic pursuits which Akbar had made so abundant. Not the least of these, for Jahāngīr, was painting.

We know of the emperor's character from several vantage points: his own memoirs (the *The emperor's* *Tūzuk-i-Jahāngīrī*, or *Jahāngīr-nāma*), contemporary accounts of Muslims at his court, the *character* diaries of visiting Europeans, and some extraordinary painted portraits. He was quixotic and impassioned, capable of excesses of both cruelty and kindness. During his rebellion, for example, when three of his followers fled camp, he had them caught, and one was flayed alive in his (Jahāngīr's) presence, an act which appalled Akbar. On another occasion, when Jahāngīr was hunting, he tells us:

> When I had got within shot of a nilgaw, suddenly a groom and two *kahār* (bearers) appeared, and the nilgaw escaped. In a great rage I ordered them to kill the groom on the spot, and to hamstring the kahars and mount them on asses and parade them through the camp, so that no one should again have the boldness to do such a thing. After this I mounted a horse and continued hunting.[8]

Such objectively observed tantrums must be balanced with other episodes, however.

> It occurred to me that however much an elephant delights in water, and it is suited to their temperament, yet in winter the cold water must affect them. I accordingly ordered the water to be made lukewarm (as warm as milk) before they (the elephants) poured it into their trunks. On other days when they poured cold water over themselves they evidently shivered, but with warm water, on the contrary, they were delighted. This usage is entirely my own.[9]

Passages such as these, and lightning fast switches of topic, make the *Tūzuk* lively and highly informative reading, for in it Jahāngīr described scientific experiments he conducted, birds and flowers he admired, important historical events, and a wide range of general observations. Throughout, however, there is none of the intense religious inquiry we sense behind Akbar; while sympathetic to, and involved with, the world of *sheikhs* and *sūfīs*, and especially with teachings of the mystic poet Sa°dī, Jahāngīr was not himself a visionary. An event of 1607 sets the tone of his approach to the world:

> On Tuesday the 4th of the month . . . I came down to the village of Bhakra. In the Ghakkar tongue *bhakra* is a jungle. The jungle was composed of clusters of flowers, white and senseless. I came the whole way from Tila to Bhakra in the middle of a riverbed, which had running water in it, with oleander flowers the color of peach-blossom. There was much of it on the banks of this river. The horsemen and men on foot who were with me were told to put bunches of the flower on their heads, and whoever did not do so had his turban taken off; a wonderful [portable] flowerbed was produced.[10]

Like Akbar, Jahāngīr had Europeans at his court; but not merely priests, for the English East India Company had been chartered, and various merchants arrived seeking trading rights, as did a number of sheer adventurers. William Hawkins, the English sea captain, was there around 1610, and because he could speak *Turkī*, the family language of the Mughals, he became an intimate drinking companion of the emperor. In his memoirs, Hawkins describes the way in which Jahāngīr (then only five years into his reign) ended his day:

> He departeth towards his private place of prayer. His prayer being ended, foure or five sorts of very well dressed and roasted meats are brought him, of which, as he pleaseth, he eateth a bit to stay his stomacke, drinking once of his strong drinke. Then he commeth forth into a private roome, where none can come but such as he himselfe nominateth (for two yeeres together I was one of his attendants here). In this place he drinketh another five cupfuls, which is the portion which the physicians alot him. This done, he eateth opium . . . and being in the height of his drinke he layeth him downe to sleepe . . . after he hath slept two houres, they awake him and bring his supper to him; at which time he is not able to feed himselfe, but it is thrust into his mouth by others; and this is about one of the clocke, and then he sleepeth the rest of the night.[11]

By the time of Jahāngīr's coronation, both his brothers, Sultān Murād and Sultān Daniyāl, had died enfeebled by alcoholism. Jahāngīr himself fell more and more under the power of inebriates, and eventually it was his wife, Nūr Jahān, who ran the government, while the emperor became unable even to continue writing the memoirs which he had so carefully recorded since his accession.

During the reign, the court was mobile. Between 1613 and 1616, the emperor moved to Ajmer, in Rājasthān, to support his son Khurram in the campaign against the Rānā of Mewar (the chief Rājput ruler, who continued to hold out against Mughal control). The campaign was successful, and the imperial establishment returned to Agra where, in 1617, Khurram was given the title Shāh Jahān ("Ruler of the World"). In late 1619, Jahāngīr moved north, to the cooler climate of Kashmir, where he became wildly enthusiastic about the variety of flowers available. Thomas Roe has described the vast size of the imperial procession on such migrations, and states that the encampments were equal in size to almost any European town. Yet whatever epicurean delights such travel had for the emperor, the effect on the countryside—which was responsible for feeding and supporting the hundreds of thousands of courtiers and camp-followers—was devastating and destructive.

In 1620, Jahāngīr was back in **Agra**, having sent Shāh Jahān to the Deccan on a military expedition. A *darbār* scene (*no. 14*) shows the emperor and his son at about the time of the prince's departure. They were never to see each other again, for Shāh Jahān also rebelled—his solution for survival among the factions forming at court as a result of the emperor's age and increasing incapacity. The prince slew his elder brother and rival Khusrau, whose own earlier rebellion against Jahāngīr had resulted in an imperial decree that he (Khusrau) be blinded. In 1626, the year before Jahāngīr's death, Shāh Jahān's second brother, Sultān Parvīz, also died, evidently of the usual vices, although contemporary scuttlebut attributed the event to Shāh Jahān. This left the throne virtually unchallenged; yet the new emperor ordered the deaths of Khusrau's sons, his dead uncle Daniyāl's sons, and his younger brother Shahriyār who had earlier been blinded and was leprosy-ridden as well. This is all mentioned here because there is a great deal beneath the surface of Shāh Jahān's reign; the surface is so controlled and highly polished, however, that it is tempting to believe the appearance to be the reality.

Shāh Jahān

Shāh Jahān was particularly intent on appropriate self-presentation to the world. Whereas Jahāngīr was willing to be shown as careworn, enjoying the harem, or in informal and private moments, Shāh Jahān attempted through the arts to present a reality so unblemished that it could exist nowhere but in the mind. The superb portrait of the old emperor by Hāshim (*no. 45*), for example, does not begin to hint at the subsurface character we find in even the small drawing of Jahāngīr (*no. 58*). And the various versions of Shāh Jahān's biography (the *Shāh Jahān-nāma*, or *Pādshāh-nāma*), written by imperial commission, not personally, are very much official texts.

Most of Shāh Jahān's artistic energies went into architecture—public proclamations of wealth and power. In the 1630s, he concentrated on the Tāj Mahal, the tomb for his beloved wife Mumtāz Mahal, who died giving birth to her fourteenth child in 1631; between 1639 and 1648, his new capital of Shāh Jahānabād (at Delhi) was in progress. In addition, he ordered many of the older red sandstone buildings in the fort at Agra to be torn down and replaced by structures in brilliant white marble inlaid with colored stones, certain indication of a lavish, highly refined and formal taste.

Unlike Akbar and Jahāngīr, Shāh Jahān was an orthodox—although not particularly strict—Muslim. Since his mother was a Hindu (the daughter of the Rājput rājā of Jodhpur), and his father was half-Rājput (Jahāngīr's mother having come from Amber, present-day Jaipur), Shāh Jahān had every reason to be sympathetic to Hindus—but he was not. He re-imposed a pilgrimage tax on non-Muslims, ordered the destruction of several Hindu temples, and openly favored Muslim nobles; the open-mindedness and intellectual appetite of his two immediate predecessors were not continued. However, as his eldest son and intended heir matured, the emperor became more lenient; for the Prince, Dārā Shikōh (*nos. 63* and *64*), was eager to investigate and reconcile Hinduism and Islam. He wrote a translation of the *Upanishads*, and commentaries on various Hindu texts, and tried to learn directly from eminent holy men; *no. 63* shows him thus occupied. Dārā, Shāh Jahān's favorite son, was given full freedom for his intellectual interests, to the detriment of the preparation necessary for his survival in the inevitable struggles for succession. Imperial status was seized by the strongest alone.

Dārā Shikōh

Shāh Jahān's reign ended in a long, deadly war among his sons (*no. 65*). All the princes were killed, with exception of the professionally pious Aurangzēb who imprisoned his father in Agra Fort and proclaimed himself emperor. Shāh Jahān lived until 1666, and probably had access to his painters during this imprisonment; he may also have used the time to piece together the *Pādshāh-nāma* manuscript, a portion of which is presently in the Royal Library at Windsor (*nos. 24–26*). Aurangzēb was not particularly interested in any of the arts. An intensely austere portrait (*no. 67*), perhaps done at the time of his coronation, shows us the man who ruled from 1658 to 1707. The latter half of this reign was spent in the Deccan, where he remained until his death, trying vainly to control the various kingdoms and predatory bands that inhabited the region and threatened his control. In doing this, he exhausted a treasury already weakened by the extravagance of his father. And the length of his rule assured that his sons would be incompetent successors, for Aurangzēb was eighty-nine when he died, and his successor, Muhammad Shāh ᶜĀlam Bahādur, at sixty-four, had never held any major responsibility. A quick turnover of generally untrained, irresponsible rulers followed, together with a thick growth of power factions, court intrigues, and the like. The unalleviated decline of the Mughal Empire, which really began at Akbar's death in 1605, formally ended in 1858. The last token emperor was exiled to Burma by the British in that year, and Her Majesty Queen Victoria became Empress of India. A quite different imperial tradition then began.

Aurangzēb

CHARACTERISTICS OF MUGHAL PAINTING

IT was under Akbar that a recognizable Mughal style was formed. While the emperor placed the Iranians Mīr Sayyid ᶜAlī and ᶜAbd as-Samad in charge of the Mughal painting studios, the works that emerged were in a new and different style which mixed Hindu (Rājput) and Muslim Indian elements with those of imperial Safavid Iran. Initially, all these ingredients seemed to be on equal footing. Iranian traits, of course, reflected the attitudes and taste with which the Mughals were most familiar; the Indian styles, however, appealed because of their novelty. With a limited palette of intense colors, little regard for fineness of technique, and immediately legible, often violently exciting compositions, they formed a contrast to the ultrasophistication and subtlety of Iranian works, in which colors were set onto the page like jewels in mounts and high drama conveyed by the raising of an eyebrow. Akbar, a youth himself, athletic and strong willed, forced the creation of a style of painting as full of physical exuberation as the life he led.

Painting under Akbar

Again, however, we are not here investigating the delights of Akbar period painting, and it must suffice simply to point out that as Akbar grew older, the paintings he demanded became subtler in composition, technique, and emotional range. He also became increasingly concerned with images of the world around him. His "invention" of portraiture, and the shift of subject away from the religious and poetic texts common to both Hindu and Muslim traditions and towards historical scenes and natural history subjects are major innovations of Akbari painting. By refinements of physical materials, Mughal painters were able to investigate the natural world in ever greater detail; by experience with new techniques of modelling, they were able to give physical substance and verity to forms; and by breaking into new ideas of the human being as a unique individual (by far the hardest development, for it involved the recognition of a completely different *weltanschauung*), they brought painting out of other-worldly realms.

FIG. 1. An Elephant. Deccani, at Ahmadnagar,
ca. 1590–95. Private Collection.

From the late sixteenth century into the mid-seventeenth, Mughal painting concentrated on naturalism, and, in particular, on portraiture. This is a brief moment of a few decades in a tradition of, at most, three hundred years, but it has served to define Mughal painting for most viewers. A quick comparison of three different paintings of the same subject—an elephant—from three different contemporary cultural complexes in India, should help to make the unorthodoxy of the Mughal style more evident.

Figure 1 from Ahmadnagar in the Deccan is in a non-Mughal Muslim Indian style very close to contemporary Iranian taste. It is a tense, superbly controlled drawing, full of vitality. The aliveness is less due to the subject than to the line, which, by twisting and turning, becoming thicker and thinner, forces our eyes continually to move over the surface. Such details as the bottom of the saddle cloth show us that the line, while suggestive of particular objects, moves quite independently of them. It is the rhythm of the line, not that of the saddle cloth, that we observe. In this way, too, the elephant becomes a generalized type; the painter's interest is not in showing a specific elephant in a particular spatial setting. *The Deccani style*

A second example (*figs. 2* and *3*) is Hindu, a painting made for one of the Rājput rājās under Mughal overlordship. The brilliance of linework and whatever sense of modelling and corporeality exists, are perhaps due to lessons learned from the Deccani and Mughal styles. However, despite the slight indication of ground, this painting, too, is a general type.

FIG. 2. A Rhinoceros Hunt. Rājput, Rajasthani, at Kota, ca. 1700. Private Collection.

FIG. 3. Detail of Fig. 2.

The Rājput style The saddle cloth is a superb, strongly colored shape, but tells us nothing of the substance of the cloth. A better detail, for our purposes here, is the eye (*fig. 3*), which swims through the head like a fish, chased, perhaps, by the wavelike ear. Such verbalization tends to kill, through suggestions of specificity, the intended generalized metaphors; but over and over again, in Hindu poetics, one encounters the idea that the subject of a work of art is to be presented in its most generalized form. Other forms and emotions, suggested much less explicitly than the earlier words implied, make the viewer aware of the degree to which every element in the universe is interrelated, part of one substance. Such a sensibility is what the Hindu artist working for a Hindu patron almost never alters; and despite the superficial Mughalization of the style seen here, it is this which makes it impossible for this work to be mistaken for a purely Mughal painting.

The Mughal example is *no. 33*, and it presents a specific elephant. The saddle cloth is the texture and weight of the material. Line does not "take-off," but transforms itself into what is being described. Every element of the picture, including the relatively naturalistic space, is meant to emphasize the uniqueness of the subject, not its universality. Within both Indian and Muslim contexts, this is a radical change of outlook.

The Mughal interest in nature Between approximately 1600 and 1660, the time span of this exhibition, Mughal painters concentrated on perfecting the techniques of naturalism. Akbar's earlier enthusiasms had been worked through, and Hindu paintings, it was now believed, provided neither the perfection of technique nor the naturalistic attitudes that the older Akbar demanded. Persian works and European prints were deemed appropriate models—and remained so throughout the further development of the Mughal style. By the 1660s, however, the Emperor Aurangzēb (r. 1658–1707), Akbar's great-grandson, like his predecessor Tahmāsp, withdrew from active artistic patronage, and many Mughal painters moved to the employ of provincial governors and nobles. Because these men were often in contact with, and receptive to, Hindu India in ways that the imperial court was not, later Mughal provincial styles—unlike the contemporary imperial tradition—are often exciting, challenging, and innovative.

It is necessary to remember that as the imperial style of painting withdrew further and further from the interests and attitudes of Hindu India (which it did steadily from the later sixteenth century), it simply cut off its own sustenance; for Hindu India was the country in which the Mughals lived. The history of later imperial Mughal painting is a story of heavy blossoms supported by shallow roots.

The years between 1600 and 1660 are approximately those of the mature Mughal style: earlier years led to the achievements of these decades, and later years sought to revive them. It is this classic moment that is being investigated in this exhibition.

PAINTING UNDER JAHĀNGĪR

As regards myself, my liking for painting and my practice in judging it have arrived at such a point that when any work is brought before me, either of deceased artists or those of the present day, without the names being told me, I say on the spur of the moment that it is the work of such and such a man. And if there be a picture containing many portraits, and each face be the work of a different master, I can discover which face is the work of each of them. If any other person has put in the eye and eyebrow of a face, I can perceive whose work the original face is, and who has painted the eye and eyebrows.[1]

EMPEROR Jahāngīr's confidence in his own visual acuity seems amply confirmed by the extraordinary quality of the works he commissioned. Unlike Akbar, who often demanded large books of both historical and poetic subject matter, Jahāngīr virtually ignored the historical, and made immediately evident his preference for small books with fewer, and thereby often finer, illustrations. Akbar's taste in the 1590s—a period which seems to be the major culmination of earlier wide-ranging and experimental stylistic developments—was for compositions tightly packed with figures and action. Manuscripts had many illustrated folios, and it was accepted, for large manuscripts, to have one painter design a composition and another do the actual painting, often with a third to add specific details, such as particular portraits. The sheer quantity of painting, and the assembly line procedure, worked to level both the quality of the painting produced and its artistic range. And this is a major problem of the later Akbar period style.

The general character of Jahāngīrī painting is quite different. Scenes are simpler and more spacious, and the predominant interest in narrative action is replaced by an investigation of the intensity of human interrelationships. Too, joint responsibility for single illustrations was discouraged, and paintings thereby became unified expressions of individual artistic sensibilities. It is tempting to attribute these changes to the change of imperial patron, yet all the elements of Jahāngīrī painting are present within the Akbar period;[2] moreover, the new trends take on major importance in the imperial studio about 1600, at a time when Jahāngīr was in rebellion and living independently in Allahabad. Thus, whether the new selectivity of subject and style was the result of early influences exerted by Jahāngīr as a prince, or of a change of direction in response to new interests of the old Emperor Akbar, is uncertain. There is clear evidence of Jahāngīr's patronage of the arts at Allahabad, however, and works commissioned there have a very specific character.

Painting at Allahabad   Between 1600 and 1604, when he was in Allahabad, Jahāngīr took for himself the title Shāh. This, by itself, was an act of rebellion, for the term had hitherto been used only by the emperor. The designation is found inscribed on several works (e.g., *no. 39*), indicating that they must have been made during these years. The *Portrait of a Courtier (no. 39)* and the manuscript of poems by Amīr Hasan Dihlavī (*no. 1*) show that a strongly Iranian element, not found in contemporary imperial works, was a major aspect of the Allahabad style. Yet another portrait (*no. 30*), inscribed with Jahāngīr's prerebellion title of Sultān Salīm, and therefore datable to approximately 1595, is also in predominantly Iranian taste. But what differentiates all these works from their source is modelling; for shading, as a means of giving physical substance and reality to forms, is not part of the Iranian tradition at this time. The early portrait (*no. 30*) is signed by Āqā Rizā, an already established artist trained in Iran, who entered Jahāngīr's employ by at least A.H. 997 = A.D. 1588–89, perhaps at the time of his arrival in India. A series of marginal drawings in the *Muraqqaᶜ-e-Gulshan*, or *Gulshan Album*, signed as well as dated 1599, proves that the artist was then copying European prints, as were, of course, many other Mughal painters of the time. Such prints were the source for the new techniques of shading which became so important for the Mughal style. The various reliably signed works by Āqā Rizā show him to have been a controlled, precise painter, making carefully balanced, highly decorative compositions. Yet he remained conservative, and deeply indebted to his training in Iran; figures seldom take on real individuality, for example, and line is expressively independent of what it ostensibly describes. Āqā Rizā was the major artist working at Allahabad, however, so his style was enormously influential on the development of the young Jahāngīr's taste.

Āqā Rizā and Abūᶜl Hasan   The painter was also the father of Abūᶜl Hasan, a man lauded above all other artists by Jahāngīr, and a comparison of works by the two is informative. *An Infant Prince (no. 28)* by Abūᶜl Hasan, presents a probing visual analysis (both formal and emotional) of the figure. With the clothing, for example, we are not aware of the movement of line per se, for both line and color have been transformed into the texture of the materials described. This is not the case with the Āqā Rizā *Portrait of a Courtier (no. 30)*, which is more concerned with surface pattern than literal descriptiveness. Also, for Āqā Rizā, shading has the character of a surface patina, whereas for Abūᶜl Hasan it is basic to our understanding of the depicted substances. Consequently, Abūᶜl Hasan's figure has a weight and density that—coupled with his extraordinary perception of personality traits—convinces us of both its reality and its individuality. This seemingly effortless naturalism is found already fully developed in Abūᶜl Hasan's earliest major work, a page from the British Library *Anwār-i-Suhailī* manuscript of 1604–10, which also contains Āqā Rizā's most brilliant and successful compositions. The shift of interest we find when comparing works by these two artists, both of them members of the Allahabad workshops, is further developed in paintings commissioned by Jahāngīr as emperor.

Once he succeeded to the throne in 1605, Jahāngīr inherited the full imperial artistic establishment. During the years of rebellion, he would certainly have been unable to patronize painters still in his father's employ. This is one reason why Āqā Rizā's presence at the prince's capital during these years as an older and highly respected, if not very exciting or innovative, representative of the Iranian tradition, substantially affected the style of paintings

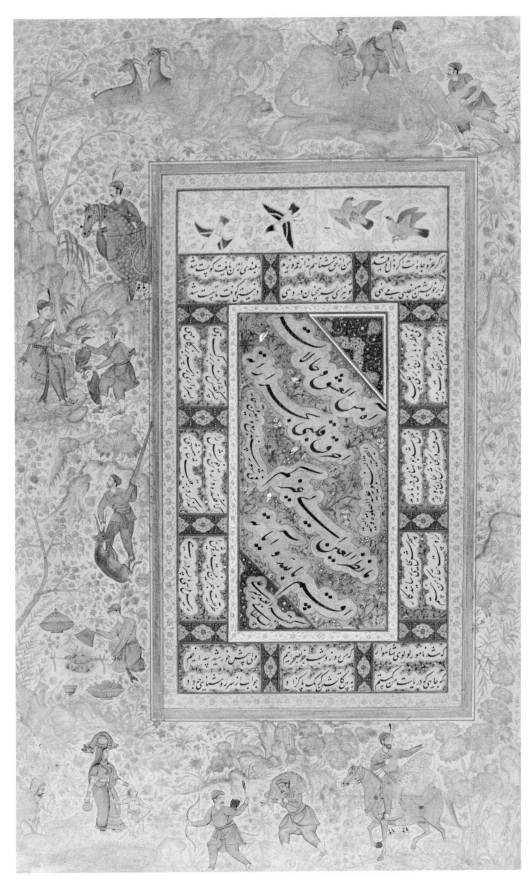

6 recto

commissioned. This is seen also in the manuscript of the *Dīwān* of Amīr Hasan Dihlavī, finished at Allahabad in 1602 (*no. 1*). Five of the fourteen illustrations are in a variant of Āqā Riżā's style, whereas the remainder are in a simplified Akbari style. We find a similar stylistic split in three other major manuscripts made in the first decade of the seventeenth century: the *Anwār-i-Suhailī* of 1604–10, already mentioned; a *Būstān* of Saʿdī, dated 1605; and a *Kulliyāt* of Saʿdī, of about 1605.³ Soon after the accession, however, painting for Jahāngīr develops an absolute stylistic consistency. The direct influence of Āqā Riżā, whose death must have occurred at about this time, goes quickly out of fashion, and is replaced by a straightforward, almost scientific naturalism.

Abūʿl Hasan was born to Jahāngīr's service, but several other major Jahāngīrī artists had earlier worked for Akbar. Manōhar, for example, was the son of Basāwan, one of the two Indian painters most esteemed by Akbar.⁴ He began painting in the 1580s, but it was a decade later before his style was fully formed. A superb, but until recently unknown, portrait of the older Akbar, with his grandsons Sulṭān Khusrau and Sulṭān Khurram (the latter would be known by his title Shāh Jahān), while too fragile for inclusion in the exhibition, is reproduced here as *fig. 11* (see page 133). Datable to about 1602, when the princes were held at court as hostages for their rebellious father, it is very different from the contemporary portraits which Āqā Riżā was making for Jahāngīr (compare *fig. 11* and *no. 30*). Instead of the Iranian artist's rather mannered study of a general princely type, this is clearly the study of individual personalities and a specific incident. Like Abūʿl Hasan, Manōhar gives three-dimensional substance to his figures, and to his contemporaries they must have had astonishing presence. And this is one aspect of the imperial tradition that Jahāngīr continues after his accession, demanding an even greater intensity of observation from his artists.

Manōhar

Yet, in the Manōhar portrait of Akbar (*fig. 11*), spatial concerns are consistent only within details; the princes, or the courtier to the left, for example, are only tenuously related to the ground beneath their feet, and there is little real sense of spatial recession. Furthermore, while the physiognomies of the men are carefully differentiated, the characterizations do not have the animation or depth that we see in works by, for example, Abūʿl Hasan. Comparing illustrations by these two artists in the *Gulistān* of Saʿdī of about 1615 (*no. 19* [above] and *no. 18* [above]), indicates that this is a continuing distinction. It seems, therefore, that Manōhar, trained during the Akbar period, could not completely adapt to the intensified demands for naturalism made by Jahāngīr, just as Āqā Riżā never really broke away from his Iranian background. And it is continually evident that the most successful Jahāngīrī painters were those who came to maturity knowing the emperor's taste. Yet if this is true, it could only be because Jahāngīr's demands were themselves new and different.

Stylistic innovations

The concern for modelling which we have seen as basic to the works of such diverse painters as Manōhar and Abūʿl Hasan, and present in illustrations by Āqā Riżā, and the accompanying desire for a sense of spatial depth within the painting, are –far more than innovations of pure technique or subject matter—evidence of a radically new outlook which Mughal painting in general promoted, and which Jahāngīrī painting developed most profoundly. It is an attitude towards space that demands a recognition of the uniqueness of the various physical forms depicted, for it stresses boundaries and separation. Neither Hindu nor Islamic artistic traditions accepted such a premise, for the arts of each were concerned with underlying unities, not with distinctness. That Mughal painters were able, for several decades, to assimilate such an alien tradition—in response, of course, to imperial interest—is testament to their perception and openmindedness.

The Gulistān of Sa'dī

The *Gulistān* of Sa'dī (*nos. 16–20*), which has been mentioned above, must have been one of the most superb of Mughal books, but only the illustrations are presently known. (They were cut from the manuscript, pasted onto new pages, and bound in albums, explaining their present odd appearance.) Here we find, perfectly exemplified, Jahāngīr's taste for the small and exquisite. It is not violent action, but gestures and glances that reveal the drama of each scene; and in this restraint and subtlety—as well as in the technical finesse—it is evident that Jahāngīr's ability to inspire the elegant and perfectly crafted work of art is fully equal to that of his Iranian predecessors. The early Iranian orientation of the emperor's taste, and the impact of Āqā Rizā, develop not into a continuation of the Iranian style, therefore, but into an expectation by Jahāngīr that his personal interest in nature and the physical world be presented with a refinement of workmanship for which Iran remained the standard of excellence.

The Albums of Jahāngīr

While a number of manuscripts made for Jahāngīr remain, including pages which must have come from the imperial copy of the *Jahāngīr-nāma* (e.g., *nos. 13–15*), the emperor preferred to commission individual paintings. Many of these are found in the extraordinary albums (*muraqqas*) which he formed, of which two large volumes remain substantially intact: the *Muraqqa'-e-Gulshan*, and the so-called *Berlin Album*. Both are further discussed in relation to several detached pages exhibited here (*nos. 5–12*).

The albums contained both paintings and calligraphies that Jahāngīr commissioned, as well as those he collected. There are Iranian, Turkish, and Deccani paintings, as well as Mughal works; European prints, and Mughal copies and adaptation of these prints (e.g., *nos. 10* and *10A*); and, in one case, a painting that seems to have been done by a European travelling in India (*no. 9*). These illustrations are surrounded by extremely beautiful borders with human figures, animals, or birds placed against floral or landscape backgrounds painted in gold. Here Mughal artists are at their most inventive; there is no hint of cliché, as we find in the endlessly repeated floral motifs in margins of the later albums made for Shāh Jahān (e.g., *nos. 35, 43,* and *51*).

Among the most superb of all muraqqa' pages is a double-sided folio in the Los Angeles County Museum (*no. 5*). On the recto—Mughal books begin at what is, to us, the back, and pages are turned from left to right—is a painting attributable to 'Abd-as-Samad, or possibly to his son, Muhammad Sharīf. The original scene was extended in the early seventeenth century (this is seen at the top, left, and bottom margins), presumably when it was mounted in the album, and it was then that the illuminated borders and calligraphies were added. The verso margins, attributed to Govardhan, well illustrate the degree to which the mature Mughal style both continued and departed from Safavid (Iranian) prototypes. It is painted with a refinement of technique (fineness of brushwork, smoothness of pigments, etc.), an intense emotional subtlety and restraint, and a sense for the miniaturistic that is due to the inspiration and ideal of traditional Iranian practices. The physical perfection of the painting of the small trays of wine and fruit is exemplary (see the detail of *no. 5* verso), and reminds us of contemporary references to the feats of Safavid painters such as Mīr Sayyid 'Alī and 'Abd-as-Samad (artists who came to India with Humāyūn, as we noted), in painting elaborate compositions on grains of rice.[5] What differentiates the Govardhan figures from Safavid works is the penetration of the portraiture; for despite similarities of technique, Jahānīgr's painter is exploring the individuality of the figures, and revealing their personalities, whereas a Persian work would concentrate on accuracy of surface and on the independent expressiveness of color and line. The result would be the creation of highly refined general types.[6]

Coupled with this resurgent interest in Iran, interest in Europe continued. Europeans came more and more frequently to the Mughal court after 1600, the year of the English East India Company's Charter. The Portuguese had been established on the west coast of India since 1510, so that awareness of Europe was no novelty; indeed, European prints and paintings seem to have been present at the Mughal court since early in Akbar's reign. In the *Darbār of Jahāngīr* (*no. 14*), for example, we find a small head of the Virgin in the architectural decoration above the emperor's throne, and a Jesuit priest among the attendants. Interest in Europe went far beyond the mere amassing of exotica, however, for the physical weight and substance of figures seen in Mughal paintings, together with the humanistic concern for true portraiture and individuality—precisely those traits of Mughal work not found in Iranian tradition—show a close observation of the technical and intellectual bases of available European works. This is not to suggest that mere availability made them influential. When one examines the difference of response in India and China to the importation at the same time of identical European prints,[7] it is quite clear that the presence of new ideas is meaningless without a basis or will for comprehension. *Europeans present at the court*

Paintings commissioned by Jahāngīr are very single-minded in focus, whereas those made for Akbar—especially early in his reign—are experimental and cover wide extremes of sensibility. The differences between works by different Jahāngīrī painters are often very subtle, for the painters worked in response to their patron, and became virtual extensions of his personality, giving a unity to the overall production of the period that is only betrayed by often unconscious quirks of technique. All the major Jahāngīrī paintings in the exhibition, for example, intend a straightforward naturalism; a belief that it is the character of the subject, not any idiosyncratic personal interpretation, that gives a painting its value. Painting was a way of exploring the external world, the reality of which was momentarily unquestioned. A particularly good example of this is the drawing of *The Dying ͨInāyat Khān* (*no. 60*), which shows a man in the final stages of opium addiction. As he was about to return from the capital to his home to die, Jahāngīr requested that he come to court to take leave and then had him sit for a portrait, so amazing was his physical condition. One of the greatest and most powerful of all drawings, it is perfect evidence of Jahāngīr's use of painting as a scientific tool.

The natural history basis of much Jahāngīrī painting is known best in the works of Ustād Mansūr; for whereas Jahāngīr praised Abūͨl Hasan above all other painters, it is Mansūr whom he mentions most frequently. Possibly the greatest work by the master is the painting of *Peafowl* (*no. 47*). Like all of Mansūr's work throughout his career, it is more a colored drawing than a painting; areas of unpainted paper—which serve to place emphasis on the color—are prominent, and there is only a minimal layering of pigment. The lines are minute, and painstakingly applied, absolutely different from the swift vitality and independent rhythms typical of Iranian line. Mansūr worked with great deliberation, to both accurately describe visual traits, and to pleasingly balance the various elements of the work. The surface brilliance (of the color, for example) coupled with the acute observation, is a perfect balance of naturalistic and formal concerns—and is thereby typical of the Jahāngīrī style. *Ustād Mansūr*

PAINTING UNDER SHĀH JAHĀN

WHILE "naturalism" and "realism" seem justifiable terms to describe the focus of painting under Jahāngīr's patronage, the style was not static; in fact, its development prepared the way for the quite different achievement of artists working for Shāh Jahān.

The Albums of Shāh Jahān

The emperor's albums give us the best insight into Shāh Jahān's taste, for the vast majority of works he commissioned were intended as album pages. When these muraqqas are compared to those of Jahāngīr, differences are at once apparent. The repertoire of motifs has diminished—most of the pages are portraits of single figures—and there is not the wide variety of source, for the illustrations are almost all contemporary Mughal works. Moreover, the range of aesthetic taste shown is far more limited. While Shāh Jahān commissioned paintings of extraordinary quality, the albums as a whole lack the obvious enthusiasm for novelty and new expressive or technical effects, and the overall vitality of perception that is so distinctive of the Jahāngīrī muraqqas. The marginal designs are good evidence of this. The borders of the *Late Shāh Jahān Album*, for example, repeat the same kind of motif that we find in the Jahāngīrī albums. Both *nos. 22* and *23 verso* show nobles set against a background drawn in gold, precisely the format of the Jahāngīrī border figures by Govardhan (*no. 5* verso). Yet while the figures are finely painted and perceptive portraits (they are among the finest marginalia in the *Late Shāh Jahān Album*), they lack the immediacy and life, the flesh-and-blood, of Govardhan's figures; the different level of rapport between figures and of ability to communicate across empty space, is one evidence of this (compare the figures at the bottom of *nos. 5* verso and *23* verso). Accurate and correctly modelled, the later figures give us a sense of an achievement well rehearsed; there is not the seeming spontaneity and feeling of new accomplishment that makes Govardhan's figures both fresh and vital. Much—but certainly not all—later Mughal painting consists of such repetition of accepted attitudes.

The new importance of technique

Other paintings allow us to examine technically new and expressively innovative aspects of Shāh Jahān period works. In the extraordinary study of *An Abyssinian* (*no. 44*) by Hāshim, there is no background to divert our attention. The technique of the work, as well as the reading of personality, is faultless. This technical perfection, however, makes purely formal qualities—the painting of the sashes and dagger at the man's waist, for example—of major visual importance, and much of the impact of the work relies on such details. A shift of emphasis from the naturalness and humanity of the subject to the perfection of the rendering slowly develops in Mughal painting from about 1610; it is the basic direction behind the evolution of painting under Jahāngīr.

A Prince Visiting a Hermitage (*no. 22*) has been attributed to Govardhan, and dated about 1635–40. In comparison with his earlier work, the figures are now so carefully modelled that a certain unnaturalness results, and we see this too in works by other painters (e.g., *no. 37* the portrait of Dārā Shikōh by Chitarman, dated 1639). While this is, in part, an overly conscious employment of a too familiar technique, it gives to the figures an undeniable vividness and formal strength that is quite a new effect. In addition, each personality is now seen more as a type than as an individually distinctive being.

A portrait of the old Shāh Jahān (*no. 45*) by Hāshim, datable to circa 1655, is an important culmination of these tendencies. Although it is painted with breathtaking technical control, the result is, nonetheless, a portrait that seems overworked, meaning simply that the technique has become so consummate and of such visual impact that it has fully assumed an expressive weight of its own; it is no longer at the service of the subject. Like a temple sculpture, this is an icon of the emperor, a work that projects his perfected general image, not his individuality. From the viewpoint of Jahāngīrī naturalism, this is a stiff, formal, cold portrait. But as painting, it is a superb and expressive work.

Technique, then, continues developing and refining itself after the Jahāngīr period, but its purpose changes. It is released from the goal of naturalism—which had, after all, been achieved—and develops virtually for its own sake. And more elaborate compositions alert us to another aspect of the new style that developed under Shāh Jahān.

A page illustrating a *Battle Scene* (*no. 25*), from the *Padshāh-nāma*, is attributable to Payāg, a painter who was almost exactly contemporary to Govardhan. The scene shows Mughal troops assembled before a distant fortification, and there is a series of portrait studies as minutely detailed and carefully defined as any works in this exhibition. The physical particularities of each man are sympathetically presented, and the textures and patterns of fabrics, horse-trappings, etc., faithfully reproduced. In this way, the work develops directly out of Jahāngīr period styles. Payāg, however, completely alters our interpretation of these details, as is evident when comparing the scene to earlier manuscript pages—the *Birth of Jahāngīr* (*no. 15*) by Bishan Dās, for example, or the page by Abūʿl Hasan in the small *Gulistān* of Saʿdī (*no. 18* above). In each of the early works, the figures are discrete, separated through carefully delineated boundaries and space from neighboring forms. The *Padshāh-nāma* illustration, on the other hand, negates any sense of the men as separate beings, for the armies are massed into large units, and, as if we were looking at flocks of birds or schools of fish, we are not primarily aware of individuals; instead, the overall group is most important. This is true, as well, of the drawing of the *Battle of Samugarh* (*no. 65*). A traditional and deeply Indian attitude, this is new to seventeenth-century Mughal painting.

Payāg

These various Shāh Jahān period works, then, all in different ways retreat from Jahāngīrī attitudes towards naturalism. And they really represent the proper culmination of the Mughal style, for which the achievements of painting under Jahāngīr were indispensable. In the Payāg *Battle Scene* (*no. 25*), for example, we relate immediately to the work by identification with the personal qualities of the carefully portrayed warriors—and we could not do this without the technical and visual skills developed by painters working for Jahāngīr. But then, by forcing us to see these details as inextricably bound to a vast, boundless entity, the elements of the painting take on a metaphoric, nonrealistic, open significance similar to what we discussed above as basic to Rājput attitudes. Less acceptable to many Western scholars than the ideals behind Jahāngīrī naturalism, these later paintings, with their spatial ambiguities and emphasis on technique, have most frequently been regarded as evidence of decline. Instead, they use all the lessons learned from the experiments and attainments of earlier Mughal painters to strongly reassert ideas that—like the later Mughals themselves— were profoundly Indian.

A changed attitude to nature

On the other hand, Mughal painting *was* in decline, for Shāh Jahān was not an involved patron. Painting was not discussed in his official biographies, which were too formal to supply us with such anecdotes and personal perceptions as we find in the *Tūzuk-i-Jahāngīrī*, his father's autobiography, and which are so helpful in understanding Jahāngīrī painting. It may well be that the new direction given to the art during his reign was in response not to the patronage of the emperor, but to that of his son, the heir-apparent, Dārā Shikōh. Many of the greatest works have Dārā as subject (*nos. 32, 33, 37, and 63–65*), and the ideas which evolved would certainly have been acceptable to the prince, who hoped to reconcile Hinduism and Islam.

CATALOGUE

The measurements given for paintings are those of the illustration exclusive of borders, unless otherwise noted, and height precedes width. Additional measurements in parenthesis, given whenever available, are for the full page. In most cases, these have been supplied by the lenders. Paintings listed under "Further Major Attributions" are those which seem to the author most certainly attributable to the particular painter, while the designation "Other Attributions" includes works whose attribution, while associated with a specific artist by tradition or scholarship, seems less reliable.

18

The Allahabad Manuscripts

From at least the early 1590s, Akbar and his son, Prince Salīm, himself a father, were in open conflict. A passage in a contemporary history written by al-Badaoni recounts an event of 1591:

In this year the Emperor's constitution became a little deranged and he suffered from stomach-ache and colic, which could by no means be removed. In this unconscious state he uttered some words which arose from suspicions of his eldest son, and accused him of giving him poison.[1]

Whether such suspicions were justified is less important for us than the fact that they were even seriously entertained, and by the end of the decade, the split and mutual distrust were even more serious. In A.H. 1008 = A.D. 1599–1600, after an unsuccessful attempt to seize the imperial treasure at Agra for his own use, Salīm went to Allahabad, where he took lands and presented them to his followers as *jāgīrs* (land holdings providing revenues through taxation). This was a flagrant act of rebellion, and Salīm furthered his designs by establishing his own court and taking the title *Shāh* ("King"). Except for a brief reconciliation in 1603, the prince remained at Allahabad until November 1604, when he returned to the court at Agra to await Akbar's certain death.

During these years, and amidst the plotting, intrigue, and occasional murder necessary to sustain his independence, Salīm led a flamboyant and dissolute life. This was nothing new within his family, of course, for both his brothers, Sultān Murād and Sultān Daniyāl, were to be dead of alcohol and drugs before Salīm's accession. Nonetheless, that it was a cause of worry to Akbar, even during the Allahabad rebellion, is reported in a supplement to the *Akbar-nāma*:

Reports arrived that the practice of indulgence in wine drinking, and of the excessive use of opium, had affected the health of the Prince Royal, Sultan Salim, and had made his temper so irritable and tyrannical, that the slightest offences were visited with the severest punishments, that pardon was never thought of, and that his adherents were struck dumb with terror. His Majesty, aware that a word of counsel spoken in season, would avail more than a thousand at a distance . . . determined to go to Allahabad, to attempt the reformation of the Prince.[2]

This was a fruitful period intellectually and artis-

tically for Salīm, however. He kept in close touch with Father Jerome Xavier and other European residents, and invited a Christian mission to come to Allahabad, which, understandably, the Jesuits could not politically manage. But there were artists at the court. In 1604, when the prince's wife, Shāh Bēgam, died, she was buried in Khusrau Bāgh, a garden designed by the painter Āqā Rizā, and decorated with calligraphic inscriptions by the noted scribe Mīr ʿAbd-allāh Kātib (whose portrait is seen in *no. 1*, fol. 187r).[3] As well, several manuscripts can be attributed to the period: the *Dīwān* of Amīr Hasan Dihlavī (*no. 1*); a *Rāj Kunvār*, copied at Allahabad in 1602–3;[4] at least part of the British Library *Anwār-i-Suhailī* of 1604–10;[5] an unidentified historical manuscript;[6] and possibly the *Dvadasa Bhāva* (*no. 2*).

Obviously, Salīm did not have access to imperial painters (as he would have had earlier) after his rebellion began, so that the character of works made at Allahabad is recognizably distinct from that of Akbar's commissions. It has been stated of the Allahabad manuscripts that "an overall stylistic unity . . . is itself a distinguishing feature of the group,"[7] whereas, in fact, the manuscripts noted above make it quite clear that two very distinct stylistic orientations were accepted. One element, seen here and not in contemporary imperial manuscripts, is a reassertion of strongly Iranian taste. This shows itself in flat, two-dimensional compositions, often brilliant in color and linework, and a relative disinterest in psychological portraiture (or, better, an inability to view human figures in other than very general terms). This is certainly a result of the presence of the important and prestigious Iranian painter Āqā Rizā. As noted elsewhere, he is mentioned in the *Tūzuk-i-Jahāngīrī* as being in Salīm's employ at this time; signed works, as well as the relative quality of his painting, make it clear that he was the major source for the revitalized interest in Iranian attitudes.

The second general stylistic element in the Allahabad manuscripts is more simply an offshoot of the imperial style. In the Amīr Hasan Dihlavī manuscript (*no. 1*), for example, fol. 15 organizes figures and landscape very differently from fol. 184. The mountains are intricate, flat, hard shapes, set against a plane of gold that is purely ornamental, for it can be read as neither land nor sky. Animals and figures are placed within cells of space, and the color is fantastic. Fol. 184, however, uses softer, naturalistically convincing color and sets the warring figures in a free, continuous space. The well-modelled forms are defined by looser brushwork, and the overall sense is of greater actuality. There is a more successful differentiation of faces and personalities, and fol. 184, therefore, incorporates more purely Mughal characteristics and innovations than fol. 15, attributed here to Mīrzā Ghulām, a disciple of Āqā Rizā.

The imperial style was itself undergoing important changes between 1600 and 1605. There was no longer the immense output of major historical and poetical manuscripts that so distinguished the 1590s. In fact, the profuse production of that decade, coupled with the uniformity of the style that had evolved, guaranteed that only the occasional illustration would be notable or exciting, and this may have caused the change of direction to fewer, smaller, and finer works.[8] This is what we find established as procedure between 1600 and 1605, and continued under Jahāngīr's rule. That it is true of both imperial works and those made at Allahabad during the years of Salīm's rebellion, suggests that the prince was not necessarily the originator of the changes, as is usually proposed. However, the concern for brilliance of line, pattern, and color—which, as a supplement to inherited representational concerns, emerges after 1605 as a new and highly important element of the Mughal style—seems to be at least partly a result of Salīm's Iranian orientation during his patronage as a prince. The results are best exemplified in the *Gulistān* of Sa̔dī manuscript of circa 1615 (*nos. 16–20*).

1 (fol. 109 verso)

I

DIWAN OF AMĪR HASAN DIHLAVĪ MANUSCRIPT

Copied at Allahabad by Mīr ῾Abd-allāh Kātib, *Mushkin Qalam* ("Musky Pen")
Dated 27th Muharram, A.H. 1011 = A.D. 1602–3
31.9 × 20.3 cm.
Lent by the Walters Art Gallery, Baltimore (W. 650)
Bibliography: Ettinghausen, *Sultans*, Pl. 8 (fol. 22v)

Najm-ad-dīn Hasan Dihlavī (1257–1336), or Hasan Sijzī Dihlavī, was a contemporary of the poet Amīr Khusrau, and both men served at the court of the Sultanate Emperor ῾Alā῾-ad-dīn Khalji (r. 1296–1316), writing mystical verse of particular intensity.[9] The present volume is a collection of *ghazals* and *rubā῾īs*, but has not been translated.

On the final colophon page of the manuscript (fol. 187r), Mīr ῾Abd-allāh, the scribe, is shown at work, as-

sisted by a youth who is burnishing paper. Such illustrations, which derive ultimately from the author's portraits found in Byzantine, classical and early Islamic manuscripts, were especially prevalent in India in the late sixteenth and early seventeenth centuries.[10] Mīr ῾Abd-allāh was the father of Muhammad Sālih, the author of one of the major histories of Shāh Jahān's reign, the *Amal-i-Sālih*.[11]

The book, contained within its original lacquer covers, has fourteen illustrations. Five (fols. 15r, 32v, 84v, 127r, 157r) are attributed here to Mīrzā Ghulām and discussed elsewhere in relation to that painter's work (see page 117). The reason why the artist, evidently a protégé of Āqā Rizā, was given such a major role in the project at a time when his style was not fully developed, is not clear, however. The final page (fol. 187r) has been attributed to Nānhā by Stuart C. Welch, but the remaining pages—on two of which Salīm is shown (fols. 41r, 109v)—have eluded definite attribution.

1 (fol. 157 recto)

1 (fol. 127 recto)

دی سوی سرو لاله رخ پیغام دادم باد را

بوشه خطا ... سوی ... پسران زاد را

تا پیش او افند مکراتیک زچشم در فشان

در بار حنی بر کنم از بهر پش افشاد را

مجنون لباس عقل و ... عشق لیلی حال زد

پند باغت شد رسوای ما در زاد را

1 (fol. 15 recto)

1 (fol. 41 recto)

1 (fol. 184 verso)

1 (fol. 187 recto)

بنخواه بر همن بسر کفت همین مینخواهم که مثل تو بر هوا راه روم و این

حالت که تو داری داشته باشم سوام کار تنک او را د عاکرد و همچنان

شد عابد با همکا مک کفت که اینست و هیچ پار متا که ازان بر همن بسر نظطور

رسید که در طلب مراد حوذ درست غرمی نموده بجدی جد نمود و غیرت

2

YOUNG WOMAN WITH A GURU

From a *Dvadasa Bhāva* manuscript (p. 44)
Circa 1600–5
16.8 × 11.2 cm. (33.4 × 21.5 cm.)
Lent by Edwin Binney 3rd
Bibliography: *Binney Collection*, no. 44

Because of the general stylistic character of the manuscript, which originally held thirteen illustrations, it has been proposed as a product of the Allahabad workshops.[12] This should be accepted only tentatively, however, until there is more information about other contemporary nonimperial styles.

The text, known as the "Twelve Existences" and reportedly translated into Persian from Sanskrit, is not otherwise known. This particular episode shows in the background a figure that has been identified as Shiva, but who is more probably Karttikeya, or Skandha, a being born from the seed of Shiva without female intervention. Known as the "chaste adolescent" and always shown young and single, Karttikeya is the power of chastity and the mastery of instinct.[13] He is thus particularly important in yogic activity, and appropriate to the subject here—an ascetic with a guru.

For other pages from the manuscript, see Sotheby 11 July 1972, Lot 45; and Soustiel, Lots 3–5.

The *Akbar-nāma* of 1604

The last of Akbar's historical manuscripts is the great *Akbar-nāma* of about 1604, a book which contains early work by several painters who came to artistic maturity under Jahāngīr and Shāh Jahān (e.g., Bālchand, Daulat, Govardhan, and Mansūr). Its basic character links it more closely to earlier Akbari manuscripts than to those of the Jahāngīr period, however; for there are many illustrated folios and scenes of often violent action predominate. Action and a sense of excitement, in fact, are so important that little attention is given to the refinement of individual figures, and painters often lapse into the repetition of character types to fill crowd scenes. We see this in both the pages shown here (*nos. 3* and *4*), but it is not characteristic of such later works as the *Jahāngīr-nāma* (e.g., *no. 15*) or the *Gulistān* of Sa'dī (*nos. 16–20*).

Two volumes of the manuscript remain; one is in the British Library (Or. 12988, which contains thirty-nine illustrations), and the other is in the Library of A. Chester Beatty, Dublin (Ms. 3, with sixty-one illustrations). The scribe is recorded as Maulānā Muhammad Husain Kashmīrī, *Zarrin Qalam*, and on fol. 145 in the British Library there is an inscription noting that work was in progress on 25 January 1604. Several detached pages are known, many of which (including the two shown here) the French dealer Demotte set into borders from an Iranian lexicon of 1608, the *Farhang-i-Jahāngīrī*.[1] For dispersed pages see: Sotheby 6 December 1967, Lot 124; Sotheby 13 July 1971, Lots 127–28, 132–34; and Sotheby 7 December 1971, Lots 187A and B; Colnaghi, *Persian and Mughal Art*, no. 86 i–iii; Blochet, *Collection Jean Pozzi*, Pls. XXVII–XXVIII; *Beach Heeramaneck*, no. 201 (by Dharm Dās); Welch, "Miniature Paintings," no. 9, fig. 12; *Welch FEM*, no. 59; and Blochet, *Catalogue of an Exhibition Held at Demotte, Inc.* (New York, 1930), nos. 166–74. Further unpublished examples are in the Metropolitan Museum of Art, New York and the Freer Gallery of Art, Washington, D.C. For discussion and reproductions of the London and Dublin volumes, see Meredith-Owens, "British Museum Manuscript," p. 94; and *Beatty Library*, vol. I, pp. 4–12 and vol. III, Pls. 6–37.

3

A MAN HANGED

From an *Akbar-nāma* manuscript
Attributed here to Miskin
Circa 1604
34 × 22.5 cm.
Lent by the Walters Art Gallery, Baltimore (W. 684B)

While the episode has not been identified, the painting can be attributed to Miskin, for it is identical in style to fols. 74B and 128B of the British Library *Akbar-nāma*. The painter was one of Akbar's greatest artists and seems to have been active from the earliest stages of Akbar's patronage. The painting here, like the London pages, seems the work of an old man (and, in fact, no later works by Miskin are known), for the artist's earlier control and precision are less in evidence. Still present, however, is his distinctive use of color (e.g., the nondescriptive area of yellow behind the central figure), and the typically weightless, carefully constructed mountain forms.

Literature: Staude, "Muskine," pp. 169–82; Glynn, "An Early Mughal Landscape Painting and Related Works," *Los*

3

Angeles County Museum of Art Bulletin 20, no. 2 (1974): 64–72 where a late work by Miskin, contemporary to the *Akbar-nāma* pages, is discussed.

4

AN EXECUTION BY ELEPHANT

From an *Akbar-nāma* manuscript
Circa 1604
34 × 22.5 cm.
Lent by the Walters Art Gallery, Baltimore (W. 684A)

While we do not know the particular event depicted, this form of death was relatively common at both Mughal and Rājput courts. Sir Thomas Roe mentions it in a letter to the Lord Bishop of Canterbury, dated 1615:

Lawes they haue none written. The Kyngs judgement byndes, Who sitts and giues sentence with much patience, once weakly, both in Capitall and Criminall causes; wher sometymes he sees the execution done by his Eliphants, with two much delight in blood.[2]

The Albums of Jahāngīr

Jahāngīr was not particularly interested in the production of illustrated manuscripts of historical subjects, as his father Akbar had been, and instead tended to commission independent pictures of personalities, events, or objects that aroused his curiosity. These were usually placed in the imperial albums (muraqqas), alongside works outside the Mughal tradition that the emperor had collected; this practice makes the albums fascinating and complete documents of Jahāngīr's artistic interests and taste. On their pages we find Persian, Mughal, and Deccani paintings and drawings, European prints, at least one European painting (*no. 9*), and Mughal copies and adaptations of all these sources. Rājput and other Hindu works, however, are conspicuously absent. The arrangement was that in turning the pages of the album, two facing pages with illustrations would be succeeded by two pages of calligraphy, and all the folios were bordered by extraordinary marginal decoration, primarily in gold: figural borders for the calligraphic pages, and floral, or abstract (e.g., arabesque) motifs for the illustrations.

Two bound volumes of the albums remain, as well as a number of detached pages. The earliest of the

4

two, known as the *Muraqqaᶜ-e-Gulshan* ("Gulshan Album"), is now in the Imperial Library, Gulistan Palace, Tehran, and the few dated pages within it are between 1599 (when Jahāngīr was still a prince) and 1609.[1] The second volume, in the Staatsbibliothek, West Berlin, contains work dated between 1609 and 1618.[2] As noted elsewhere, Iran was a major dispersal point for Mughal works, and the *Berlin Album* as well came from there. It was obtained in 1860–61 by Brugsch Pasha, an Egyptologist who accompanied Freiherr von Minutoli's embassy to Iran.[3]

The general character of the marginal decoration had been established late in Akbar's reign, for it is found in several of the great imperial manuscripts of the 1590s: the *Bahāristān* of Jāmīᶜ, in the Bodleian Library; the British Library *Khamsa* of Nizāmī; or the *Dīwān* of Amīr Khusrau Dihlavī in Baltimore,

5 recto

4   THE ALBUMS OF JAHĀNGĪR

5 verso

for example.[4] The immediate source for such designs is found in Safavid imperial manuscripts, although Iranian works inevitably subordinate the figural representations to an overall decorative scheme.[5] In the Mughal margins, on the other hand, the figures become increasingly prominent, and are eventually made spatially independent of the flat gold background by being highly colored and modelled. Many of the greatest Mughal portraits are found among the Jahāngīrī album borders which include signed margins by such major artists as Basāwan, Āqā Rizā, Daulat, Bālchand, Govardhan, and Bishan Dās.[6]

Among the marginalia of the Tehran volume is a series of portraits by Daulat showing artists at work (some are reproduced here as *figs. 4* and *8–10*).[7] While artists' portraits were occasionally made for Akbar and several studies of painters appear on central panels of the *Berlin Album*,[8] this is the first coordinated series and is evidence of the importance given to the artist as a personality under Jahāngīr. Later, we find further recognition of this in the Windsor *Padshāh-nāma*, where artists are shown among figures attending darbārs.[9]

The majority of the detached album pages can be attributed to the earliest years of the seventeenth century, and it thus seems probable that they were removed at some point from the Tehran volume.

Literature: Kühnel and Goetz, *Indian Book Painting*; Wilkinson and Gray, "Indian Paintings"; Godard, "Marges"; Beach, "The Gulshan Album"; Goetz, "Early Muraqqas," *Marg*; Ettinghausen, "New Pictorial Evidence."

5

[Recto] HUNTING SCENE

Attributed to ʿAbd as-Samad and Muhammad Sharīf
Dated A.H. 999 = A.D. 1591

[Verso: Margins]

Attributed to Govardhan
Circa 1610

From an Album of Jahāngīr
41 × 23.8 cm. (full page)
Provenance: Heeramaneck Collection
Lent by the Los Angeles County Museum of Art: The Nasli and Alice Heeramaneck Collection (L.69.24.220)
Bibliography: *Beach Heeramaneck*, no. 198

ʿAbd as-Samad, an Iranian painter who returned to India with Humāyūn in 1555, was still painting in the 1590s,

for a signed page is in the British Library *Khamsa* of Nizāmī of 1595.[10] The flattened space, the absence of convincingly portraitlike characterizations, and the interest in decorative and minute detail, are all typically Iranian traits; while the dark tonalities and the densely packed mountain forms, together with the heavy outlining, point to ʿAbd as-Samad's authorship. The painting has been extended in size along its edges (this is especially clear along the bottom and left margins), presumably to make it identical in size and proportions to the Jahāngīrī album page signed by the same artist in the Freer Gallery of Art.[11] Both works have an identical arrangement of calligraphic panels and illumination at top and bottom and identical margins, and must have been facing pages in the original album. The Freer painting is dated 1588.

There are several inscriptions on the painting, most of which have been heavily rubbed. At the bottom right of the initial surface (above the swans) is a signature found in identical form as a marginal notation on a page from the "Ardeshir" *Khamsa* of Nizāmī of about 1585: *amal-i-murīd dar chahār martaba-yi-ikhlās pāy bar jā Sharīf* ("the work of the disciple in the four stages of sincerity, with foot in place, Sharīf").[12] This evidently attributes the painting to Muhammad Sharīf, the son of ʿAbd as-Samad, and a confidant of Prince Salīm.[13] From what little we know of Sharīf's work as a painter, however,[14] it seems most unlikely that he is fully responsible for the painting seen here.

The verso margins contain some of the most sensitive of Mughal portraits and can be attributed to Govardhan on the basis of signed border figures dated 1609 in the Berlin muraqqaʿ.[15] Govardhan's work is discussed elsewhere.

6

[Recto] CALLIGRAPHY

Signed by Mīr ʿAlī al-Sultānī
Iranian, dated 1537

[Recto: Margins]

Attributed to Āqā Rizā
Circa 1604

[Verso] A BUFFALO FIGHTING A LIONESS

Attributed here to Farrukh
Circa 1595–1600

From an Album of Jahāngīr
43 × 26.5 cm. (full page)
Lent by The Nelson Gallery–Atkins Museum, Kansas City: Nelson Fund (48.12/2)

5 verso (detail)

6 verso

7 verso

7 recto

Bibliography: *Welch AMI*, no. 27; Nelson Gallery–Atkins Museum, *Handbook*, 2d ed. (Kansas City, 1973), vol. 2, p. 145; Los Angeles County Museum, *The Art of Greater India* (exhibition catalogue), 1959, no. 99

The majority of the calligraphies on the Jahāngīrī muraqqaᶜ pages are by Mīr ᶜAlī al-Sultānī, a sixteenth-century Iranian calligrapher, although border illuminations—and in this case the panel of birds above—were added by Mughal artists.

Āqā Riżā, whose style is discussed separately, is best known for his work in the British Library *Anwār-i-Suhailī* manuscript of 1604–10;[16] the margins here—first attributed to the artist by Stuart C. Welch—are in identical style.

There is a series of *nim qalam* (lightly colored) drawings of animals in the albums, at least several of which are by one artist.[17] That he can be identified as Farrukh is suggested by a comparison with fol. 123 of the *Khamsa* of Nizāmī of 1595.[18] Dr. Anand Krishna believes Farrukh to be the same man as the painter Farrukh Chela.[19]

Color plate facing text page 24.

7

[*Recto*] A YOUNG PRINCE WITH AN OLD MAN AND AN ATTENDANT

Circa 1600

[*Verso*] CALLIGRAPHY

Signed by Mīr ᶜAlī
Iranian, circa 1540

[*Verso: Margins*]

Circa 1605

From an Album of Jahāngīr
42.2 × 26.7 cm. (full page)
Lent by The Nelson Gallery–Atkins Museum, Kansas City: Nelson Fund (48.12/1)

The recto illustration is further evidence of the importance of Iranian taste in Jahāngīr's studio, for the elements of the subject (a youth, an old man, a book of verse, a flowering tree) are found constantly in Iran as evocations of artistic sensibility and the brevity of life. In addition, the figures are clearly general types and not actual observed portraits. Such scenes were most popular before the emperor's accession to the throne, when the painter Āqā Riżā's influence was strongest. In style, the page seems close to paintings signed by Jaganāth in the *Gulshan Album*, and to a detached muraqqaᶜ leaf in the Freer Gallery of Art.[20]

8

WOMAN NURSING A CHILD

From an Album of Jahāngīr
Circa 1590
40 × 24.8 cm. (full page)
Provenance: Kevorkian Collection
Lent by Edwin Binney 3rd
Bibliography: *Binney Collection*, no. 51; *Welch FEM*, no. 58 (color)

Scenes showing women nursing, playing musical instruments, conversing, or simply lost in thought, are found frequently in the muraqqas. All seem to be inspired by European sources, although these have yet to be identified. One such group of works was executed by three painters working in close relationship to each other: Kesu Dās, Basāwan, and Manōhar; their works of this type are datable to circa 1590 on the basis of known dated paintings.[21] It is often extremely difficult to attribute unsigned paintings in this idiom by means of visual characteristics alone. The present example, for instance, has traits of both Manōhar (e.g., the lack of background depth) and Basāwan (e.g., the softness of the modelling of the clothing). It has been attributed to the latter artist by Stuart C. Welch.

9

MADONNA AND CHILD WITH ANGELS

From an Album of Jahāngīr
Circa 1595–1600
42 × 26.5 cm. (full page)
Provenance: Helen Temple Cooke Collection
Lent by the Fogg Art Museum, Harvard University: Gift—John Goelet (1958.233)

Any European able to paint or draw was of great interest to Jahāngīr. Sir Thomas Roe, whom we have mentioned as the official ambassador of James I of England, was at the Mughal court between 1615 and 1618, and wrote in his diaries as follows:

At night I went to the *Durbarr* to visitt the king. So soone as I came in hee sent Asaph chan to mee: that hee heard I had in my house an excellent Paynter, and desiered hee might see some of his works. I replyed, according to truth, that ther was none but a young man, a Merchant, that for his exercise did with a pen draw some figures, but very meanly, far from the Arte of paynting. The king replyed that I should not feare that hee would take any man from mee by forse: that hee would neither doe mee Injurie nor suffer any other; and prayed that hee might see that man and his woorke, whatsoeuer it was.[22]

Roe's reference is to one Robert Hewes (or Hughes). A second British painter, named Hatfield, actually painted a

9

10 recto

10 verso

portrait of the emperor, who granted him a sitting.[23]

Jahāngīr's interest in European works preceded his accession. In 1595, the third Jesuit Embassy had also included a painter, and a contemporary chronicler noted of Prince Salīm that:

As the Fathers had brought with them a Portuguese painter, the Prince straightaway ordered him to make a copy of the picture of Our Lady which they had brought from Goa.[24]

The present painting seems to be such a European copy, for there is nothing Mughal about the page, other than the margins. Nonetheless, the modelling and coloring, the effects of light on cloth, and the combination of architectural and landscape setting, would have been of sufficient novelty and interest to the Mughals to offset the obvious deficiencies in quality. The work is a loose prototype for the composition and formal concerns seen in *no. 8*.

10

[*Recto*] JOSEPH TELLING HIS DREAM TO HIS FATHER

Attributed to Kesu Dās
Circa 1590

[*Verso*] CALLIGRAPHY

Signed by Mīr ᶜAlī
Iranian, circa 1540

[*Verso: Margins*]

Circa 1602

From an Album of Jahāngīr
42.2 × 26.5 cm. (full page)
Provenance: Heeramaneck Collection
Lent by the St. Louis Art Museum: Gift of J. Lionburger Davis (37–403 : 52)
Bibliography: Beach, "European Source," fig. 5; Beach, "Kesu Das," fig. 10

Several Mughal copies and adaptations of an engraving by Georg Pencz, *Joseph Telling His Dream to His Father*, dated 1544 (*no. 10A*), are known.[25] The present work is the later of two versions made by Kesu Dās, the earlier being in the A. Chester Beatty Library, Dublin;[26] it may be that this is an illustration made specifically for Salīm, who is known to have requested copies of paintings owned by his father. Here Kesu retained the original arrangement of the figures, although the rather intricate modelling of the clothing in the print is simplified (note, in particular, the figure to the left). Moreover, the background has been opened up to include the favorite Mughal device of distant mountains. The birds at the top were

IOA

added to lengthen the proportions of the illustration so that it would match the facing page.

The verso marginal figures can be attributed to an artist who worked for Jahāngīr at Allahabad and was responsible for fol. 41 of the Walters Art Gallery *Dīwān* of Amīr Hasan Dihlavī of 1602 (*no. 1*).

IOA

JOSEPH TELLING HIS DREAM TO HIS FATHER

By Georg Pencz
German, dated 1544
Engraving
10.9 × 7.3 cm.
Lent by the Museum of Fine Arts, Boston: Harvey D. Parker Collection (P2354)

II

12

58 THE ALBUMS OF JAHĀNGĪR

11

CALLIGRAPHY

Signed by Mīr ʿAlī
Iranian, circa 1540

[*Margins*]

Circa 1605

From an Album of Jahāngīr
42 × 26.5 cm. (full page)
Provenance: Helen Temple Cooke Collection
Lent by the Fogg Art Museum, Harvard University:
Gift—John Goelet (1958.187)

The figures along the right border, including a crucifixion, were adapted from unidentified European sources.

12

CALLIGRAPHY

Signed by Mīr ʿAlī
Iranian, circa 1540

[*Margins*]

Circa 1602

From an Album of Jahāngīr
42 × 26.8 cm. (full page)
Provenance: Helen Temple Cooke Collection
Lent by the Museum of Fine Arts, Springfield: Gift of Mrs. Roselle L. Shields (59 Ms. 46)
Bibliography: Walter B. Denny, *The Image and the Word: Islamic Painting and Calligraphy* (Springfield, Mass., 1976), no. 19

The style of the marginal figures is in the tradition of the Iranian artist Āqā Rizā, but can be tentatively attributed to the painter identified as Ghulām, who is discussed elsewhere in this catalogue.

Additional Jahāngīr Album Pages

A Youth on Horseback Giving Wine to a Youth in a Treehouse

Freer Gallery of Art, Washington, D.C. (54.116)

The painting is in the style of *no. 7* recto, and may be by the same artist. The marginal figures on the reverse show men preparing books.

A Chained Elephant

Freer Gallery of Art, Washington, D.C. (56.12)

The central *nim qalam* drawing, which relates closely to *no. 6* verso, is surrounded by extremely beautiful marginal designs showing fantastic animals, close in style to Iranian prototypes. The border figures on the reverse are adaptations from European prints, including Georg Pencz' *Geometry*, from his series of the *Seven Liberal Arts* (see Beach, "The Gulshan Album," no. 7a).

Mongol Chief and Attendants

Freer Gallery of Art, Washington, D.C. (52.2)

The border figures on the reverse are also drawn from European sources.

Jamshīd Writing on the Rock

Inscribed to ʿAbd as-Samad
Dated 1588
Freer Gallery of Art, Washington, D.C. (63.4)

Because of size, and the character of the inscriptions and designs bordering the illustration, this page almost certainly faced *no. 5* recto. The margins, on the reverse, show figures involved with astrological calculations.

Unhappy Lady

Museum of Fine Arts, Boston (14.688)
Bibliography: *Coomaraswamy Boston*, no. LXXXII, Pl. XXXIX

Marginalia

Musée Guimet, Paris
Bibliography: *Stchoukine Louvre*, no. 44, Pl. V; Kühnel and Goetz, *Indian Book Painting*, opposite p. 46; Marteau and Vever, *Miniatures Persanes*, vol. II, no. 237, Pl. CLXVII; Welch, *Indian Drawings*, no. 13

Prince Reading

Present location unknown
Bibliography: Kühnel and Goetz, *Indian Book Painting*, opposite p. 46; Marteau and Vever, *Miniatures Persanes*, vol. II, no. 236, Pl. CLXVII

Throne Scene

Attributed to Farrukh Beg
Collection of Otto Sohn-Rethel, Düsseldorf
Bibliography: Kühnel, "Miniaturen Otto Sohn-Rethel," figs. 2–4; Skelton, "Farrokh," fig. 12

The Kühnel article also reproduces sections of the reverse margins.

Marginalia

Collection of Otto Sohn-Rethel, Düsseldorf
Bibliography: Kühnel, "Miniaturen Otto Sohn-Rethel," fig. 1

13

The *Jahāngīr-nāma*

The *Tūzuk-i-Jahāngīrī*, or *Jahāngīr-nāma*, was written personally by the emperor, and covers the years from his accession to the nineteenth year of his reign (1605–24); the last two years, however, were transcribed by Muᶜtamad Khān, for, from 1622 on, Jahāngīr was too weak and addled with drink to continue unaided.

A full imperial illustrated manuscript of the *Jahāngīr-nāma* has not survived, although several known paintings (listed below) were probably intended for inclusion in it. The emperor made reference to the work in his memoirs. In the year 1612, for example, he wrote

Muqarrab Khān . . . went with diligence to Goa, and remaining there for some time, took at the price the Franks asked for them the rareties he met with at that port. . . . When he returned . . . he produced before me one by one the things and rareties he had brought. . . . I both described them and ordered that painters should draw them in the Jahāngīr-nāma, so that the amazement that arose from hearing of them might be increased.[1]

The passage is important for several reasons. It indicates not only that work on the book had begun by at least the seventh year of the reign, but also that the volume may have been very different in character from the *Akbar-nāma*. Unlike his father, Jahāngīr did not wish to record simply the great historical events; rather, his memoirs—illustrations no less than text—presented his interests as well as his actions. It was a very personal work, and thus akin in this respect, to an earlier work—Bābur's autobiography, the *Bābur-nāma*. The illustrated version may therefore have had the character of an album of pictures, rather than that of a highly coordinated manuscript. If this is the case, then one of the intended paintings might be *The Death of ᶜInāyat Khān*, an illustration in the Bodleian Library of an event which Jahāngīr described in detail, and for which an extremely powerful preparatory drawing is included here (see *no. 60*). Another intended painting might be the portrait of a *Turkey* by Mansūr, in the Victoria and Albert Museum, for such a bird was among the "rareties" brought from Goa by Muqarrab Khān. A definite *Jahāngīr-nāma* page showing the arrival of the bird at court is in the Rampur State Library.

Two further comments should be made about the *Jahāngīr-nāma* paintings. Several bear inscriptions giving painters' names. Usually added at a later date, these are generally questionable; a few are reattributed in the list below. Furthermore, many of the illustrations have been considerably retouched, and this both lowers the quality which we perceive and confuses our recognition of authenticity.

13

JAHĀNGĪR ENTERTAINING SHEIKHS

From a *Jahāngīr-nāma* manuscript
Inscribed: *amal-i-Abūᶜl Hasan* ("work of Abūᶜl Hasan")
Circa 1615–20
32.6 × 19.4 cm. (55.2 × 34.9 cm.)
Provenance: A. C. Ardeshir Collection
Lent by Edwin Binney 3rd
Bibliography: *Binney Collection*, no. 52

The event represented is uncertain, although Edwin Binney 3rd has suggested that the setting is the Shalimar Gardens in Kashmir.

Since portions of the illustration have been repainted (note the face of the emperor), and the surface is well worn, a judgment of the validity of the attribution is difficult. A peculiarity of the work is the prominence of half-shadowed figures, especially at the bottom, an experimental motif known in other Abūᶜl Hasan paintings (e.g., *no. 27*). The use of the name Abūᶜl Hasan without the title of *Nādir-al-Zamān* would suggest a date before at least 1618, after which the honorific was constantly used. On the other hand, the very specific chiaroscuro device of showing a single source of illumination for the shadowed figures (in this case the candlestick) is otherwise known—and very popular—only in the 1630s and later (see *no. 52*).

On the reverse (not exhibited) is a panel of calligraphy dated A.H. 1016 = A.D. 1607–8 and signed by ᶜImād al-Husainī.

14

DARBĀR OF JAHĀNGĪR

From a *Jahāngīr-nāma* manuscript
Inscribed: *amal-i-kamtarīn khānazādān* ("done by the most humble of the slave-born"), and attributed here to Manōhar
Circa 1620
34.5 × 19.5 cm.
Provenance: Goloubev Collection
Lent by the Museum of Fine Arts, Boston: Francis Bartlett Donation of 1912 and Picture Fund (14.654)
Bibliography: Sarre and Martin, *München Ausstellung*, Pl. 38; Martin, *Miniature Paintings*, Pl. 216; Marteau and Vever, *Miniatures Persanes*, vol. II, Pl. 234 (where a key to an identifi-

14

cation of the figures is given); Schulz, *Miniaturmalerei*, Pl. 193; Gluck and Diez, *Kunst*, p. 518; *Coomaraswamy Boston*, no. LXXIV, Pl. XXXIV; *Coomaraswamy Goloubev*, no. 122; *Welch AMI*, no. 30; *Welch IMP*, Pl. 17 (color)

A darbār was an official audience, a time when the nobility gathered in the imperial presence to witness the enactment of court business. William Hawkins, an English sea captain who gained access to Jahāngīr's private quarters, left a description of one of these events:

Then at three of the clocke, all the nobles in generall (that be in Agra and are well) resort unto the court, the king comming forth in open audience, sitting in his seat royall, and every man standing in his degree before him, his chiefest sort of the nobles standing within a red rayle, and the rest without. . . . In the middest of the place, right before the King, standeth one of his sheriffes together with his master hangman . . . and others with all sorts of whips being there, readie to do what the King commandeth. . . . The King heareth all causes in this place, and stayeth some two hours every day. . . . Then departeth towards his private place of prayer.²

Known paintings of darbārs commemorate specific events. That this gathering can be dated 1619 can be established by the presence and age of the young prince to Jahāngīr's left. An inscription tells us that he is Shāh Shujāᶜ, second son of Prince Khurram (Shāh Jahān), next to whom he stands. Shujāᶜ, whom we also see as a child in *no. 28*, was born in 1616, but it was not until 1619 that he came with the imperial party to Agra, the setting of this scene. Between April and October of that year, Jahāngīr remained at the capital together with Khurram, whose mother had just died. Both men then proceeded to Lahore, and Khurram almost immediately departed for the Deccan. He never again saw his father.

The scene is a carefully constructed composition, built by tracing and arranging pre-existing portraits of the various nobles to be included; this would account both for discrepancies in size of the individual figures and the rather unnatural spatial character. Of particular interest is the figure of the Jesuit priest at the lower left. Inscribed simply "padre," it is probably Father Corsi, the major priest in attendance at the court at this time. In addition, there is a small head of the Virgin Mary painted on the wall above Jahāngīr's throne. European Christian and secular themes were widely used as decoration in both public and private areas of Mughal palaces.³

The inscription states that the painter (it had previously, but wrongly, been thought that the reference was to "painters") was a *khānazādān*, or "house-born" artist, one born into imperial service. While he is not explicitly named, the work can be attributed to Manōhar and is elsewhere discussed with that artist's work.

15

THE BIRTH OF JAHĀNGĪR

From a *Jahāngīr-nāma* manuscript
Attributed to Bishan Dās
Circa 1620
26.4 × 16.4 cm.
Provenance: Goloubev Collection
Lent by the Museum of Fine Arts, Boston: Francis Bartlett Donation of 1912 and Picture Fund (14.657)
Bibliography: *Coomaraswamy Boston*, no. III, Pls. III–IV; *Coomaraswamy Goloubev*, no. 113, Pl. 68; *Welch AMI*, no. 26; *Welch IMP*, Pl. 16

"The unique pearl of the Caliphate emerged from the shell of the womb, and arrived at the shore of existence," wrote Abūᶜl Fazl of the birth of Sultān Salīm, who would become Jahāngīr. "The star of auspiciousness rose from the horizon of fortune."⁴ It was an event of particular importance, because, except for the birth and quick death of twin boys in 1564, Akbar was childless. Various remedies were attempted, of course. Finally, hearing of the saintly Sheikh Salīm Chishtī, Akbar sent his wife to Fathepur, just outside Agra, to pass the term of a new pregnancy under the holy man's protection. The birth on 30 August 1569 was successful, and the infant was named Salīm, in the Sheikh's honor.

In this painting, the child is shown aureoled, and this seems a certain identification of the episode. Such a halo would have been inappropriate, during Jahāngīr's lifetime, for one of his own sons. Here it is a retrospective comment on the child's future imperial status. The empress, in the pavilion, was the Rājput Maryam-uz-Zamanī, daughter of Bhārmal, the Hindu rājā of Amber (Jaipur); this accounts for her dark color. The elder woman enthroned at her side is probably Hamīda Bānū Bēgam, who bore Akbar in 1542, at the age of fourteen. The emperor himself, by custom, was forbidden to see his son for several days. Below, well outside the purdah quarters where the harem was secluded, astrologers are casting the child's horoscope.

The painting has been attributed to Bishan Dās and is further discussed with that painter's work.

Additional Probable *Jahāngīr-nāma* Pages

Celebrations at the Accession of Jahāngīr

Academy of Sciences, Leningrad
Bibliography: Ivanova et al., *Albom Indiyskikh*, Pls. 7 and 32 (both in color)

This was referred to by Jahāngīr as having been completed in 1618 by Abūᶜl Hasan, by whom it is signed, and placed as the frontispiece of the *Jahāngīr-nāma* (*Tūzuk*, vol. II, p. 20).

Jahāngīr Watching a Snake and Spider Fight
> Rampur State Library
> Bibliography: *Brown*, Pl. XIX

The event is described in *Tūzuk*, vol. I, p. 117, and occurred in 1607–8.

Jahāngīr Weighs Prince Khurram
> British Library
> Bibliography: Barrett and Gray, *Painting*, p. 103; *Welch IMP*, Pl. 18 (color)

This may illustrate the ceremony in 1607–8, described in *Tūzuk*, vol. I, p. 115.

Jahāngīr Punishes Prince Khusrau
> Rampur State Library
> Bibliography: *Brown*, pp. 137–38, Pl. XLIX

Percy Brown identified the scene as the capture of Kaukab, a noble youth who ran off with a *sannyāsī*. Instead, it quite clearly shows an episode in Jahāngīr's contest with his eldest son, Khusrau, and exactly illustrates the following passage:

On Thursday, Muharram 3rd, 1015 = 1605–06, in Mirza Kamran's garden, they brought Khusrau before me with his hands tied and chains on his legs. . . . They made Husain Beg stand on his right hand and ʿAbdu-r Rahim on his left. Khusrau stood weeping and trembling between them. . . . (I) handed over Khusrau in chains, and ordered these two villains to be put in the skins of an ox and an ass. . . . (*Tūzuk*, vol. I, pp. 68–69.)

Jahāngīr in the Shrine at Ajmer
> Staatliche Museen, Berlin
> Bibliography: Anand and Goetz, *Miniaturen*, Pl. 6 (color)

The painting is attributed here to Daulat and discussed further with that artist's work.

Jahāngīr Celebrates the Festival of *Āb-pāshī*
> Rampur State Library
> Bibliography: *Brown*, frontispiece (color)

The emperor mentions the festival twice in his memoirs (*Tūzuk*, vol. I, pp. 265 and 281, dated 1614 and 1615). The painting is inscribed *amal-i-Govardhan* ("work of Govardhan"), but is here attributed instead to Anant, whose dark tonalities, odd shifts of scale, and distinctive figure types with unnaturally angular gestures can be found in the British Library *Anwār-i-Suhailī* manuscript (see Wilkinson, *Lights*, Pl. XIV).

Jahāngīr Visiting the Shrine at Ajmer
> Rampur State Library
> Bibliography: *Brown*, Pl. XX

Jahāngīr Dispensing Food at Ajmer
> Prince of Wales Museum, Bombay
> Bibliography: Bussagli and Sivaramamurti, *5000 Years*, fig. 368 (color)

This represents the episode described in *Tūzuk*, vol. I, p. 256.

Jahāngīr Giving Books to Sheikhs
> Freer Gallery of Art, Washington, D.C.
> Bibliography: Ettinghausen, "Emperor," fig. 10

Jahāngīr Shoots a Lioness
> Indian Museum, Calcutta
> Bibliography: *Brown*, Pl. XLII (color); Das, "Mughal Royal Hunt," pp. 1–5

As identified by Aśok Das, this illustrates an occurrence during the visit of Karan Singh of Mewar in 1615 (*Tūzuk*, vol. I, p. 287). The scene is attributed here to Nānhā and is discussed with that painter's work.

Jahāngīr Converses with Gosain Jadrūp
> Musée Guimet, Paris
> Bibliography: *Stchoukine Louvre*, Pl. VII; Coomaraswamy, "Portrait," pp. 389–91

Between 1616 and 1620, Jahāngīr had a number of interviews with this noted *sannyāsī*. See *Tūzuk*, vol. I, p. 355; vol. II, pp. 49, 52, and 104–5.

Jahāngīr Visiting Akbar's Tomb
> A. Chester Beatty Library, Dublin
> Bibliography: Wilkinson, *Mughal Painting*, Pl. 5 (color)

See also *Tūzuk*, vol. II, p. 101 (dated 1619–20).

Jahāngīr in Darbār
> Keir Collection
> Bibliography: *Robinson ed., Keir*, V.79

The painting has been considerably reworked, so that a judgment of the inscription naming Manōhar as author of any original portions is difficult.

Jahāngīr in Darbār
> Academy of Sciences, Leningrad
> Bibliography: Grek, *Indiyskikh Miniatyur*, Pl. 12 (color)

Jahāngīr at the *Jharoka* Window
> Private Collection
> Bibliography: Sotheby 23 March 1973, Lot 6 (color)

There is an inscription giving a credible attribution to *Nādir-al-Zamān*.

Procession
> Rampur State Library
> Bibliography: *Brown*, Pl. XXXI (color)

The inscription naming Manōhar should be disregarded. The work is attributed here to Bishan Dās and is further discussed with that artist's work.

Additional pages are reportedly in the Rampur State Library and the Imperial Library, Tehran.

15

The *Gulistān* of Saʿdī

One of Jahāngīr's greatest books has come down to us only in severely mutilated form. At some point, probably in the early nineteenth century, illustrations were cut from an imperial copy of the *Gulistān* ("Rose Garden") of the thirteenth-century mystic poet Saʿdī, and mounted on album pages. The presentations are so literal and exact in detail, however, that most of the scenes can still be easily identified; they come from Chapter I, "The Manners of Kings." The illustrations vary somewhat in style and proportion, but their single source seems unquestionable.

The *Gulistān* is a series of stories, often earthy and sometimes ribald, that are meant to be immediately entertaining, but also to provide rules of conduct, and even initiation into mystic attitudes.[1] A simple example would be the illustration to Chapter I, Story 13, shown in *no. 18* below, in which a naked dervish attracts the attention of a king. The ruler offers him a bag of coins, telling him to spread his skirt that he might catch the gold as it falls from the balcony. The dervish protests that his rag covering is too small, whereupon the king offers him a robe as well—the incident we see here. The dervish, however, soon spends the gift and returns for more, whereupon the king protests angrily at the holy man's heedless squandering of the boon. And upon this slender frame, which carefully delineates the character of kings and dervishes, is built a discussion of the unimportance of property to those who have renounced the world (e.g., dervishes), and the unworthiness of anger (in kings and gift-givers).

The manuscript can be immediately compared to two other Saʿdī books: a *Kulliyāt*, of circa 1605, formerly in the collection of the Marquess of Bute; and a *Būstān*, dated 1605, once in the possession of Baron Maurice de Rothschild.[2] Both are now owned privately in Iran. While the illustrations of the group shown here are smaller in size and later in date, they are finer in quality than the 1605 works. Many pages in each, moreover, were executed by the same artists. Two later Saʿdī manuscripts, a *Gulistān* and a *Būstān*, both dated 1629,[3] may have been modelled on the present examples, for the unusual format using small, horizontal illustrations, is similar.

The pages in the Walters Art Gallery (*nos. 16–18*) come from an important album formed by at least 1830,[4] whereas the other pages are mounted on album leaves of different sizes. One further illustration was also formerly in the Rothschild Collection.[5]

16

[*Above*] THE PADSHĀH AND THE SLAVE GIRL

6.2 × 12.6 cm.

[*Below*] THE SALVATION OF ONE BROTHER

Inscribed: "done by the slave of the court, Daulat"
6.6 × 12.4 cm.

From a *Gulistān* of Saʿdī manuscript
Circa 1610–15
29.5 × 19 cm. (full page)
Lent by the Walters Art Gallery, Baltimore (W. 668, fol. 36v)
Bibliography: Gray et al., *R.A. Arts of India and Pakistan*, no. 695, Pl. 133

The episode shown at the top is from Chapter 1, Story 40, and concerns a Chinese slave girl who refuses the advances of a king, and is then given to an extraordinarily ugly negro slave as punishment. The other scene (Chapter 1, Story 35) relates the tale of two brothers, only one of whom can be saved from drowning. The choice is made to help the man whose past good deeds are known to a passenger of the boat.

The inscription, which has also been read "by a master 'Friend of the Court,'" appears just above the waterline, a hidden placement which, like the verbal formula used, is typical of Daulat. The painter's style, of which this is a superb example, is discussed separately.

17

[*Above*] A YOUTH'S ECSTATIC TRANCE

6.3 × 12.2 cm.

[*Middle*] THE KING AND THE TROOPER

6.3 × 12.2 cm.

[*Below*] SAʿDĪ IN THE GARDEN

Attributed here to Daulat
4.7 × 12.2 cm.

From a *Gulistān* of Saʿdī manuscript
Circa 1610–15
29.5 × 19 cm. (full page)
Lent by the Walters Art Gallery, Baltimore (W. 668, fol. 48v)
Bibliography: Ettinghausen, *Sultans*, Pl. 10

16

17

The middle episode is related in Chapter 1, Story 9, and tells of a trooper who comes to the bed of a dying king to announce the defeat of his enemies. Rather than rejoicing, the king chooses to think of the ignorance and folly of existence. The lower scene, with its specific reference to the tools of book making, and to a garden, must illustrate one of the introductory passages, "The Cause for Composing the *Gulistān*."

The painting at the top seems to be by an artist who was responsible for at least two paintings in both the Bute *Kulliyāt* and the Rothschild *Būstan* of 1605.[6] These are works that are compositionally more complex but which show the same immaculate surface and penchant for "moon-faced," rather characterless youths.

18

[*Above*] A PRINCE, A YOUTH, AND A SAGE

Attributed here to Abūʿl Hasan
6.3 × 12.4 cm.

[*Below*] THE KING AND THE DERVISH

6.6 × 12.4 cm.

From a *Gulistān* of Saʿdī manuscript
Circa 1610–15
29.5 × 19 cm. (full page)
Lent by the Walters Art Gallery, Baltimore (W. 668, fol. 49)

The upper painting, the subject of which has not yet been identified,[7] is an early and superb work by Abūʿl Hasan; it can be best compared to his page in the 1604–10 *Anwār-i-Suhailī* manuscript and to the *Squirrels in a Plane Tree* of about 1610–15.[8] The quiet sympathy and depth with which he explores personalities, and his avoidance of purely surface effects, are typical. For example, the artist of the lower illustration (the story has been discussed on p. 66), makes the patterns of the robes of the king and his attendants, and of the architectural decoration, clear, strong, and flat. It is a concern for surface pattern making that also determines the placement of the flowering tree in the center. Abūʿl Hasan, however, avoids such effects, and undermines the potential visual brilliance of such details as the striped robe at the lower right of his painting, through modelling, and an actual toning down of color. For that artist, formal concerns, however superbly handled, never take precedence over naturalism.

Color plate facing text page 32.

19

19

[*Above*] THE UNDOING OF THE ILL-NATURED *WAZĪR*

Attributed to Manōhar
6.3 × 8.9 cm.

[*Below*] A FRAUDULENT PILGRIM REJECTED FROM COURT

6.2 × 8.8 cm.

From a *Gulistān* of Saʿdī manuscript
Circa 1610–15
Lent Anonymously
Bibliography: *Welch AMI*, no. 25 A and B; Welch, "Miniature Paintings," no. 15, fig. 18 A and B

The first illustration shows a prisoner saved from punishment by the more benign of the king's two *wazīrs*

20

19 (detail)

27 (detail)

(Chapter 1, Story 1), and the second tells of an imposter sent from the ruler's presence (Chapter 1, Story 32). Both allow discussions on the occasional propriety of falsehood.

The scene placed above is attributable to Manōhar, a painter whose style came to maturity in the later Akbar period and whose interests did not include the intense personal interactions and character studies found on other folios of this book. In this regard, a comparison of the figure of the elderly standing man seen here, presumably Saʿdī himself, with the figure of the poet in *no. 17* [below], by Daulat, or *no. 27*, by Abūʾl Hasan, is informative. The guard at the left seems to be a portrait of a leading courtier, Mahābat Khān.[9]

It has been suggested that the painting found below is by Mīrzā Ghulām,[10] an artist discussed elsewhere. It is an attribution not accepted here.

20

A PRISONER CHASTISED

From a *Gulistān* of Saʿdī manuscript
Circa 1610–15
7.6 × 12.5 cm. (35.8 × 28.1 cm.)
Lent by Edwin Binney 3rd
Bibliography: Colnaghi, *Persian and Mughal Art*, no. 89ii

The subject, which has not been definitely identified, would seem to be similar to that in *no. 19* [above].

The Albums of Shāh Jahān

The majority of the paintings made for Jahāngīr and Shāh Jahān were placed in albums (*muraqqas*). Increasing Mughal interest in the natural world, in flowers, portraits, and historical events, meant both that painting no longer served merely to illustrate traditional texts, and that the format of a manuscript was no longer uniquely appropriate. This does not imply that text and calligraphy became less important, however. So great was the visual epicureanism of the time that writing too was elaborately mounted for visual, rather than primarily narrative, appreciation (e.g., *nos. 5* verso, *23* recto).

The earliest reference to a Mughal album is given in the *Āʿīn-i-Akbarī*, the official account of Akbar's rule, where it is stated that:

His Majesty himself sat for his likeness, and also ordered to have the likenesses taken of all the grandees of the realm. An immense album was thus formed.[1]

There is no evidence that this album remains intact, although possible dispersed pages are known in abundance.[2] The superb muraqqas made for Jahāngīr were begun before his accession, and are elsewhere discussed. It was customary, in fact, for the princes to commission such compilations (usually including earlier, as well as contemporary, works); early seventeenth-century albums assembled for both Khurram and Dārā Shikōh survive (see below).

Among the most prevalent of the Mughal paintings found in European and American collections are pages thought to come from the albums of Shāh Jahān, for the majority of the illustrations are of men important to that emperor's rule, and the marginal designs accord perfectly in type with contemporary architectural decoration. Moreover, there are frontispiece pages associated with the albums (e.g., *no. 21*), some of which bear inscriptions to the emperor.

It is the margins, really, that define the Shāh Jahān album pages. Most are floral (e.g., *no. 35*), or show very formal abstract designs (e.g., *no. 23* recto), and forms tend to be outlined with a heavy, even line of gold that is visually similar to the effect of jewels inlaid into jade, for example.[3] This is very different from the lively naturalism of Jahāngīrī muraqqaᶜ folios (e.g., *nos. 5–12*). If we compare the placement of the animals and birds in *nos. 9* and *23* recto, we find that the Shāh Jahān margins arrange the animals according to an abstract, predetermined system, whereas the Jahāngīrī borders allow them a seemingly random placement that stresses their unpredictability and animation.

There are three major assemblages of album paintings associated with Shāh Jahān that remain intact: the *Minto*, *Wantage*, and *Kevorkian Albums*. The first of these contains a brilliant series of paintings with signatures or marginal attributions to virtually all the major painters of the period under consideration here. And that these inscriptions are reliable is confirmed by comparisons with other works assignable to each painter. Pages from the *Minto Album* are essential to the check lists of authentic works provided in this catalogue.

The *Wantage* and *Kevorkian Albums*, on the other hand, each contain a majority of late paintings; works which, on grounds of style, seem to have been made roughly about 1800, for similar heavily shaded forms, dull color, and rather spongy surfaces—not seventeenth-century characteristics—are found in works made in Delhi (often for British patronage) at the time.[4]

The *Minto Album* is named for the Earl of Minto, who served as Governor General of India between 1807 and 1813 when this album may have been acquired. The *Kevorkian* and *Wantage Albums* appeared in Britain at later dates, and there is no information as to their routes of exit from India. Given the date when the *Minto Album* became available for purchase (presumably), and the fact that so much copying of imperial Mughal work was done around 1800, it seems likely that various albums and manuscripts were removed from the palace libraries during the chaos of declining imperial control. Some works may have been sold directly; others were broken up. The core of such volumes as the *Kevorkian* and *Wantage Albums* was augmented by careful, then modern, copies of original pages and eventually sold as complete imperial albums. While the dispersal of the Mughal imperial collections in the early nineteenth century certainly brought many Indian works to England and Europe, perhaps an even more important route was through Tehran. Iran served as repository for much of the loot wrested from India by various predators, beginning with Nādir Shāh in 1739; and it was from Iran that many of the greatest Mughal works were acquired for European collections.[5]

In addition to these three albums, there is a fourth,

now dispersed: the so-called *Late Shāh Jahān Album*. It differs from the *Minto Album* as its borders are largely figural (e.g., *no. 22*); because it concentrates on portraits of the elderly emperor and nobles of the mid-seventeenth century, it seems to be a volume assembled late in Shāh Jahān's reign. Unlike the Jahāngīrī muraqqas, the figural marginalia are not confined to pages of calligraphy; instead, the borders often show men associated with the central personage and comment on the main panel. It sometimes seems, as well, that the border figures are by the same hand as the central illustration (e.g., *no. 36*). This, together with the fact that they are often virtual continuations of the central scene, produces an odd—sometimes unsatisfactory—visual effect; the contrast between illustration and border found in the Jahāngīrī album pages provides a greater visual richness. Furthermore, the later marginal figures generally lack the extraordinary warmth and sympathy of the best Jahāngīrī borders, for they are no longer experimental and innovative, but in a well-accepted and established mode. An exception, however, is the superb border by Payāg seen in *no. 22*.

There are also many dispersed pages with floral borders (e.g., *no. 51*), but whether these relate specifically to the above albums, or to other separated groupings, is presently uncertain. One difficulty in the study of these pages is the result of the activity of the late French dealer Demotte, who frequently (and often crudely) inserted loose paintings into Shāh Jahān album borders to increase their value. An example of this is seen here in *no. 43*. Furthermore, floral marginal decoration of similar type was continued on paintings of post-Shāh Jahān period date.[6]

21

SHAMSA

> Probably from an Album of Shāh Jahān
> Circa 1640–50
> 38 × 27.4 cm. (full page)
> Provenance: Rothschild Collection
> Anonymous Loan
> Bibliography: Colnaghi, *Persian and Mughal Art*, no. 97

A *shamsa*, a term derived from the Arabic *shams* ("sun"), sometimes containing in the center the name of the owner or patron, is often placed as the first page of an album or manuscript. Another such page from a Shāh Jahān album is reproduced in *Welch IMP*, Pl. 30 (color), while further

examples—identical in style—are found in the Windsor *Padshāh-nāma* manuscript.

Color plate facing text page 128 and cover.

22

A PRINCE VISITING A HERMITAGE

> From the *Late Shāh Jahān Album*
> Attributed here to Govardhan, with marginal figures attributed here to Payāg
> Circa 1635–40
> 37.5 × 25.4 cm. (full page)
> Provenance: John Dolliver MacDonald Collection
> Lent by the Cleveland Museum of Art: Purchase from the Andrew R. and Martha Holden Jennings Fund (71.79)

It is, perhaps, to be expected that both emperors and princes were continually fascinated by religious mendicants and ascetics, men whose worlds were so totally different from life at court. Jahāngīr, for example, wrote in amazement of the sage Jadrūp:

> God Almighty has granted him an unusual grace, a lofty understanding, an exalted nature, and sharp intellectual powers, with a God-given knowledge and a heart free from the attachments of the world, so that, putting behind his back the world and all that is in it, he sits content in the corner of solitude and without wants. He has chosen of worldly goods half a *gaz* of old cotton like a woman's veil, and a piece of earthenware from which to drink water, and in winter and summer and the rainy season lives naked. . . . He has made a hole in which he can turn round with a hundred difficulties and tortures, with a passage such that a suckling could hardly be put through it.[7]

The present scene, whose participants have not been identified, shows a similar sage outside his cave, visited by a prince.

The particularly lively border figures are attributable to Payāg, and both that artist and Govardhan are discussed elsewhere.

23

[*Recto*] CALLIGRAPHY

> Inscribed to "al-Fakhr, al-Muzahib"

[*Recto: Margins*]

> Circa 1645

[*Verso*] SHĀH JAHĀN HOLDING A JEWEL

> Circa 1635

> From the *Late Shāh Jahān Album*
> 36.7 × 23.8 cm. (full page)

23 recto

22

Provenance: Heeramaneck Collection
Lent by the Los Angeles County Museum of Art: The Nasli
and Alice Heeramaneck Collection (L.69.24.224)
Bibliography: *Beach Heeramaneck*, no. 218

The motif of Shāh Jahān holding a jewel is common. His passion for precious stones was well known, and it even seems that his painters frequently tried to fabricate artistic equivalents for the brilliance of the jewels he admired. Paintings such as this, or *no. 45* from the same album, for example, are immensely controlled in technique, in the application of color and line to paper, but lack qualities of warmth and sympathy. The humanistic concerns of Jahāngīr and the use of painting as a way to explore the physical world have been replaced by painting as the creation of beautiful, jewel-like objects. This development, of course, returns Mughal painting to more traditional pathways, for the acceptance of the primary importance of human individuality—basic to Jahāngīrī works— was neither Muslim nor Hindu, but a Mughal aberration.

The recto borders, animals against floral arabesques, are among the most beautiful of Mughal margins. More formal than their Jahāngīrī predecessors (e.g., *no. 9*), the animals are placed symmetrically, and the flowers heavily outlined with gold, cancelling any naturalistic sense.

While the *Late Shāh Jahān Album* is usually identified by its figural borders, the recto margins here indicate that abstract and floral ornament were used as well. A folio with similar margins is in an American private collection.

Color plate facing text page 72.

Selected List of Major Albums
Containing Mughal Paintings
Datable between 1600 and 1660

Muraqqaᶜ-e-Gulshan
    See page 43 ff.

Berlin Album
    See page 43 ff.

Sultān Khurram Album
    Dispersed
    Bibliography: Sotheby 15 June 1959, Lot 118; Sotheby 1 December 1969, Lots 126–32; Sotheby 7 December 1970, Lots 104–8; *Binney Collection*, no. 49; Grube, *Islamic Paintings*, nos. 239–40, Pl. LIII (color); *Robinson ed., Keir*, V.60; Welch, *Indian Drawings*, no. 7 (color)

A muraqqaᶜ of twenty pages, purchased by Hagop Kevorkian at Sotheby's in 1959. Inscriptions reveal that it was made for Prince Khurram before his accession as Shāh Jahān, and it includes calligraphies by Khurram, dated A.H. 1020 = A.D. 1611–12.

Minto Album
    A. Chester Beatty Library, Dublin, and the Victoria and Albert Museum, London

The album was sold from the collection of the Earl of Minto in 1925 at Sotheby's, and had presumably been inherited from an ancestor, who served as governor-general of India from 1807 to 1813. It contained forty double sided pages, of which the nineteen in the Beatty Library have been fully catalogued (*Beatty Library*, vol. I, pp. 27–33, and vol. III, Pls. 53–65). The remaining portion, in the Victoria and Albert Museum, is listed below in sequence of accession number (I.M. 8–1925 to 28–1925):

Tīmūr, Bābur and Humāyūn, by Govardhan
    Bibliography: Welch, *Indian Drawings*, no. 17, verso
Jahāngīr receiving Sultān Parvīz, by Manōhar
    Bibliography: *BM*, no. 111
An aged Mullā, by Farrukh Beg
    Bibliography: Skelton, "Farrokh," fig. 7
A Dervish, by Farrukh Beg
    Bibliography: Skelton, "Farrokh," fig. 10
Prince Khurram riding, by Manōhar
    Bibliography: Archer, *Indische Miniaturen*, Pl. 5
Three younger sons of Shāh Jahān, by Bālchand
    Bibliography: Deneck, *Indian Art*, Pl. 34
Prince Khurram in his twenty-fifth year, by Abūᶜl Hasan,
    Nādir-al-Zamān
    Bibliography: Gascoigne, *Great Moghuls*, p. 186
Shāh Shujāᶜ, by Lālchand
ᶜAbdullāh Khān, Firuz Jāng, with the head of Khān Jahān Lodī,
    by Abūᶜl Hasan, *Nādir-al-Zamān*
Shāh Jahān in 1631, by Bichitr
    Bibliography: *Welch AMI*, no. 43
Shāh Jahān riding with Dārā Shikōh, by Govardhan
    Bibliography: *Welch AMI*, no. 42; Stchoukine, *Peinture Indienne*, Pl. 36; *BM*, no. 139
Dārā Shikōh in 1645, by Chitarman
ᶜAbdullāh Khān Uzbeq hawking, by Abūᶜl Hasan,
    Nādir-al-Zamān
Malik ᶜAmbar, by Mīr Hāshim
Sultān Muhammad Qutb Shāh of Golconda, by Hāshim
    Bibliography: *BM*, no. 131
A Zebra, by Ustād Mansūr
    Bibliography: Archer, *Indian Miniatures*, Pl. 26
Zūlfiqār Khān Turkman, by Nānhā
    Bibliography: Skelton, "Motif," Pl. LXXXVIII
Muhammad ᶜAlī Beg, by Mīr Hāshim
    Bibliography: *BM*, no. 130
Āsaf Khān, by Bichitr
    Bibliography: Hambly and Swaan, *Cities*, fig. 64; *BM*, no. 152; Archer, *Indian Miniatures*, Pl. 27; Stchoukine, *Peinture Indienne*, Pl. 38
Dhobī, Singer, and Musician, by Bichitr
    Bibliography: Stchoukine, *Peinture Indienne*, Pl. 44
Prince Salīm as a youth, by Bichitr
    Bibliography: Hambly and Swaan, *Cities*, fig. 47

Wantage Album
    Victoria and Albert Museum, London

According to the account of Stanley Clarke (*Wantage Bequest*, "Prefatory Note"), the album of thirty-six double sided folios (some with illustrations on both sides), was purchased in London

23 verso

during the 1867–68 season by Baron Overstone, who presented it to his daughter, the Honourable Harriet Lindsay (later Lady Wantage), on her thirty-first birthday in 1868. In 1920, it was bequeathed to the nation.

The album contains some pictures which seem to be datable to the first half of the seventeenth century; the majority are additions of about 1800. Whether the borders are seventeenth century or later has not yet been properly determined. Because the album has been published, no list is given here (see *Wantage Bequest*).

Kevorkian Album

Metropolitan Museum of Art, New York, and the Freer Gallery of Art, Washington, D.C.

Consisting of forty-six double sided folios and four illuminated rosettes, of the same size and stylistic range as the *Wantage Album*, the album was bought in Scotland for £100 in the late 1920s, and sold to Hagop Kevorkian (Sotheby 12 December 1929) for £10,000. Soon thereafter, it was the subject of an extensive legal battle (see B. Hollander, *The International Law of Art* [London, 1959], pp. 112–13 and 170–71).

In the following list of *Kevorkian Album* pages, those marked FGA are in the Freer Gallery of Art.

Dancing dervishes
    Bibliography: Grube, *Classical Style*, no. 100
Akbar with a falcon, and Jahāngīr, inscribed to Bālchand
    Bibliography: Dimand, *Handbook*, fig. 225
Khwāja Jahān and a youth fallen from a tree, inscribed to
    Āqā Rizā
    Bibliography: *Dimand Bulletin*, p. 95
Equestrian portrait of Shāh Jahān, inscribed to Payāg
    Bibliography: Dimand, *Handbook*, fig. 228; Dimand,
    Indian Miniature Painting, cover (color)
Akbar with a lion and heifer, inscribed to Govardhan
Jahāngīr and Itimād-ad-daula, inscribed to Manōhar
    Bibliography: *Dimand Bulletin*, p. 96
Jahāngīr shooting at head of Malik ʿAmbar, inscribed to
    Abūʿl Hasan; reverse: Vulture, inscribed to Mansūr (FGA)
Jahāngīr with a globe (FGA)
Shāh Jahān with a globe, inscribed to Hāshim (FGA)
Shāh Jahān standing, inscribed to Chitarman
    Bibliography: R. Craven, *Miniatures and Small Sculptures
    from India* (Gainesville, Florida, 1966), no. 82
Equestrian portrait of Shāh Jahān, inscribed to Govardhan;
    reverse: Bird, inscribed to Abūʿl Hasan, *Nādir-al-Zamān*
    (FGA)
ʿAbdullāh Khān, Firūz Jang, inscribed to Muhammad ʿAlam;
    reverse: Vulture, inscribed to Mansūr
Sheikh Hasan Chishtī, inscribed to Bichitr
    Bibliography: *Dimand Bulletin*, p. 99
Shāh Tahmāsp, inscribed to Farrukh Beg; reverse: Bird,
    inscribed to Mansūr (FGA)
Muhammad ʿAlī Beg, inscribed to Hāshim; reverse: Game
    Fowl, inscribed to Mansūr
Dhobī, singer and musician, inscribed to Bichitr; reverse:
    Bird on flowering tree, inscribed to Farrukh Beg (FGA)
Humāyūn under an umbrella; reverse: Two deer, inscribed to
    Mansūr (FGA)
Hājjī Husain Bukhārī, inscribed to Mansūr
    Bibliography: *Dimand Bulletin*, p. 98
Four portraits, inscribed to Bālchand, Murād, etc.

Qulīj Khān, inscribed to Lālchand
Nasrat-i-Jang, inscribed to Murād
Sultān Daniyāl, inscribed to Manōhar
    Bibliography: Skelton, "Two Mughal Lion Hunts," p. 39
Ibrāhīm ʿAdil Shāh, inscribed to Hāshim
Itimād-ad-daula, inscribed to Bālchand (FGA)
Muhammad Khān Walī, inscribed to Hāshim
Two lovers, inscribed to Govardhan
Jahāngīr enthroned with a child, inscribed to Nānhā
Jān Nisār, inscribed to Bālchand
Khān Khānān, inscribed to Hāshim (FGA)
Rājā Vikramājīt, inscribed to Bichitr
Rājā Bhim Singh, inscribed to Nānhā
Mahābat Khān, inscribed to Manōhar
Sayyid Saʿīd Khān, inscribed to Nānhā
Sayyid Khān Jahān, inscribed to Lālchand
Jādūn Rāī Deccanī, inscribed to Hāshim
Rājā Surāj Singh, inscribed to Bishan Dās
Sar Rāi Chanda, inscribed to Govardhan
    Bibliography: Dimand, *Handbook*, p. 97
Man with a bear, inscribed to Govardhan
    Bibliography: *Dimand Bulletin*, p. 101
Man with a bear, inscribed to Govardhan
Saint with a lion
    Bibliography: *Dimand Bulletin*, p. 101
A Nilgae, inscribed to Mansūr
Two vultures, inscribed to Mansūr
A Hornbill, inscribed to Mansūr
    Bibliography: *Dimand Bulletin*, p. 100; *Welch AMI*, no. 37
Long-tailed bird, inscribed to Abūʿl Hasan, *Nādir-al-Zamān*
    Bibliography: *Dimand Bulletin*, p. 100
Bird on a rock, inscribed to Mansūr
A Buck

Late Shāh Jahān Album

Dispersed

According to F. R. Martin, the album was dispersed in Paris about 1909 (Martin, *Miniature Paintings*, p. 85). Traditionally it was thought to have been taken from Delhi in 1739 by Nādir Shāh, and, like much of the loot removed from India in the eighteenth century, it eventually entered the Iranian imperial collections. In the late nineteenth century, it was taken to Russia by a brother of the Iranian Shāh Nāsir-ud-dīn, and he sold it to the Armenian dealer who brought it to Paris. Only about a third of the original album can now be accounted for, and known pages are listed here (see also *nos. 22, 23, 36, and 45*):

The elderly Akbar—Collection of Prince Sadruddin Agha
    Khān (ex-Cartier Collection)
    Bibliography: Welch, "Mughal and Deccani Miniature
    Paintings," no. 17, fig. 17; *Brown*, Pl. XXVI
A Nobleman—Beatty Library
    Bibliography: *Beatty Library*, vol. III, Pl. 67
Shāh Daulat, by Dilwarat—Beatty Library
    Bibliography: *Beatty Library*, vol. III, Pl. 68
Dervish, musician and soldier—Beatty Library
    Bibliography: *Beatty Library*, vol. III, Pl. 69
Rustam Khān, by Hūnhar—Beatty Library
    Bibliography: *Beatty Library*, vol. III, Pl. 71
Khān Daurān, *Nasrat-i-Jang*—Beatty Library
    Bibliography: *Beatty Library*, vol. III, Pl. 72
Sayyid Hidāyat Allāh, by Daulat—Present location unknown
    (ex-Rothschild Collection)

Bibliography: Colnaghi, *Persian and Mughal Art*, no. 122;
Brown, Pl. XXVII
Shāh Shujāᶜ, by Hūnhar—Present location unknown
(ex-Pozzi Collection)
Bibliography: *Collection Jean Pozzi* (sales catalogue),
Palais Galliéra, Paris, 5 December 1970, Lot 22
Akbar and Shāh Jahān—Musée Guimet, Paris
Bibliography: Marteau and Vever, *Miniatures Persanes*,
vol. II, Pl. 160
Antelope, by Murād—Present location unknown
(ex-de Béarn Collection)
Bibliography: Marteau and Vever, *Miniatures Persanes*,
vol. II, Pl. 164
Bābur and Humāyūn (double page)—Present location
unknown (ex-Demotte Collection)
Bibliography: Martin, *Miniature Paintings*, Pls. 211–12
The elderly Akbar—Present location unknown
(ex-Demotte Collection)
Bibliography: Martin, *Miniature Paintings*, Pl. 213
Tīmūr, Bābur, and Humāyūn, by Hāshim—Present location
uncertain (ex-Demotte and ex-de Béarn Collections)
Bibliography: Martin, *Miniature Paintings*, Pl. 214;
Marteau and Vever, *Miniatures Persanes*, vol. II,
Pl. CLVIII
Sultān Murād IV—Present location uncertain (ex-Demotte
and ex-de Béarn Collections)
Bibliography: Martin, *Miniature Paintings*, Pl. 215;
Marteau and Vever, *Miniatures Persanes*, vol. II, Pl. CLXIII
Akbar, Jahāngīr, and Shāh Jahān—Present location uncertain
(ex-de Béarn Collection)
Bibliography: Marteau and Vever, *Miniatures Persanes*,
vol. II, Pl. CLIX
Two Mullās—Musée Guimet, Paris
Bibliography: *Stchoukine Louvre*, Pl. XIII
Bābur—Musée Guimet, Paris
Bibliography: *Stchoukine Louvre*, Pl. XIV
A Visit to ascetics—Musée Guimet, Paris
Bibliography: *Stchoukine Louvre*, Pl. XV; Bussagli, *Indian
Miniatures*, fig. 63
The elderly Jahāngīr—Present location uncertain
(ex-Demotte and ex-Heeramaneck Collections)
Bibliography: Stchoukine, "Portraits III," fig. 72
Shāh Nawāz Khān, by Rām Dās—Edwin Binney 3rd
Collection
Bibliography: *Binney Collection*, no. 62
Rāo Chattar Sāl of Bundī—Kraus Collection
Bibliography: Grube, *Islamic Paintings*, no. 249
Shāh Jahān with Khajar Khizr—Present location unknown
Bibliography: Sotheby 1 December 1969, Lot 151
Shāh Jahān standing—Present location unknown
(ex-Rothschild Collection)
Bibliography: Colnaghi, *Persian and Mughal Art*, no. 120
Akbar and Jahāngīr—Present location unknown
(ex-Rothschild Collection)
Bibliography: Colnaghi, *Persian and Mughal Art*, no. 119
The elderly Shāh Jahān—Present location unknown
(ex-Rothschild Collection)
Bibliography: Colnaghi, *Persian and Mughal Art*, no. 121
Shāh Jahān and child—Present location unknown
(ex-Heeramaneck Collection)
Portrait of a Rājput—Present location unknown
(ex-Heeramaneck Collection)
Holy Men, attributed to Govardhan—Musée Guimet, Paris
(ex-Sevadjian Collection)

Rājā Bhim Singh of Udaipur—Museum of Fine Arts, Boston
(60.172)
The elderly Shāh Jahān holding a jewel—Ralph Benkaim
Collection
ᶜAlā al-Mulk Tunī, Fāzil Khān—Cleveland Museum of Art
(45.168)
Bibliography: Hollis, "Portrait of a Nobleman,"
pp. 180–85
Portrait of a Courtier—Museum of Fine Arts, Boston
(60.171)
A Nobleman, by Payāg—Metropolitan Museum of Art,
New York

See also: *Beatty Library*, Ms. 7, nos. 21, 23–24, 27–34, 37–38;
Marteau and Vever, *Miniatures Persanes*, vol. II, Pl. 159.

Dārā Shikōh Album
India Office Library, London

Prince Dārā Shikōh presented this muraqqaᶜ to his wife, Nādira
Banu Bēgam, in A.H. 1051 = A.D. 1641–42. It chiefly contains
paintings of flora and fauna, with some portraits, European
prints, and miscellaneous studies. For published folios see: *Brown*,
Pls. XXII, LV (figs. 1, 2); Smith, *History*, frontispiece, Pl. B;
Binyon and Arnold, *Court Painters*, Pls. XXIII, XXXI; S.
Crowe, S. Haywood, and S. Jellicoe, *Gardens of Mughal India*
(London, 1972), pp. 12–13 and p. 188.

Add. 18801
British Library

According to Vincent Smith (Smith, *History*, p. 195), there is an
inscription in the album recording its "pious donation" in
A.H. 1072 = A.D. 1661–62. It contains works by Chitarman,
Muhammad Nādir of Samarkand, Mīr Hāshim, and others.
Pages have been reproduced in Martin, *Miniature Paintings*, Pls.
184–97 and fig. 42.

Leningrad Album
Academy of Sciences, Leningrad

This is an extensive compilation of seventeenth and eighteenth-
century paintings, including many of the greatest Mughal works.
The album has been fully published (see Ivanova, et al., *Albom
Indiyskikh*). According to Russian sources, it was bought in
Tehran and later offered to the Russian museums by Czar
Nicholas II.
    For further pages asserted to be from this album see Fondation
Custodia, no. 178, Pl. 68; and Soustiel and David, *Miniatures de
l'Inde*, no. 15.

Nāsir-ud-dīn Album
Imperial Library, Gulistan Palace, Tehran

Yedda Godard has reported that this album belonged to Khusrau
Khān Nā-kām of Kurdistan in 1826, but was registered in the
Gulistan Palace Library by 1844 where it was restored and re-
bound by Shāh Nāsir-ud-dīn. It may well be that this is a compi-
lation made at the same time as the *Leningrad Album*, which is
believed to have come to Russia from Iran, as did the *Late Shāh
Jahān Album*. For a catalogue of the complete muraqqaᶜ see
Godard, "Album."

The *Padshāh-nāma*

While the *Jahāngīr-nāma* is a thoughtful, intensely personal memoir, the *Padshāh-nāma* (or *Shāh Jahān-nāma*) is an official state biography, limited to the events and decisions of Shāh Jahān's life as prince and emperor. As we would expect, the illustrations are almost solely of darbārs, processions, and military campaigns.

There are several different contemporary histories of the emperor's rule. The earliest was commissioned in 1634 (the eighth regnal year) from Muhammad Amīn Qazwīnī and finished in 1646; his text, entitled *Padshāh-nāma*, covered the first ten years of the reign. ᶜAbd-al-Hamīd Lāhorī, the author of the most famous *Padshāh-nāma* (the illustrated version in the Royal Library, Windsor Castle), used Qazwīnī as the basis for the first part of his work, but added another volume devoted to the second ten years (1636–46); a completion of the text, up to the year 1656, was made as a third volume by Muhammad Wāris.[1] It is to ᶜAbd-al-Hamīd Lāhorī's text that the illustrations in this exhibition reportedly relate.[2]

The Windsor Castle manuscript contains forty-four illustrations, some of which are signed by Bālchand, Lālchand, Rām Dās, Murād, Bichitr, Bola, ᶜĀbid, Payāg, and Mīr Dust.[3] According to a colophon, the writing of this copy, by Muhammad ᶜAmīn of Meshhed, was completed in 1657–58, and a seal reveals that in 1776 the book was in the collection of Asaf Jah, the Wazīr of Lucknow. With seven exceptions, all the illustrations depict scenes from the first ten years of the reign, and these carefully follow the sequence of ᶜAbd-al-Hamīd Lāhorī's narrative (and, therefore, that of Qazwīnī also). Of the seven exceptions, four pages show Shāh Jahān with Jahāngīr, and obviously refer to events preaccession; three (including the frontispiece portrait) show the emperor as an old man. These seven paintings (with the exception of the frontispiece) may have been placed at random within the text.

Several separate paintings are so close to the Windsor *Padshāh-nāma* in size and character that they may well have been intended for inclusion in further, now missing, volumes of that copy. A list of these is provided below, and here the identifiable events are either preaccession, or after the tenth regnal year.

There are further problems relating to the manuscript, especially when trying to determine the date of the illustrations. As noted, the copying (i.e., writing out) of the Windsor volume was completed at the end of the emperor's reign (i.e., 1657–58). Moreover, ᶜAbd-al-Hamīd Lāhorī could not have begun to write his text until at least 1646, since his source is the Qazwīnī version, only completed in that year. Yet, while none of the Windsor pages is specifically dated, there are indications that the illustrations may have been begun at the very beginning of Shāh Jahān's rule. Three of the dispersed pages listed below are inscribed with execution dates that seem to read 1628, 1635, and 1639; this, together with the style of various illustrations, suggests strongly that at least some paintings used in the manuscript were begun before that particular copy of the text was written. In each of the three dated pages, moreover, the date of execution (even when judged by the style alone) seems immediately to follow the date of the event. It is very likely, therefore, that the Windsor text was illustrated by already existing paintings, perhaps made for a copy of the initial history by Qazwīnī, later rendered obsolete by the completion of ᶜAbd-al-Hamīd Lāhorī's version. In the events surrounding the seizure of the throne by Aurangzēb and the imprisonment of Shāh Jahān, this great imperial copy may never have been properly finished.

There are a number of further illustrations that have long been thought to be eighteenth-century insertions, perhaps made at Lucknow during the manuscript's residency there. Recent assertions have been made that the book is completely of Shāh Jahān's time, however, and the manuscript is now in the process of being fully published by Robert Skelton of the Victoria and Albert Museum.

24

SHĀH JAHĀN ENTHRONED

From a *Padshāh-nāma* manuscript
Inscribed: *raqam-walad-i-Āqā Rizā ᶜĀbid* ("by ᶜĀbid, son of Āqā Rizā")
Dated "23 shaban in the regnal year of Shāh Jahān 13" = 19 Dec. 1639
36.9 × 24.6 cm. (55.2 × 34.9 cm.)
Provenance: A. C. Ardeshir Collection
Lent by Edwin Binney 3rd
Bibliography: *Binney Collection*, no. 58

Of major interest in this work is the throne upon which the emperor sits. It is shown also in a portrait of Shāh

24

Jahān attributed to Abū'l Hasan,[4] and has long been considered a contemporary representation of the great Peacock Throne commissioned by the emperor at his accession, and finished and inaugurated only in 1634. A passage by the French traveller and physician, François Bernier, who travelled in India between 1656–68, not only described the throne but gives a vivid sense of a darbār:

Never did I witeness a more extraordinary scene. The King [i.e., Aurangzēb] appeared seated upon his throne, at the end of the great hall, in the most magnificent attire. His vest was of white and delicately flowered satin, with a silk and gold embroidery of the finest texture. The turban, of gold cloth, had an aigrette whose base was composed of diamonds of an extraordinary size and value, besides an Oriental topaz, which may be pronounced unparalleled, exhibiting a lustre like the sun. A necklace of immense pearls, suspended from his neck, reached to the stomach, in the same manner as many of the *Gentiles* wear their strings of beads. The throne was supported by six massy feet, said to be of solid gold, sprinkled over with rubies, emeralds, and diamonds. I cannot tell you with accuracy the number or value of this vast collection of precious stones, because no person may approach sufficiently near to reckon them, or judge their water and clearness; but I can assure you that there is a confusion of diamonds, as well as other jewels, and that the throne, to the best of my recollection, is valued at four *Kourours* of *Roupies*. I observed that a *Lecque* is one hundred thousand *roupies*, and that a *Kourour* is a hundred *Lecques*; so that the throne is estimated as forty millions of *roupies*, worth sixty millions of pounds or thereabouts. It was constructed by *Chah-Jehan*, the father of *Aurang-Zebe*, for the purpose of displaying the immense quantity of precious stones accumulated successively in the treasury from the spoils of ancient Rajas . . . and the annual presents to the Monarch, which every *Omrah* [i.e., noble] is bound to make on certain festivals. The construction and workmanship of the throne are not worthy of the materials; but two peacocks, covered with jewels and pearls, are well conceived and executed. They were made by a workman of astonishing powers, a *Frenchman* by birth . . . who, after defrauding several of the Princes of *Europe*, by means of false gems, which he fabricated with particular skill, sought refuge at the *Great Mogol's* court, where he made his fortune.[5]

A further description is given by Jean-Baptiste Tavernier, a French jeweller, who wrote about 1665:

The principal throne . . . resembles in form and size our camp beds; that is to say, it is about six feet long and four wide. Upon the four feet, which are very massive . . . are fixed the four bars which support the base of the throne, and upon these bars are ranged twelve columns, which sustain the canopy . . . above the canopy, which is a quadrangular-shaped dome, there is a peacock with elevated tail made of blue sapphires and other coloured stones, the body of gold inlaid with precious stones, having a large ruby in front of the breast, whence hangs a pear-shaped pearl of 50 carats or thereabouts. . . . On both sides of the pea-

cock there is a large bouquet of the same height as the bird, consisting of many kinds of flowers made of gold inlaid with precious stones. . . . In my opinion the most costly point about the magnificent canopy throne is that the twelve columns supporting the canopy are surrounded with beautiful rows of pearls, which are round and of fine water.[6]

In the *Padshāh-nāma* of 'Abd-al-Hamīd Lāhorī, however, for the eighth regnal year, the following description is given:

The outside of the canopy was to be of enamel work with occasional gems, the inside was to be thickly set with rubies, garnets, and other jewels, and it was to be supported by twelve emerald columns. On the top of each pillar there were to be two peacocks thick set with gems, and between each two peacocks a tree set with rubies and diamonds, emeralds, and pearls.[7]

Thus, there is no concurrence, among these three independent and equally reliable observers, about the importance of the twelve columns (for Bernier does not mention them), or whether they were made of pearls or emeralds; nor about the number of feet. They all do agree, however, about the presence of peacocks, even if not about their number or arrangement. It seems clear, nevertheless, that the present throne is not the legendary Peacock Throne, and that consequently the form and design of that quintessentially Mughal object remain elusive. (The throne was taken by Nādir Shāh at his sack of Delhi in 1739, and some of the jewels can now be found in the relatively modern and uninventive "Peacock Throne," included with the Iranian crown jewels.)

The inscribed date on the painting, 1639, with the additional information that it took two years to execute, allows us to date and identify the probable episode commemorated. The figures surrounding the emperor include Dārā Shikōh who is presenting a *sarpech*, or turban ornament, Sultān Murād, and Rājā Gaj Singh of Marwar (to the right, wearing a white turban). From December 1636, Gaj Singh was at Jodhpur on leave from imperial service, returning to court at Agra the following November and receiving a robe of honor in January 1638. He was then sent to Kabul with Shāh Shujā', to help protect Qandahar from anticipated Iranian attacks. In May 1638, he died,[8] and this darbār must therefore date from late 1637 or early 1638, exactly the date inscriptionally indicated for the scene. It is possible that the prince standing to the emperor's left and holding a tray of jewels is Shujā'. The same man is found in the Bodleian Library *Shāh Jahān Receiving a Prince*, listed below.

The bottom portion has been slightly restored. (See also the discussion of the painter 'Ābid.)

25 (detail)

25

BATTLE SCENE

From a *Padshāh-nāma* manuscript
Attributed to Payāg
Circa 1640
34.3 × 23.9 cm.
Provenance: Pozzi Collection
Anonymous Loan
Bibliography: *Welch FEM*, no. 66; *Welch IMP*, Pl. 33 (color);
Blochet, *Collection Jean Pozzi*, Pl. 35.

The magnificence of the massed Mughal troops, contrasting with the stunted, blackened trees and decaying corpses of the mid-ground, provides one of the most evocative and moody of Mughal battle pictures. The scene has long been associated with the siege of Qandahar, a major—if unsuccessful—series of battles during the early 1650s, whereby Shāh Jahān sought to regain the fortress and lands that separated Mughal India from Safavid Persia. There are several reasons to question this identification, however. The *Padshāh-nāma* manuscripts as a group, avoided extended mention of events that were not reinforcements of Mughal prestige, and Qandahar was a decidedly gloomy episode. Moreover, the chief noble (bottom center), identified by S. C. Welch as Dārā Shikōh, the leader of the expedition of 1653, seems to be a Rājput, for his *jāma* ("coat") is tied under his left arm, a Rājput (Hindu) fashion (compare this figure to the portrait of the prince in *no. 64*).

The central figure among the three men at the bottom right, however, may be Khān Daurān, a major figure in various battle scenes of the Windsor manuscript.[9] He was primarily stationed in the Deccan, but in 1638, immediately following the fall of Qandahar to the Mughals, was sent to Kabul with Shāh Shujā' to provide added

26

protection. Since the setting here is clearly northern (the background mountains are snow-capped), it may be an episode from these years that is shown.

Like some other dispersed pages of this group, the illustration has been mounted on an eighteenth-century album page.[10] See also the discussion elsewhere of works by Payāg.

26
ATTENDANT FIGURES

From a *Padshāh-nāma* manuscript
Mid-seventeenth century
37.5 × 22 cm.
Lent by the Art Institute of Chicago: Kate S. Buckingham Fund (1975.555)

This is the left half of a double page composition, showing courtiers attending a darbār, or reception.

Selected Dispersed *Padshāh-nāma* pages

Shāh Jahān in Darbār with Mahābat Khān and a Sheikh
Inscribed: *raqam-i-ᶜĀbid, barādar-i-Nādir-al-Zamān Mashhadī dar sana-i 2* [?] *bi-itmān rasīd* ("by ᶜĀbid, brother of Nādir-al-Zamān of Meshhed. In the year 2 [?] it was finished")
Dated (?) 1628–29
Vever Collection
Bibliography: Marteau and Vever, *Miniatures Persanes*, vol. II, no. 229, Pl. CLXI

By the age of the child, Sultān Murād (b. 1624), and of the emperor, this superb work would seem to be a coronation portrait; considering the prominence of Mahābat Khān, shown paying homage, there are two possible episodes as its basis. In 1627, after Jahāngīr's death, when Shāh Jahān was enroute to the capital, he stopped at Ajmer, appointed Mahābat Khān its governor, and granted him four lacs of rupees (Khan, *Maasir-ul Umara*, vol. II, p. 20). Later, on 4 February 1628, Mahābat Khān was appointed *Khān-i-khānān* ("Commander-in-Chief") and "shaikhs and sayyids . . . all partook of generous bounty. . . ." (Saksena, *History*, p. 63.) The conspicuous absence of the three elder princes, and their grandfather Āsaf Khān, all of whom arrived at court only three weeks later, is important in considering the date of the event shown.

A further discussion of ᶜĀbid is given below.

The Surrender of Qandahar
Musée Guimet, Paris
Bibliography: Blochet, *Catalogue*, Pl. XXXIX; J. Auboyer, *Rarities of the Musée Guimet* (New York, 1975), fig. 69

An event of the eleventh regnal year (= A.D. 1637–38), the coveted fortress at Qandahar was turned over to the Mughals by its Persian governor, ᶜAlī Mardān Khān. It was then put in charge of Qulīj Khān, the major Mughal equestrian figure shown here.

A Persian Embassy
Attributed here to Payāg
Bodleian Library, Oxford (Ouseley Add. 173, No. 13)
Bibliography: Binyon and Arnold, *Court Painters*, Pl. XXXVI; *Brown*, p. 87ff., Pl. XXIV

The reception of the Persian Ambassador Muhammad ᶜAlī Beg in 1630–31 is shown on fol. 97v of the Windsor manuscript, so that this scene could only show the later embassy of Yādgār Beg, who arrived in India immediately following the fall of Qandahar in 1638; this date is confirmed by the ages of the princes. This is the right half of a double page composition (see next listing), and can be attributed to Payāg.

A Persian Embassy
Collection of Sita Ram Sahu, Benares

This is unquestionably the left half of the Bodleian page listed above, for the design, subject, and style are continuous.

Shāh Jahān Receiving a Prince
Attributed here to ᶜĀbid
Dated 1635
Bodleian Library, Oxford (Ouseley Add. 173)
Bibliography: Binyon and Arnold, *Court Painters*, Pl. XXI

The young prince, shown arriving at the gates to the sanctum of the darbār hall, is seen also in *no. 24*. It is possibly Shāh Shujāᶜ. The illustration is evidently dated 1635, and a signature has been read as Muhammad (Gray et al., *R.A. Arts of India and Pakistan*, no. 763). It is very likely that the correct reading is Muhammad ᶜĀbid, whose style the work closely resembles.

Attendant Figures
Indian Museum, Calcutta
Bibliography: *Brown*, Pls. XLVI–XLVIII

This is the left portion of a double page composition. There is no known reason to accept the identification of the scene by Brown as the marriage celebrations of Prince Khurram.

Shāh Jahān Entertaining a Party of Mullās
Attributed to Murād
Freer Gallery of Art, Washington, D.C. (42.17 & 18)
Bibliography: Gascoigne, *Great Moghuls*, p. 200; *Welch IMP*, Pls. 31 and 32 (color)

While the episode has not been definitely identified, this full double page composition is by the painter of the Windsor *Padshāh-nāma* fols. 123v and 124r, to whom other of the manuscript pages can also be given. Stuart C. Welch has identified the artist as Murād.

Additional dispersed *Padshāh-nāma* pages may be in the Bharat Kala Bhavan, Benares, and the Academy of Sciences, Leningrad.

ᶜĀbid

Only three paintings with definite signatures or contemporary attributions to ᶜĀbid are known, but these make clear that—at his best—he was among the very greatest Mughal artists. The inscriptions tell us that he was the son of Āqā Riżā and the brother of Abūᶜl Hasan, *Nādir-al-Zamān*. All works attributed to him at present, however, are of the Shāh Jahān period, although we must assume he was active earlier as well.

Considering this scarcity of recognized works, there is little that can be said of his style. The Vever Collection *Shāh Jahān in Darbār* reveals him to have been equal to his brother as a portraitist. The Windsor *Padshāh-nāma* illustration of the *Death of Khān Jahān Lodī* further indicates that he was in the vanguard of the continuing development of the Mughal style. It is a superb example of the combination of technical perfection and intensely observed detail (of textures, materials, portraits, gestures), with consciously irrational and mannered spatial relationships, that moves the style away from the scientific attitude toward realism that developed under Jahāngīr.

ᶜĀbid's paintings often contain unexpected observations that heighten their narrative impact. The *Death of Khān Jahān Lodī* is described with vivid and unusual combinations of color that intensify the chilling immediacy of the central act of decapitation. The Vever *Darbār* shows a silent, secretively grinning sheikh, revealing far more of the man than the subject alone would warrant.

For the painting by ᶜĀbid in the exhibition, see *no. 24.*

Further Major Attributions to ᶜĀbid

Shāh Jahān in Darbār with Mahābat Khān and a Sheikh

Probably from the Windsor *Padshāh-nāma* manuscript
Inscribed: *raqam-i-ᶜĀbid barādar-i-Nādir-al-Zamān Mashhadī dar sana-i 2* [?] *bi-itmān rasīd* ("by ᶜĀbid, brother of Nādir-al-Zamān of Meshhed. In the year 2 [?] it was finished")
Dated (?) 1628–29

Vever Collection
Bibliography: Marteau and Vever, *Miniatures Persanes*, vol. II, no. 229, Pl. CLXI

This superb page is discussed above in the check list of dispersed *Padshāh-nāma* pages.

The Death of Khān Jahān Lodī

From the Windsor *Padshāh-nāma* manuscript, fol. 93v
Signed by ᶜĀbid
Royal Library, Windsor Castle
Bibliography: *Welch AMI*, fig. 4

Jahāngīr in Darbār with Prince Khurram

From the Windsor *Padshāh-nāma* manuscript, fol. 191v
Royal Library, Windsor Castle

The scene is not in sequence with the historical events of Shāh Jahān's reign, so it is difficult to know the exact event it depicts. There is no signature, but the even line-up of figures at the bottom, and the grinning, highly characterized faces are trademarks of the artist; additionally, the dense, evenly textured, and minute details of the upper half are further seen in such signed paintings as *no. 24*, exhibited here.

Shāh Jahān Receiving a Prince

Probably from the Windsor *Padshāh-nāma* manuscript
Dated (?) 1635
Bodleian Library, Oxford (Ouseley Add. 173)
Bibliography: Binyon and Arnold, *Court Painters*, Pl. XXI

It has been stated that this page is dated 1635 and signed by Muhammad (Gray et al., *R.A. Arts of India and Pakistan*, no. 763). It is more likely that the signature reads Muhammad ᶜĀbid whose style the work closely resembles.

Shāh Jahān

From the *Wantage Album*
Signed by Muhammad ᶜĀbid
Victoria and Albert Museum, London (223–1921 I.M.)

Shāh Jahān Beneath a Baldaquin

Fondation Custodia, Paris (1972–T.63)
Bibliography: Fondation Custodia, no. 173, Pl. 69

Unsigned, this accords in style with Windsor *Padshāh-nāma* fol. 191v and the Binney *Darbār* (*no. 24*), for in all three the portraits have become softer, almost hazy. Given the explicitly dated Binney work, this would seem to indicate a late phase of ᶜĀbid's style.

Abūʿl Hasan, *Nādir-al-Zamān*

In his memoirs, under the year 1618, the Emperor Jahāngīr wrote:

On this day Abuʿl Hasan, the painter, who has been honored with the title *Nadiruʿl Zaman*, drew the picture of my accession as the frontispiece to the *Jahangir-nama*, and brought it to me. As it was worthy of all praise, he received endless favors. His work was perfect, and his picture was one of the *chefs-d'œuvres* of the age. At the present time he has no rival or equal.... His father, Aqa Riza, of Herat, at the time when I was a prince, joined my service. There is, however, no comparison between his work and that of his father.... My connection is based on my having reared him, till his art arrived at this rank. Truly he has become *Nadiruʿl Zaman* ("the wonder of the age").[1]

No other painter received such extensive homage from the emperor, and the passage is important evidence that Abūʿl Hasan's father, the Iranian artist Āqā Riżā, had entered the service of Prince Salīm, the future Jahāngīr, by the time of Abūʿl Hasan's birth. Moreover, a drawing of *St. John* (copied from an engraving by Albrecht Dürer), made by Abūʿl Hasan in A.H. 1009 = A.D. 1600–1601, "in my thirteenth year," allows us to date his birth to A.H. 997 = A.D. 1588–89. A portrait of the artist (*fig. 4*) in the margins of the *Muraqqaʿ-e-Gulshan*, further informs us that he was left-handed. Beyond this, however—and it is more factual knowledge than we have of any other major Mughal painter—all we know of the artist is what can be learned from his paintings.

Jahāngīr noted distinct differences between the work of Abūʿl Hasan and that of his father, and we have already compared *nos. 28* and *30* in this exhibition. The earliest fully mature painting by the younger artist is found in a manuscript of the *Anwār-i-Suhailī* finished in 1610, and now in the British Library. Alongside the single page signed by Abūʿl Hasan (who added to his name, in sign of humility, *khāk-i-astān-i-Riżā*, "dust of the threshhold of Riżā") are several pages signed by his father. The difference in the work of the two men is, even here, instantly apparent. Although both make carefully arranged compositions that are closely related to contemporary Iranian manuscripts such as the *Anwār-i-Suhailī* of 1593 painted at Isfahan by Sādiqi,[2] Abūʿl Hasan is already less concerned with purely ornamental effects. This is seen best in his treatment of robes and cloth, where the lines follow the natural texture and fall of

FIG. 4. Portrait of Abūʿl Hasan. By Daulat, ca. 1605–9. From the *Muraqqaʿ-e-Gulshan*. Imperial Library, Tehran. After Y. Godard, "Marges," fig. 11.

the fabric, rather than serve as an excuse for surface pattern making—as is the case in his father's work. Too, his faces are individually characterized, sympathetically observed, and expressive, whereas Āqā Riżā tends to use standard impersonal Safavid formulae which he dresses up with newly fashionable techniques of shading. Abūʿl Hasan's naturalism, his brilliance of technique, and his intense sympathy for the subject presented, are already apparent in his *Anwār-i-Suhailī* page, although this remains closely derived from his father's way of painting.

The study of European prints, known already in Abūʿl Hasan's earliest identified work, the drawing of *St. John*, was an important ingredient in the distinctive style which the younger man evolved. In the Dürer copy, for example, Abūʿl Hasan was even more extreme in his experimentation with the novel technique of shading than the source would have warranted. His later works are particularly notable for giving a sense of substance and mass through the play of light on rounded surfaces, and for dark shadowed backgrounds (e.g., *nos. 13* and *27–29*). Āqā Riżā, who is known to have copied European works in the same years, repeated European motifs and techniques, but without fundamentally altering his already formed style, itself a conservative reiteration of established devices. Abū᾽l Hasan, merely a novice, used these new ideas as means for presenting more effectively a world he observed directly.

The *St. John* is dated 1600–1601, and the *Anwār-i-Suhailī* bears a terminal date of 1610 (although two of Āqā Riẓā's illustrations are independently inscribed with the date A.H. 1012 = A.D. 1603–4, meaning that we cannot be sure of the exact date of Abū᾽l Hasan's contribution). A superb page from the fragmentary *Gulistān* of Saʿdī (*no. 18* [above]) of circa 1610–15 can be attributed to Abū᾽l Hasan on the basis of his *Anwār-i-Suhailī* page, and the famous *Squirrels in a Plane Tree* of about 1610.

Two further works of about 1615 are included in the exhibition. The first, the left half of a double page composition, shows the poet Saʿdī, Mughal nobles, and Muslim rulers, presumably in attendance on Jahāngīr (*no. 27*). It is signed Abū᾽l Hasan, a form of signature used only before the grant of the title *Nādir-al-Zamān* in about 1618. The second painting is a small portrait of the infant Shāh Shujāʿ (*no. 28*) and is based on an English portrait type. Such works were brought to the court in 1615 by Sir Thomas Roe and quickly became fashionable.[3] Here the acceptance of a child as subject, as well as the device of placing fruit in his lap, has no precedent in the Mughal tradition, but was a popular English motif.[4] Both illustrations, in fact, show a continuing interest in European paintings and prints, although in different ways. *No. 27* makes it evident through the heavy modelling and shading of the attendant figures.

There is less abundant material for a judgment of Abū᾽l Hasan's work after about 1620. Richard Ettinghausen has shown that a signed allegorical portrait, *Jahāngīr's Dream of Shāh ʿAbbās' Visit*, in the Freer Gallery of Art, is datable between 1618 and 1622. It is one of the artist's most formal and highly finished works, although there is no reason to assume that this was a general stylistic development. More troublesome is a group of well-known portraits identified as showing *Shāh Jahān on the Peacock Throne*, for at least two of the paintings—one of which is inscribed to Abū᾽l Hasan, *Nādir-al-Zamān*—seem to be later copies, probably made about 1800. In addition, the painted throne conforms to none of the many contemporary verbal descriptions of it (see catalogue entry for *no. 24*).

One of the most reliable of the portraits signed by Abū᾽l Hasan of Shāh Jahān as emperor is in the Walters Art Gallery, Baltimore (*no. 29*). Again, the aliveness of both observation and modelling, especially evident in the hem of the robe, links it clearly to the *Anwār-i-Suhailī* page, making us aware of how consistent Abū᾽l Hasan's style remained throughout his career.

A comparison of the *Portrait of Shāh Jahān* (*no. 29*) with a double portrait by his contemporary Bichitr, *Shāh Shujāʿ with Gaj Singh of Marwar* (*no. 34*), may further clarify Abū᾽l Hasan's style. Bichitr rejoices in building and contrasting intricate patterns and in setting down intense bright colors bounded by sharply defined contours. Abū᾽l Hasan, however, with no less technical control, aims at broader surface effects: his colors are darker, more subdued, less instantly brilliant, and his use of line much softer. What this produces, in works by Abū᾽l Hasan, is an initial concentration on the subject portrayed, rather than an immediate impression of surface brilliance. Moreover, Abū᾽l Hasan's portraits are among the most penetrating in Mughal art.

There is no evidence yet that Abū᾽l Hasan painted beyond the first years of Shāh Jahān's reign, despite the fact that he was relatively young (about forty) at the time of the emperor's accession.

27

THE PRESENTATION OF A BOOK

Inscribed by Abū᾽l Hasan
Circa 1616
18 × 13 cm. (29.5 × 19 cm.)
Lent by the Walters Art Gallery, Baltimore (W. 668, fol. 37)
Bibliography: Ettinghausen, *Sultans*, Pl. 11; Ettinghausen, "Emperor," pp. 110–11, fig. 2

Eight men surround the stooped figure of the thirteenth-century poet Saʿdī, who is presenting a book to someone, presumably Jahāngīr, who would have been found on a page to the right. In addition to the poet, other men are identified by inscription: Khwāja Jahān (d. 1620), at the upper right; Mīrzā Ṣādiq al-Husainī, lower right, who here fulfills his function as *bakshī* ("registrar"), to which he was appointed in 1615; Bāyazīd Yildirim, left foreground, the Ottoman Sultan defeated by Tīmūr; and, in the right foreground, the Shāh of Iran.

Clearly, this is not to be interpreted as an actual *darbār*, for the participants are not contemporary. Instead, as Richard Ettinghausen has shown, this is a statement of Jahāngīr's preference for men of religious rather than political importance, and, in particular, of his devotion to the mystic poet, Saʿdī. More difficult to determine, however, is the date. The presence of two Mughal courtiers suggests that 1615–20 (between the appointment of one and the death of the other) would be proper; while the signature, naming Abūʿl Hasan without his title of *Nādir-al-Zamān*, would encourage a date prior to 1618. There is no reason to doubt the signature, as Ettinghausen has done, for the style is that of the painter at his most typical and most observant. How this left half relates to the *Darbār of Jahāngīr* in the Freer Gallery of Art is problematical. The Freer painting compositionally completes the Baltimore page; it is the same size, and both were found together in an important album formed in the nineteenth century. There is, however, a discrepancy in the size of the figures, although this is not unknown in double page compositions, even by the same painter. The Freer painting, as Ettinghausen has argued, is datable to 1615–16.

Color plate facing text page 88.

Detail on page 70.

28

AN INFANT PRINCE

Inscribed: *raqam-banda be-ikhlās Nādir-al-Zamān* ("work of the slave Nādir-al-Zamān")
Circa 1617
9.3 × 5.3 cm.
Anonymous Loan
Bibliography: *Welch AMI*, no. 31

Stuart C. Welch has suggested that this might be Shāh Shujāʿ, the second son of Shāh Jahān, born in 1616, and an inscribed portrait of the young prince in about 1619 is found in the Boston *Darbār of Jahāngīr (no. 14)*. As a child, Shujāʿ remained at his grandfather's court, and Jahāngīr recounts an incident when, at the age of four, Shujāʿ fell from a palace window onto a *farrash*, or "carpet spreader," working on the ground below. "Then weakness overcame him, and he could speak no more," the emperor wrote in the *Tūzuk-i-Jahāngīrī*.

I was lying down when this alarming news reached me, and ran out in a state of bewilderment. When I saw him in this state my senses forsook me, and for a long time holding him in my affectionate embrace I was distracted with this favour from Allah. When a child of four years of age falls headlong from a place . . . and no harm happens to his limbs, it is a cause for amazement. Having performed my prostrations for this fresh act of goodness, I distributed alms.[5]

This child, with regular and handsome features, seems not to be the same infant shown in an uninscribed portrait formerly in the Rothschild Collection, and identified by Stchoukine as Shujāʿ.[6] The latter may be Prince Murād Bakhsh.[7]

29

SHĀH JAHĀN ENTHRONED

Inscribed: *amal-i-Abūʿl Hasan al-Mashhadī, Nādir-al-Zamān* ("the work of Abūʿl Hasan of Meshhed, *Nādir-al-Zamān*")
7.7 × 6 cm. (29.3 × 19 cm.)
Lent by the Walters Art Gallery, Baltimore (W. 668, fol. 45)

The inscription on this superb small portrait is of particular interest, for the term *al-Mashhadī* indicates that the city of Meshhed was considered the family home of the painter, and therefore of his father Āqā Rizā. The matter is considered further in the discussion of the latter painter's style.

More amusing, but presently of unknown significance, is the decoration carefully detailed on the throne. In portraits of both Jahāngīr and Shāh Jahān, a symbolic lion and lamb (or goat, sheep, etc.) is sometimes shown, proclaiming the peacefulness of the particular emperor's rule

27

29

(e.g., *no. 45*). Here, on the front panel to the left, a recumbent lion is seen with an ox; but to the right, the lion seems to be lying on his back with his paws in the air.

The emperor appears to be the same age as in an accession portrait in the *Padshāh-nāma*,[8] thus allowing us a basis for dating the work.

Further Major Attributions to Abūʿl Hasan, *Nādir-al-Zamān*

St. John

> Inscribed by Abūʿl Hasan
> Dated A.H. 1009 = A.D. 1600–1601, "in my thirteenth year"
> Ashmolean Museum, Oxford: Reitlinger Collection
> Bibliography: Gray et al., *R.A. Arts of India and Pakistan*, no. 665, Pl. 128

This figure is copied from the *Crucifixion*, dated 1511, in the *Engraved Passion* by Dürer (see W. L. Strauss, *The Complete Engravings, Etchings, and Drypoints of Albrecht Dürer* [New York, 1972], no. 53). However, it is difficult to establish whether the Dürer print, or one of the various later copies was used by the Mughal artist.

Anwār-i-Suhailī Manuscript (fol. 41b)

> Inscribed: *amal-i-Abūʿl Hasan khāk-i-astān-i-Rizā* ("work of Abūʿl Hasan, dust of the threshhold of Rizā")
> Dated 1604–10
> British Library (Or. Add. 18579)
> Bibliography: Wilkinson, *Lights*, Pl. 6; Coomaraswamy, "Notes," pp. 206–7

Seated Lady under a Tree

> From the *Leningrad Album*
> Inscribed to Abūʿl Hasan, son of Āqā Rizā
> Circa 1605–10
> Academy of Sciences, Leningrad
> Bibliography: Ivanova et al., *Albom Indiyskikh*, Pl. 12

Seated Lady under a Tree

> From the *Leningrad Album*
> Inscribed to Abūʿl Hasan
> Circa 1605–10
> Academy of Sciences, Leningrad
> Bibliography: Ivanova et al., *Albom Indiyskikh*, Pl. 13

The above two works are variant adaptations of a European source, perhaps after Martin de Vos.

Būstān of Saʿdī Manuscript (fol. 67v)

> Attributed here to Abūʿl Hasan
> Dated 1605
> Private Collection (ex-Rothschild and Goelet Collections)
> Bibliography: Stchoukine, "Un Bustan de Saʿdi," fig. 4

Fol. 67v, and possibly a second page, show Abūʿl Hasan's style just prior to the 1604–10 *Anwār-i-Suhailī*. Other artists to whom pages can be attributed include Āqā Rizā, Mīrzā Ghulām, Sūr Dās, Daulat, Govardhan, and Padarāth.

Squirrels in a Plane Tree

> Attributed to Abūʿl Hasan, *Nādir-al-Zamān*
> Circa 1610
> India Office Library, London
> Bibliography: *Welch AMI*, no. 35 (color); *Welch IMP*, Pl. 25 (color); Archer, *Indian Miniatures*, Pl. 25 (color); Wilkinson, *Mughal Painting*, Pl. 6 (color)

According to Toby Falk, the reverse of the painting which is mounted on an eighteenth-century album leaf, bears the following inscription: *amal-i-nādir-al-ʿasr nādir-al-zamān* ("the work of *Nādir-al-ʿAsr, Nādir-al-Zamān*"). Nādir-al-ʿAsr was a title given to the painter Ustād Mansūr; it has been suggested by Aśok Das that this is a collaborative effort of that artist and Abūʿl Hasan (see Das, "Mansur," p. 39). The style, however, does not accord with Mansūr's distinctively methodical line-work and thin pigments.

Portrait of a Lady with a Rifle

> Inscribed: "work of Abūʿl Hasan"
> Circa 1612–15
> Rampur State Library

It has been suggested plausibly that this is a portrait of Nūr Jahān, whom Jahāngīr married in 1611, and whose exploits as a shot were often mentioned in the *Tūzuk-i-Jahāngīrī* as in vol. I, p. 375, for example.

Darbār of Jahāngīr (right half)

> Inscribed to Abūʿl Hasan
> Circa 1615–16
> Freer Gallery of Art, Washington, D.C. (46.28)
> Bibliography: Ettinghausen, *Sultans*, Pl. 11; Ettinghausen, "Emperor," fig. 3; Stchoukine, "Portraits III," pp. 233–39

Prince Khurram (Shāh Jahān)

> From the *Minto Album*
> Inscribed to *Nādir-al-Zamān*
> Dated 1615–16
> Victoria and Albert Museum, London
> Bibliography: Gascoigne, *Great Moghuls*, p. 186; Stchoukine, *Peinture Indienne*, Pl. XXXII

An inscription by Shāh Jahān notes that this is a "good portrait of me in my 25th year" (i.e., after his twenty-fourth birthday). The work should therefore be dated A.D. 1615–16 (= A.H. 1024), as the future emperor was born in A.D. 1592 (= A.H. 1000). Since the subject is titled Shāh Jahān, a designation only granted in 1617, and the painter called by his honorific, *Nādir-al-Zamān*, the inscription must have been added at a later date.

Elderly Couple

> From the *Leningrad Album*
> Inscribed: "work of Abūʿl Hasan"
> Circa 1615–20

Academy of Sciences, Leningrad
Bibliography: Ivanova et al., *Albom Indiyskikh*, Pl. 9

A Pilgrim

Inscribed: "work of Nādir-al-Zamān"
Circa 1615–20
Private Collection
Bibliography: Colnaghi, *Persian and Mughal Art*, no. 93

Head of Christ

From the *Minto Album*
Inscribed by Abūᶜl Hasan, "servant of Jahāngīr Shāh" (on painting); "the work of Nādir-al-Zamān" (on border)
Circa 1615–20
A. Chester Beatty Library, Dublin (Ms. 7, No. 12)
Bibliography: Gascoigne, *Great Moghuls*, p. 114 (color)

Jahāngīr Shooting the Head of Malik ᶜAmbar

From the *Minto Album*
Inscribed by Abūᶜl Hasan
Circa 1615–20
A. Chester Beatty Library, Dublin (Ms. 7, No. 15)
Bibliography: Gascoigne, *Great Moghuls*, p. 153; *Beatty Library*, vol. III, Pl. 62

Celebrations at the Accession of Jahāngīr

From the *Jahāngīr-nāma* and the *Leningrad Album*
Inscribed to Abūᶜl Hasan
Datable to 1618
Academy of Sciences, Leningrad
Bibliography: Ivanova et al., *Albom Indiyskikh*, Pl. 7 (color)

Jahāngīr's Dream of Shāh ᶜAbbās' Visit

Inscribed by Abūᶜl Hasan, *Nādir-al-Zamān*, son of Āqā Rizā
Circa 1618–22
Freer Gallery of Art, Washington, D.C. (45.9)
Bibliography: Ettinghausen, *Sultans*, Pl. 12; *Welch IMP*, Pl. 21 (color)

Jassa Jām

From the *Berlin Album* (p. 23a)
Inscribed: *Nādir-al-Zamān*
Circa 1618
Staatsbibliothek, West Berlin
Bibliography: Kühnel and Goetz, *Indian Book Painting*, Pl. 37

At the end of the twelfth regnal year (= A.D. 1618), Jahāngīr records in the *Tūzuk*: "On this day the Jam zamindar had the good fortune to kiss the ground. He presented 50 horses, 100 muhrs, and 100 rupees. His name is Jassa, and Jam is his title. . . . He is one of the chief zamindars of Gujarat, and, indeed, he is one of the noted rajas of India. . . . I gave him a dress of honour." (*Tūzuk*, vol. I, p. 443.) It is presumably this meeting that the portrait commemorates.

Jahāngīr at the *Jharoka* Window

From the *Jahāngīr-nāma*

Inscribed to *Nādir-al-Zamān*
Circa 1620
Private Collection
Bibliography: Sotheby 23 March 1973, Lot 6 (color)

Jahāngīr with a Portrait of Akbar

Inscribed to *Nādir-al-Zamān* (in part)
Musée Guimet, Paris
Bibliography: *Stchoukine Louvre*, Pl. VI; Arnold and Grohmann, *Islamic Book*, Pl. 83; *Welch AMI*, no. 29; Krishna, "Problems of a Portrait," pp. 392–94

Other Attributions

A Bullock Chariot

Inscribed: "work of Abūᶜl Hasan"
Present location unknown
Bibliography: Mehta, *Studies*, pp. 63ff., Pl. 27

Neptune

Inscribed: "work of Abūᶜl Hasan, son of Rizā"
Collection of Jagdish Goenka
Bibliography: Singh, "European Themes," Pl. 35 (color)

Equestian Figure and Falconer

From the *Leningrad Album*
Inscribed to *Nādir-al-Zamān*
Academy of Sciences, Leningrad
Bibliography: Ivanov et al., *Albom Indiyskikh*, Pl. 14

At least three major full versions of this work are known, the others being in the Rampur State Library (*Brown*, Pl. IX) and the British Museum (Martin, *Miniature Paintings*, Pl. 177). Moreover, a later drawing is in the Museum of Fine Arts, Boston (*Coomaraswamy Boston*, Pl. XXX).

Harem Scene

From the *Nāsir-ud-dīn Album*
Inscribed: "work of Abūᶜl Hasan"
Imperial Library, Tehran
Bibliography: Godard, "Album," p. 214ff. and fig. 79

Prince Giving Wine to a Young Woman

Inscribed to *Nādir-al-Zamān*
Walters Art Gallery, Baltimore (W. 668, fol. 40v)

The lower portions of the figures have been completely repainted, but the faces are intact, and the attribution seems plausible. From the same album as *nos. 16–18, 27,* and *29* in this exhibition.

Jahāngīr Holding a Book

Inscribed to Abūᶜl Hasan
Metropolitan Museum of Art, New York

Spotted Forktail

From the *Kevorkian Album*
Inscribed to *Nādir-al-Zamān*
Metropolitan Museum of Art, New York
Bibliography: *Dimand Bulletin*, p. 100

A second version of this work, also from the *Kevorkian Album* but with an inscription naming Ustād Mansūr, is in the Freer Gallery of Art. Both seem to be of the early nineteenth century, as does the portrait listed above.

Wounded Buck

Private Collection
Bibliography: Welch and Beach, *Gods*, no. 10; Welch, *Mughal and Deccan Miniature Painting*, no. 14, fig. 15

An attribution to Abūʿl Hasan has been proposed by Stuart C. Welch and Robert Skelton; see also *no. 69*.

Shāh Jahān Standing

From the *Leningrad Album*
Inscribed to *Nādir-al-Zamān*
Imperial Library, Tehran
Bibliography: Godard, "Album," pp. 218ff., and fig. 81

Jahāngīr Holding an Orb

From the *Kevorkian Album*
Inscribed to *Nādir-al-Zamān*
Freer Gallery of Art, Washington, D.C.

A late copy of this composition, now in a private collection, is inscribed with the information that the scene represents Jahāngīr's victory over the rebellious Shāh Jahān in 1623 (see Christie's 11 July 1974, Lot 81). A pounce, or pattern, for the composition is in the Freer Gallery of Art.

Jahāngīr Standing on a Globe Shooting Poverty

Los Angeles County Museum of Art
Bibliography: Kahlenberg, "Mughal Patka," Pl. XCII

While the work is not signed and is later in date, it is almost certainly based on a now lost composition by Abūʿl Hasan, and is an important addition to the iconography of Jahāngīrī allegorical portraits.

Shāh Jahān

Inscribed to *Nādir-al-Zamān*
Private Collection
Bibliography: Sotheby 23 March 1973, Lot 3

A closely related portrait is in the British Library (Gray et al., *R.A. Arts of India and Pakistan*, no. 753, Pl. 136), and both bear the date of the first regnal year (=A.D. 1628). Such portraits commemorating the emperor's accession must have been turned out in quantity.

Shāh Jahān on the Peacock Throne

Inscribed to *Nādir-al-Zamān*
Metropolitan Museum of Art, New York
Bibliography: Hambly and Swaan, *Cities*, p. 75

There are three identical versions of the painting. This, and its counterpart in the *Wantage Album* (*Wantage Bequest*, no. 16, Pl. 10) seem to be based on a third composition, possibly the unsigned painting formerly in the Rothschild Collection (Colnaghi, *Persian and Mughal Art*, no. 95). The throne, despite a traditional identification, does not follow contemporary descriptions of the Peacock Throne (see text accompanying *no. 24*).

Āqā Rizā

Jahāngīr referred very briefly to Āqā Rizā, during his discussion of Abūʿl Hasan in the *Tūzuk-i-Jahāngīrī*:

His [Abūʿl Hasan's] father, Aqa Riza of Herat (or Merv) at the time when I was a prince, joined my service. There is, however, no comparison between his work and that of his father.[1]

The statement is more in praise of Abūʿl Hasan than purposely derogatory to Āqā Rizā, but it establishes the elder man as an important personality, whatever our view of the visual rewards of his work. He brought to India direct knowledge of the most current Iranian artistic styles; he served as a painter for Prince Salīm and is therefore important to an investigation of Salīm's taste and patronage before the imperial workshops came under his control; and, of course, he was enormously influential as the father and presumably early teacher of Abūʿl Hasan and, as various inscriptions inform us, of ʿĀbid.

We know that Āqā Rizā was in India by the time of Abūʿl Hasan's birth in 1588–89, and his earliest known works are probably two pages in the *Muraqqaʿ-e-Gulshan* which are almost purely Iranian. They indicate that Āqā Rizā was a thoroughly trained Safavid (Iranian) painter at the time of his arrival at the Mughal court, and it is informative to see what happens to his style under Mughal impact. Jahāngīr's memoirs state that he came from Herat, or Merv, but inscriptions on two paintings refer to Abūʿl Hasan as *al-Mashhadī* ("of Meshhed"). As one of these inscriptions is by Abūʿl Hasan himself, and the other by ʿĀbid, the Meshhed affiliation of the family seems unquestionable.[2] And indeed, the great *Haft Aurang* of *Jāmī* manuscript, made at Meshhed between 1556 and 1565,[3] is a perfect stylistic source for the

Muraqqaᶜ-e-Gulshan pages by Āqā Rizā referred to above.

We have no definite information on the painter's activities before his appearance in India, however, nor do we know why he left Iran. It seems that he is not to be identified with either Maulānā Muhammad Rizā of Meshhed, or Muhammad Rizā of Meshhed, the pupil of Mīr Sayyid Ahmad, both known from contemporary texts.[4] That he is also distinct from the late sixteenth-century Iranian court painter Āqā Rizā has long been accepted,[5] although the seeming commonness of the name has caused considerable confusion.

Āqā Rizā's Iranian origins are also clear in the *Portrait of a Courtier (no. 30)*, for the pose, such details as the bench, and the languorous mood are duplicated in innumerable Safavid illustrations. What defines the work as Mughal is the degree of modelling in the face, and, of course, the inscription. This latter refers to Āqā Rizā as *murīd* ("disciple"), a term found in inscriptions by both Āqā Rizā and the young Abūᶜl Hasan and used by Mughal courtiers to indicate their subservience to the wisdom of the emperor (or in this case, the prince).[6] Above this, the name Sultān Salīm appears in gold, so there can be no doubt to whom the painter is paying homage. That Salīm is titled Sultān allows us to date the illustration before 1599–1600, at which point the rebellious prince took the title *Shāh*.

The major paintings by Āqā Rizā are in an *Anwār-i-Suhailī* manuscript in the British Library which has an inscription stating that it was finished in 1610. Two of Āqā Rizā's illustrations, however, are independently inscribed with the date 1604. The book, which was thus begun for Jahāngīr before his accession, has two types of illustration: works of a very Iranian character by Āqā Rizā and painters under his influence (e.g., Abūᶜl Hasan and Mīrzā Ghulām); and paintings of a more typically Mughal type by Bishan Dās, Anant, Nānhā, etc. The first group is distinguished by brilliant mineral colors, frequent use of gold, carefully organized surface patterns, general spatial flatness, and a detailed, miniaturistic technique; the others tend to show softer earth colors and looser brushwork, traits current in imperial Mughal works. This same stylistic range is found in other major manuscripts made at the same time (see *no. 1*), and serves to emphasize Āqā Rizā's distance from mainstream Mughal tradition. It may have been this inability to adapt, even more than the quality

of individual illustrations, that caused Jahāngīr's comments on the painter's work.

The margins of a page from one of Jahāngīr's albums (*no. 6 recto*) show this phase of Āqā Rizā's style, for, while unsigned, the figures are identical to those in the *Anwār-i-Suhailī*. It is a superbly decorative border and shows episodes that occurred during a hunt. Individual faces are defined and modelled far more smoothly than in *Portrait of a Courtier (no. 30)*, and the overall action has an immediacy that was not present in Āqā Rizā's earliest work. This development came about through the painter's increasing familiarity with Mughal attitudes and through his study of European prints; fol. 105 of the *Muraqqaᶜ-e-Gulshan*, for example, signed by Āqā Rizā and dated A.H. 1008 = A.D. 1599–1600, uses European motifs in the margins. Nonetheless, despite the surface "Mughalization" of the painter's work, the figures lack individuality or interior life. A comparison of *no. 6 recto* with the marginal figures by Govardhan (*no. 5 verso*) makes clear the degree to which Āqā Rizā was unable to go beyond traditional attitudes to human form. This is no judgment on the painting per se; it is simply that the meaning of the figures does not accord with contemporary Mughal imperial ideas.

The Iranian orientation of Āqā Rizā's style was an important ingredient in the evolution of Prince Salīm's taste; it may be that such innovations as the marginal designs found on imperial manuscripts of the mid-1590s, as well as on the earliest Jahāngīr album pages, were due to ideas introduced by Āqā Rizā. His specific influence, however, is not found after about 1605, and it seems that his style went quickly out of date once Jahāngīr had the full imperial workshops at his command. That Āqā Rizā's activity was not confined simply to painting is shown by his reported responsibility for the design of Khusrau Bāgh, the garden at Allahabad in which Salīm's wife, Shāh Bēgam, was buried in 1604.[7]

Literature: Chaghtai, "Aqa Riza"; Goetz, "Early Muraqqas," *Marg*, pp. 39–41.

30

PORTRAIT OF A COURTIER

Inscribed: *Raqam-i-Āqā Rizā murīd ba-ikhlās* ("work of the devoted disciple, Āqā Rizā")
Circa 1595

14.4 × 7.8 cm.
Provenance: Goloubev Collection
Lent by the Museum of Fine Arts, Boston: Francis Bartlett
Donation of 1912 and Picture Fund (14.609)
Bibliography: *Coomaraswamy Boston*, no. XL, Pl. XXI;
Martin, *Miniature Paintings*, fig. 29

The motif of a prince or courtier seated under a willow or blossoming tree had a particularly extensive life. Originating in Iran, it passed into Mughal India, as we see here, to the Deccan, Rajasthan, and the Panjab Hills.[8]

Further Major Attributions to Āqā Rizā

A Prince Watching Ladies Bathing
From the *Muraqqaᶜ-e-Gulshan*
Inscribed to Āqā Rizā
Circa 1580–90
Imperial Library, Tehran
Bibliography: Hajek, *Indian Miniatures*, Pl. 23 (color)

Court Scene
From the *Muraqqaᶜ-e-Gulshan*
Inscribed: "work of Rizā, disciple (*murīd*) of Padshāh Salīm"
Circa 1580–90
Imperial Library, Tehran
Bibliography: *BWG*, no. 236, Pl. CIV

Prince with a Falcon Kneeling before Sheikh Salīm Chishtī
From the *Muraqqaᶜ-e-Gulshan*
Inscribed: "work of the devoted disciple, Āqā Rizā"
Imperial Library, Tehran
Literature: Goetz, "Early Muraqqas," *Marg*, p. 39

Muraqqaᶜ-e-Gulshan (fols. 29, 105, 145, 152)
Inscribed to Āqā Rizā
Circa 1600
Imperial Library, Tehran
Bibliography: Godard, "Marges," pp. 13ff., and figs. 1–8

These are all marginal illustrations. Fol. 105, which is dated A.H. 1008 = A.D. 1599–1600, contains adaptations of European prints.

Portrait of a Head Gardener
Inscribed: "work of the devout and true servant of Shāh Salīm, Āqā Rizā"
Circa 1600
Collection of Edwin Binney 3rd
Bibliography: *Binney Collection*, no. 42

Būstān of Saᶜdī Manuscript (fol. 169)
Dated 1605

Private Collection (ex-Rothschild and Goelet Collections)
Bibliography: *Welch AMI*, no. 24

The page has been attributed to Āqā Rizā by Stuart C. Welch. See also Stchoukine, "Un Bustan di Saᶜdi."

Anwār-i-Suhailī Manuscript
(fols. 21a, 36a, 40b, 54b, 331b)
Inscribed to Āqā Rizā
Dated 1604–10
British Library (Add. 18579)
Bibliography: Wilkinson, *Lights*, Pls. III–V, VII, XXIX;
Coomaraswamy, "Notes," pp. 202–12 and fig. 11

The signatures (or inscriptions) vary on each folio: 21a reads *amal-i-Muhammad Rizā murīd* ("work of the disciple Muhammad Rizā"); 36a is *amal-i-Āqā Muhammad Rizā, murīd Padshāh* ("work of the emperor's disciple Āqā Muhammad Rizā"); 54b is *amal-i-Muhammad Rizā ba-ikhlās murīd* ("work of the devoted disciple Muhammad Rizā"); while 40b and 331b are inscribed in the margins simply *Āqā Rizā*. One further page (see Wilkinson, *Lights*, Pl. II) can be attributed to the artist as well.

30

Other Attributions

Man Piping

> Museum of Fine Arts, Boston (14.610)
> Bibliography: *Coomaraswamy Boston*, no. XLI, Pl. XXI;
> Martin, *Miniature Paintings*, fig. 30

Gentleman with a Gold Wine Cup

> Fogg Art Museum, Harvard University, Cambridge
> (1921.33)
> Bibliography: Schroeder, *Fogg Persian Miniatures*, no. XIX

Seated Youth

> Museum für Völkerkunde, Berlin
> Bibliography: Schulz, *Miniaturmalerei*, vol. II, Pl. 147c

The attribution was proposed by Eric Schroeder in *Fogg Persian Miniatures*, p. 111.

Khwāja Jahān and a Youth Fallen from a Tree

> From the *Kevorkian Album*
> Metropolitan Museum of Art, New York
> Bibliography: *Dimand Bulletin*, p. 95

A second version of this composition, of late date and in the *Wantage Album*, is inscribed to Farrukh Beg (*Wantage Bequest*, no. 5, Pl. 4).

Soz u Godaz of Nauᶜī Manuscript

> Bibliothèque Nationale, Paris
> Literature: Goetz, "Early Muraqqas," *Marg*, p. 39

Shāh-nāma Manuscript

> Bayerisches Staatsbibliothek, Munich (Cod. Pers. 10)
> Literature: Goetz, "Early Muraqqas," *Marg*, p. 39

Lovers Picnicking

> Keir Collection
> Bibliography: *Robinson ed., Keir*, V.49

Bālchand

That Bālchand had duties at the Mughal court in addition to his activities as painter is shown on fol. 72 verso of the Windsor *Padshāh-nāma*, where, in a darbār scene datable (as an event) to about 1635, he is depicted presiding over jewels and precious objects being distributed or received by the emperor (*fig. 6*). Likewise, on fol. 43 verso, we find him present as Jahāngīr bids farewell to Prince Khurram departing for his campaign against the Rānā of Mewar in 1614 (*fig. 5*). Bālchand, shown as a man of about thirty, is a seemingly meek attendant in the latter scene and is dressed in modest Hindu garb. On fol. 72 verso, however, he has become elderly and white haired and is dressed in Mughal fashion (Hindus tied their coats

FIGS. 5 (left) and 6 (below). Portraits of Bālchand. By Bālchand, ca. 1635–40. From the Windsor *Padshāh-nāma* ms. (fols. 43v and 72v, details). The Royal Library, Windsor.

31 (detail)

34 (detail)

under the left arm, Muslims under the right). Thus, besides the clues which these portraits provide about Bālchand as a personality, they evidence the careful regard that most Mughal painters had for the historical and physical correctness of their illustrations, for fol. 43 verso was painted well after the actual event (and probably in the mid-1630s). The object which Bālchand holds, a rectangular board with a red border, may be a support for works being presented for imperial inspection; in any case, it is certainly a reference to his professional activity.[1]

Bālchand's style can be characterized by a comparison of his *Royal Lovers on a Terrace* (*no. 31*), showing Shāh Shujāᶜ and his wife, with a portrait of the same prince seated with Rāja Gaj Singh of Marwar, by Bichitr (*no. 34*). Besides Shuja's presence in each, the major figures are surrounded by elaborately decorated bolsters, rugs, etc. It is not only because of the subject that the Bālchand work is so much more emotionally rich: it is characteristic of the painter that the major interest is the intensity of human relationships. This element is made even more important by the quiet and unobtrusiveness of Bālchand's style; in this he distinguishes himself from the painter Govardhan, whose interests are otherwise very similar. The Bichitr work, on the other hand, is concerned with surface values; it is hard, brilliant, and coldly formal. Whereas Bālchand opens up the background to aid the romantic, evocative mood, Bichitr puts a solid plane of color behind the figures, forcing his technique into even greater prominence. He uses the subject to display this technique, while Bālchand, reversing the procedure, uses his equally superb technical skills to place the human values of the subject foremost.

Royal Lovers on a Terrace is datable to about 1633, for it and a matching work, showing Dārā Shikōh, were probably painted for the marriages of the two princes in that year.[2] Bālchand's earliest important work is a lightly colored drawing of extreme emotional as well as technical sensitivity, in the British Library *Nafahāt-al-Uns* manuscript of 1603. When seen together with a page from a *Dīwān* of Hafiz of about 1610, also in the British Library and attributed here to Bālchand, it is evident that the focus of interest in the painter's mature works was already present at the beginning of his career, and that his technique became more and more able to explore and reveal subsurface emotional currents.

Almost all of Bālchand's known illustrations before the 1630s are more colored drawings than paintings; one exception is a rather unsuccessful page from a *Shāh-nāma* manuscript of about 1610. From the mid-1630s, however, richness of technique becomes an increasingly expressive element in the artist's work. This may not be due to a conscious shift of emphasis but is more probably the result of the character of his commissions, which were inherently formal darbār scenes and portraits. It may also be a result of renewed contact with his brother, Payāg. Bālchand's early works have little in common with those of Payāg, but his illustrations in the *Padshāh-nāma* and the *Gulistān* of Saᶜdī rival his brother's in ability to create a luxuriously rich surface, to give sheen to textiles, or to model forms. At this point, the two men clearly worked closely together, although Bālchand remains more emotionally restrained.

31

ROYAL LOVERS ON A TERRACE

Inscribed: *amal-i-Bālchand* ("work of Bālchand")
Circa 1633
22.5 × 13.1 cm.
Anonymous Loan
Bibliography: *Welch FEM*, no. 65; *Welch IMP*, Pl. 35; Beach, "Rajput Painting," fig. 1

In the mid-seventeenth century, François Bernier, a French traveller in the Mughal Empire, observed of Shāh Shujāᶜ:

Sultan Shuja, the second son of the *Great Mogol*, resembled in many characteristic traits his brother *Dara*; but he was more discreet, firmer of purpose, and excelled him in conduct and address. . . . He was, nevertheless, too much a slave to his pleasures; and once surrounded by his women, who were exceedingly numerous, he would pass whole days and nights in dancing, singing, and drinking wine·. . . the business of government therefore often languished, and the affections of his subjects were in a great measure alienated.[3]

Royal Lovers on a Terrace, however, shows the prince at an earlier and more innocent age, for it seems to have been painted in 1633, at the time of Shuja's marriage to the daughter of Mīrzā Rustam Safavī (Mīr Rustam of Qandahar). This was an event that followed, by only a few days, the wedding of his brother, the heir apparent, Dārā Shikōh. Matching portraits were probably painted of the two princes at this time, for a compositionally identical work, showing Dārā and his consort, was formerly in the Museum of Fine Arts, Boston.[4]

For additional portraits of Shujāᶜ see *nos. 14, 28,* and *34*.

31

32

32

DĀRĀ SHIKŌH

> Attributed to Bālchand
> Circa 1639
> 3.49 × 2.86 cm.
> Anonymous Loan

Small oval portraits, a form inspired by English miniatures brought to India by Sir Thomas Roe,[5] remained popular throughout the seventeenth century. For another example, see *no. 64*. The work has been attributed to Bālchand by Stuart C. Welch.

Further Major Attributions to Bālchand

Bahāristān of Jāmiᶜ Manuscript (fol. no. unknown)
> Dated 1595
> Bodleian Library, Oxford (Elliott 254)

Akbar-nāma Manuscript (fols. 152b, 153)
> Inscribed to Bālchand
> Dated 1604
> A. Chester Beatty Library, Dublin (Ms. 3)
> Bibliography: *Beatty Library*, vol. III, Pl. 24

Nafahāt-al-Uns Manuscript (fol. 315a)
> Inscribed to Bālchand
> Dated 1603
> British Library (Or. 1362)

Shāh-nāma Manuscript (fol. no. unknown)
> Inscribed: *Bālchand*
> Circa 1610
> Present location unknown (ex-Rothschild Collection)
> Bibliography: Colnaghi, *Persian and Mughal Art*, no. 88ii

Dīwān of Hafīz Manuscript (fol. 42r)
> Attributed here to Bālchand
> Circa 1610

> British Library (Or. 7573)
> Bibliography: Barrett and Gray, *Painting in India*, p. 100 (color)

Berlin Album (p. 13b)
> Inscribed to Bālchand
> Circa 1609–18
> Staatsbibliothek, Berlin
> Bibliography: Kühnel and Goetz, *Indian Book Painting*, Pl. 38

Shāh Jahān and his Sons
> From the *Minto Album*
> Inscribed: "servant of the royal court, Bālchand"
> Circa 1628–30
> A. Chester Beatty Library, Dublin (Ms. 7, No. 10)

Three Younger Sons of Shāh Jahān
> From the *Minto Album*
> Inscribed: "work of Bālchand"
> Circa 1637
> Victoria and Albert Museum, London
> Bibliography: Deneck, *Indian Art*, fig. 34 (color)

Āsaf Khān
> From the *Wantage Album*
> Inscribed: "work of Bālchand"
> Circa 1640
> Victoria and Albert Museum, London
> Bibliography: *BM*, no. 128

If the identification is correct, this would seem to be a post-humous portrait. Āsaf Khān is shown as he would have appeared about 1615, whereas the style of the work is that of Bālchand's later years.

Padshāh-nāma Manuscript (fols. 43v, 72v, 134v)
> Inscribed to Bālchand
> Circa 1635–40
> Royal Library, Windsor Castle

Given the ages of the princes, fol. 72v could not be dated before about 1635, while fol. 43v showing Jahāngīr with Khurram is in identical style. Fol. 134v which depicts an event of 1611 (see *Tūzuk*, vol. I, pp. 185–86), is very similar in treatment of landscape to the *Three Younger Sons of Shāh Jahān* of about 1637. All three pages are distinctly more elaborate in visual effect than Bālchand's simple and direct style of pre-1633, and show the painter's increasing stylistic kinship with his brother Payāg.

Jān Nisār Khān
> From the *Kevorkian Album*
> Inscribed: "work of Bālchand"
> Circa 1640
> Metropolitan Museum of Art, New York

The title, Jān Nisar Khān, was granted to Hidāyat Ullāh, Fidāᶜī Khān, in 1640, and six years later he was sent as ambassador to Iran. This, as well as the elaborately worked technical finesse of the portrait, would place the date of execution late in Bālchand's career. There is a marginal attribution, and a microscopic signature on the sword scabbard.

Gulistān of Sa°dī Manuscript (fol. no. uncertain)

Inscribed: "work of Bālchand"
Circa 1640
Private collection (formerly Collection of the Marquess of Bute)

Other Attributions

Jahāngīr

A. Chester Beatty Library, Dublin (Ms. 45, No. 1)

A signature has been read as Bālchand by Robert Skelton.

Jahāngīr

Private Collection
Bibliography: Sotheby 26 March 1973, Lot 3

Shāh Jahān

From the *Wantage Album*
Victoria and Albert Museum, London
Bibliography: *Wantage Bequest*, no. 15, Pl. 9

Shāh Jahān with a Child

Victoria and Albert Museum, London
Bibliography: Gray et al., *R.A. Arts of India and Pakistan*, no. 754, Pl. 136

The attribution has been suggested by Stuart C. Welch (*Welch FEM*, p. 109).

Akbar with Jahāngīr

From the *Kevorkian Album*
Metropolitan Museum of Art, New York
Bibliography: Dimand, *Handbook*, fig. 225

There are several versions of this composition; one in Prague, signed "work of Bālchand Mīr Ghulām," is the earliest.

Akbar, Jahāngīr, and Shāh Jahān

From the *Nāsir-ud-dīn Album*
Imperial Library, Tehran
Bibliography: Godard, "Album," no. 2, fig. 64

Shāh Shujā° (?)

From the *Nāsir-ud-dīn Album*
Imperial Library, Tehran
Bibliography: Godard, "Album," no. 41, fig. 91

Bāqir Khān

India Office Library, London (Johnson Album 25, fol. 9)
Bibliography: Arnold and Grohmann, *Islamic Book*, Pl. 88

Bāqir Khān

From the *Nāsir-ud-dīn Album*
Imperial Library, Tehran
Bibliography: Godard, "Album," no. 19, fig. 75

Mīrzā Abū Tālib

Present location unknown
Bibliography: Maggs Brothers, Ltd., *Oriental Miniatures and Illumination, Bulletin No. 22* (London, 1974), Lot 2

Madonna

Museum of Ethnology, Berlin (I.C. 24338, p. 12b)
Literature: Kühnel and Goetz, *Indian Book Painting*, p. 12

Itimād-ad-daula

From the *Kevorkian Album*
Freer Gallery of Art, Washington, D.C.

Several versions of this portrait are known, including one other in the Freer Gallery. All are late; no early prototype is presently known.

Bichitr

The earliest works definitely ascribable to Bichitr are in a fully mature—if rather experimental—style, and these are followed almost immediately by the series of brilliant portraits for which he is best known. A self-portrait (*fig. 7*) included in the well-known painting *Jahāngīr Preferring a Sūfī Sheikh to Kings*, datable to circa 1620 and in the Freer Gallery of Art, shows a man of no more than thirty. That this is a self-portrait can no longer be doubted. From the later Jahāngīr period, the inclusion within an audience scene of a man holding a painting, or the board on which a painting was presented for viewing by the emperor, is accepted custom; examples, several of them inscribed, are known in both the *Jahāngīr-nāma* and *Padshāh-nāma* manuscripts (see *figs. 5, 6, and 13*).[1] Bichitr's clothing informs us that he was a Hindu, and his age implies that he may have been painting professionally for ten or fifteen years. Since the Freer illustration is the earliest signed work known by the painter, however, we have no firm knowledge of the early development of his style.

There is a major group of portraits by Bichitr that can be dated in the 1630s. One of these is inscribed by the emperor, "a good portrait of me in my fortieth year," giving us the date of 1631; Shāh Jahān was

FIG. 7. Portrait of Bichitr. By Bichitr, ca. 1615–20. Detail from *Jahāngīr Preferring a Sūfī Sheikh to Kings*. Courtesy of the Smithsonian Institution, Freer Gallery of Art, Washington, D.C.

born on 5 January 1592. Others are often datable by the age of the subject, or by the occasion. In general—although there are notable exceptions—Mughal portraits can be historically placed on the basis of such information. For example, *Shāh Shujāᶜ Enthroned with Mahārāja Gaj Singh of Marwar* (*no. 34*) represents an event of 1638. Gaj Singh, who ruled Marwar (better known by the name of its capital, Jodhpur) between 1619 and 1638, had first attended a Mughal darbār with his father in 1615. He fought on the imperialist side against Prince Khurram during the rebellion of 1624, but was reconciled when the prince ascended the throne in 1628. In 1633, he was nominated to be governor of the Deccan, and in January of 1638 was called to Lahore by the emperor, to join Shāh Shujā's Qandahar campaign. He returned to Agra and died there on 6 May 1638.² The painting would seem to be a commemoration of the rājā's association with the Mughal prince who was his cousin. (The emperor's mother was a Jodhpuri.) Its date is confirmed by Shujā's age (he is noticeably older than in *Royal*

Lovers on a Terrace, no. 31) and the painting's style.

Shāh Shujāᶜ Enthroned with Mahārāja Gaj Singh of Marwar is easily compared with another almost contemporary portrait of the Mughal prince, *Royal Lovers on a Terrace*, to which we have just referred. This latter work was painted by Bālchand, and both show figures seated against bolsters on a rug under a canopy. While in the Bālchand portrait Shujāᶜ is younger and handsomer, the major difference is one of technique and expressive effect. Bichitr paints with a brilliant, but hard line; his colors and patterns are bold and assertive, and the effect is of cold formality. This is typical of the majority of his works, although it is seen here to an almost exaggerated degree. The Bālchand painting, on the other hand, is as soft as flesh and silk, a quality we could never associate with Bichitr. The open misty background, subdued colors, and intense sympathetic portraiture are equally typical of Bālchand, for the difference in style cannot be explained merely by the obvious difference in subject and occasion.

Dārā Shikōh on a Pink Elephant (*no. 33*) can be dated to circa 1630 on the basis of the prince's age, for he is younger than in the portrait (formerly in Boston) made at the time of his wedding in 1633.³ Here, instead of clearly bounded shapes and bright color, Bichitr uses heavy shading for the figure on the right, and a nonlinear *pointilliste* technique for the background. This manner of constructing distant landscapes was in general currency at the time; it is found also in *nos. 31* and *43*. Bichitr's interest in modelling through the use of shadow derives from his interest in European prints and paintings, for he is known to have copied motifs from Dürer and a *Portrait of James I* by John de Critz (see below). Cast shadows are found as well in the portrait of *Āsaf Khān*, from the *Minto Album*, painted about 1628–30, and the portrait of Iᶜtabār Khān. The *Minto Album Āsaf Khān* is a perfect transition from what seems the softer, more romantic, and openly innovative style of Bichitr's early works, to the technically immaculate, emotionally restrained paintings made after 1630.

Bichitr continued painting into the 1640s, at least; two firmly datable portraits of that decade are listed below. Stuart C. Welch has suggested that the *Darbār of Aurangzēb* (*no. 67*) is by the artist, as well as *Episode in a Bazaar* (*no. 35*).

करति महाराज श्रीमसिंह

करति महाराजा श्री सिंह

34

33

DĀRĀ SHIKŌH ON A PINK ELEPHANT

Attributed to Bichitr
Circa 1628–30
24.6 × 34.3 cm.
Provenance: Kevorkian Collection
Anonymous Loan
Bibliography: *Welch FEM*, no. 64

Elephants were frequently among presentation gifts made to and by the emperor, and portraits of favorites among these animals were common.[4] A Deccani ruler, Ibrāhīm ʿAdil Shāh of Bijapur (r. 1580–1627), was so devoted to elephants that he wrote in the *Kitāb-i-Nauras*, an anthology of poetry:

Having separated from Atash Khan [his chief elephant] I am feeling the anguish of burning fire. My sad plight is such that the exemplary heat of the Day of Resurrection with its acute intensity is nothing in comparison with it.[5]

The princely rider is the young Dārā Shikōh, who is shown at about the same age in an oval portrait in Paris.[6]
Color plate facing text page 176.

34

SHĀH SHUJAʿ ENTHRONED WITH MAHĀRĀJA GAJ SINGH OF MARWAR

Attributed to Bichitr
Circa 1638
25.2 × 18.5 cm.
Provenance: Heeramaneck Collection
Lent by the Los Angeles County Museum of Art: Nasli and Alice Heeramaneck Collection (L.69.24.246)
Bibliography: *Welch AMI*, no. 44 (color); *Beach Heeramaneck*, no. 216

Shāh Jahān Enthroned (*no. 24*) also depicts an event related to the meeting of these two men in 1638. The two inscriptions in *devanāgarī* script are of later date, and probably added when the picture was in a Rājput collection. The identification given the right figure is erroneous, for it is clearly Shujāʿ, and not Rājā Jai Singh (of Amber) as labelled.[7]
Detail on page 97.

35

EPISODE IN A BAZAAR

Attributed to Bichitr
Circa 1650–60

19.4 × 13.6 cm. (36.5 × 24.7 cm.)
Provenance: Rothschild Collection
Anonymous Loan
Bibliography: Colnaghi, *Persian and Mughal Art*, no. 109 (not reproduced)

The painting, which is unfinished, nonetheless presents extremely perceptive portraits of merchants in the stall of a covered bazaar. The work relates closely to the *Darbār of Aurangzēb* (*no. 67*) and an *Equestrian Figure* (listed below). Stuart C. Welch has attributed all three illustrations to Bichitr whose name is found in a late inscription on the latter work.

Further Major Attributions to Bichitr

Jahāngīr Preferring a Sūfī Sheikh to Kings

Inscribed to Bichitr
Circa 1615–20
Freer Gallery of Art, Washington, D.C. (45.15)
Bibliography: Ettinghausen, *Sultans*, Pl. 14; Ettinghausen, "Emperor"; *Welch IMP*, Pl. 22

Ettinghausen has dated this work to 1625 on the basis of the emperor's age and condition, and because of the absence of Shāh ʿAbbās I among the attendant kings; the Iranian ruler was out of favor after the seizure of Qandahar in 1622. Jahāngīr, however, does not appear older than in the portrait of 1619 (*no. 14*). Furthermore, the presence and choice of attendants may be less consciously controlled than Ettinghausen implies, for otherwise it is impossible to explain the inclusion of Bichitr himself alongside James I and an Ottoman Sultān. The figure at the lower left (reproduced here as *fig. 7*) follows a recognized formula for artists' portraits, and it may therefore be that the symbolism is looser than has been believed; this is discussed above.

There are several reasons to propose an earlier date. The *sūfī* holy man, Sheikh Husain Ajmerī, died about 1620, and Jahāngīr's stay at Ajmer between 1613 and 1616 marked the height of his interest in the Ajmerī shrine (as shown especially in the given list of *Jahāngīr-nāma* illustrations). The Ottoman figure, copied from an unidentified European print, also appears in a darbār of about 1615 (*no. 27*), while the portrait of James I must have been copied from a painting given to Jahāngīr by Sir Thomas Roe, who arrived at the Mughal court in 1615, when it was at Ajmer. The source for Bichitr's figure is a painting by the English king's official painter, John de Critz (for one of several examples see R. Strong, *The Elizabethan Image* [London, 1969], no. 174), and it would not be surprising to find it copied immediately, before its novelty had waned. Moreover, there is the question of style. This is a work that is alive and vital in a manner not associated with the mature Bichitr. And despite the immediate impact of brilliance which the work gives, there are passages—the putti, for example—that show a slight uncertainty in such matters as modelling; this too suggests that this is an early work by the painter.

I'tabār Khān

Inscribed: "work of Bichitr"
Circa 1623
Musée Guimet, Paris
Bibliography: *Stchoukine Louvre*, no. 38, Pl. IX

I'tabār Khān Khwājasarā, who had earlier served as guardian for the rebellious Prince Khusrau, was in charge of the capital province of Agra, together with its fort and treasury, when Prince Khurram attempted to seize power there during his rebellion (Khan, *Maasir-ul Umara*, vol. I, pp. 704–5). The Khān's bravery, in spite of his extreme age, was rewarded by Jahāngīr in 1623 at a ceremony by the lake at Fathepur-Sikri, the background of this portrait (*Tūzuk*, vol. I, pp. 257–58).

Prince and Sages in a Garden

From the *Minto Album*
Inscribed to Bichitr
Circa 1625–30
A. Chester Beatty Library, Dublin
Bibliography: *Beatty Library*, vol. III, Pl. 58; *Welch IMP*, Pl. 36

The proper dating of this work depends on the identification of the prince. S. C. Welch has recently proposed that it is Dārā Shikōh about 1640–50, but other known representations of Dārā in those years show him bearded (e.g., *no. 64*). He appears to be the same man who is shown in a drawing in the Victoria and Albert Museum (see P. Rawson, *Drawing* [London, 1969], pp. 262–63), a work stylistically datable to 1625–30 (see Bichitr, n. 4). Moreover, the rough technique of this illustration is comparable to Bichitr's early paintings rather than to his highly controlled and refined later works.

Āsaf Khān

From the *Minto Album*
Circa 1628–30
Victoria and Albert Museum, London
Bibliography: Stchoukine, *Peinture Indienne*, Pl. 38; Archer, *Indian Miniatures*, Pl. 27 (color)

Padshāh-nāma Manuscript (fol. 50v)

Inscribed to Bichitr
Circa 1630
Royal Library, Windsor Castle
Bibliography: Gascoigne, *Great Moghuls*, p. 145 (color)

The scene is that of the arrival of the three oldest sons of Shāh Jahān, together with their grandfather, Āsaf Khān, at court at Agra on 27 February 1628, during the celebrations of accession. The style of the work accords with the dated imperial portrait of 1631 (listed immediately below).

Shāh Jahān

From the *Minto Album*
Inscribed to Bichitr
Dated 1631
Victoria and Albert Museum, London
Bibliography: *Welch AMI*, no. 43

The inscription, in the imperial hand, states that this is Shāh Jahān in his fortieth year, meaning just after his thirty-ninth birthday early in 1631.

Prince Salīm as a Young Man

From the *Minto Album*
Inscribed to Bichitr
Circa 1635
Victoria and Albert Museum, London
Bibliography: Hambly and Swaan, *Cities*, p. 72 (color)

The reason for the published identification as Salīm is unknown. It bears no physical resemblance to the prince.

Muhammad Rizā Kashmīrī

From the *Minto Album*
Inscribed to Bichitr
Circa 1635
A. Chester Beatty Library, Dublin
Bibliography: *Beatty Library*, vol. III, Pl. 60

A Sheikh Holding an Orb

From the *Minto Album*
Inscribed to Bichitr, "servant of the royal court"
Circa 1635
A. Chester Beatty Library, Dublin
Bibliography: Gascoigne, *Great Moghuls*, p. 61 (color); *Beatty Library*, vol. I, frontispiece (color)

Shāh Jahān

From the *Minto Album*
Inscribed to Bichitr
Circa 1635
A. Chester Beatty Library, Dublin
Bibliography: *Beatty Library*, vol. III, Pl. 63

The angels at the top are copied from Dürer, *The Madonna Crowned by Two Angels*, dated 1518. (See W. L. Strauss, *The Complete Engravings, Etchings, and Drypoints of Albrecht Dürer* [New York, 1972], no. 87.)

Akbar, Jahāngīr and Shāh Jahān

From the *Minto Album*
Inscribed to Bichitr
Circa 1635–40
A. Chester Beatty Library, Dublin
Bibliography: *Beatty Library*, vol. III, Pl. 65

An alternate version, of superb quality but with no signature, is in a private collection (see Sotheby 1 December 1969, Lot 152).

Jahāngīr Holding an Orb

From the *Minto Album*
Inscribed to Bichitr, "servant of the royal court"
Circa 1635
A. Chester Beatty Library, Dublin
Bibliography: *Beatty Library*, vol. III, Pl. 57

Musician, Archer and Dhobī

From the *Minto Album*
Inscribed to Bichitr
Circa 1630–40
Victoria and Albert Museum, London
Reproduced: Stchoukine, *Peinture Indienne*, Pl. XLIV

The archer at the upper right is identical to a figure in another *Minto Album* page, *A Group of Servants*, by Govardhan (*Beatty Library*, vol. III, frontispiece). In the latter work he is without his weapon but is given duties as a singer. This appears to be a conscious attempt by Bichitr to create a work in Govardhan's style. A late version is in the *Kevorkian Album*.

Hājjī Muhammad Khān Qudsī

Inscribed to Bichitr
Dated 1645
Present location unknown (ex-Collection J. B. Macauley)
Bibliography: Macauley, "Mughal Art," Pl. 11, fig. C

A full version of this sketch is reproduced in *Brown*, Pl. LXI, fig. 1.

Shāh Jahān and a Courtier

Inscribed to Bichitr, "servant of the royal court"
Circa 1645
Vever Collection
Bibliography: Stchoukine, *Peinture Indienne*, Pl. XXXIX

Other Attributions

Equestrian Figure

Fondation Custodia, Paris
Bibliography: Fondation Custodia, frontispiece; van Berge, Gahlin, and van Hasselt, "Mughal Miniatures," no. 21, Pl. 13

As reported in the publications above, an eighteenth-century inscription attributes this work to *Bichitr rāī Shāh Jahānī*. A superb painting, the connection with Bichitr is tentative.

Shāh Jahān Choosing a Jewel

Present location unknown (ex-Ardeshir Collection)
Bibliography: Sotheby 26 March 1973, Lot 27

Rājā Vikramājīt

From the *Kevorkian Album*
Metropolitan Museum of Art, New York

Prince and Sages on a Terrace

Present location unknown (ex-Ardeshir Collection)
Bibliography: Sotheby 26 March 1973, Lot 20

Shāh Jahān with Sons and Āsaf Khān

Present location unknown
Bibliography: Christie's 25 June 1969, Lot 57

A Prince

From the *Nāsir-ud-dīn Album*
Imperial Library, Tehran
Bibliography: Godard, "Album," fig. 77

Standing Woman

From the *Nāsir-ud-dīn Album*
Imperial Library, Tehran
Bibliography: Godard, "Album," fig. 107

Sūfīs and Poets

A. Chester Beatty Library, Dublin, and Heeramaneck Collection
Bibliography: Ettinghausen, "Emperor," p. 119 and n. 66, figs. 4 and 5

Tarbiat Khān

Present location unknown (ex-Ardeshir Collection)
Bibliography: Sotheby 10 July 1973, Lot 33

Six Sages

Collection of Edwin Binney 3rd
Bibliography: *Binney Collection*, no. 60

Bishan Dās

Bishan Dās's career inevitably divides itself into two parts. In 1613, he was chosen to accompany the embassy of Khān ᶜĀlam to the court of the Safavid Shāh ᶜAbbās at Isfahan. Jahāngīr, anxious to persuade his Iranian rival of the wealth and power of the Mughals, arranged for the mission to be ostentatiously grand, and its success, in this regard, is related in a contemporary Iranian account:

The highly placed King Salim Shah, Ruler of Hindustan, sent Mirza Barkhurdar, entitled Khan ᶜAlam, who is a great noble of that court and is styled *bhai* or brother by that Shah, as Ambassador.... The day when Khan ᶜAlam entered Qazvin, the writer . . . was present in the city, and himself beheld the great magnificence of the Ambassador's train. He also made enquiries of the old men, who had beheld other embassies in the days gone by, and all were agreed that from the beginning of this divine dynasty no Ambassador ever came from India or Rum with such splendid and lavish equipments . . . he had with him 1000 royal servants, his own private servants, and 200 falconers and hunters. He also had mighty elephants with golden ornaments and turrets of innumerable kinds, and Indian animals . . . many singing birds, and beautiful *palkis*.[1]

Khān ʿĀlam remained until A.H. 1029 = A.D. 1620, and upon his return was lavished with honors. Jahāngīr mentions this event in a passage of interest to us:

At the time when I sent Khan ʿAlam to Persia, I had sent with him a painter of the name of Bishan Das, who was unequalled in his age for taking likenesses, to take the portraits of the Shah and the chief men of his state, and bring them. He had drawn the likenesses of most of them, and especially had taken that of my brother the Shah exceedingly well, so that when I showed it to any of his servants, they said it was exceedingly well drawn.[2]

The emperor further notes of the events of the embassy's return that "Bishan Das, the painter, was rewarded with the gift of an elephant."[3] What is important at this point, however, is simply to realize that Bishan Dās was absent from India during the middle, artistically rich, years of Jahāngīr's reign.

A famous group of pictures, attributed traditionally and by inscription to Bishan Dās, relates to this trip, for it includes paintings of the meeting of Khān ʿĀlam and Shāh ʿAbbās as well as portraits of the Shāh and members of his family. One such illustration, from the *Late Shāh Jahān Album*, is included here (*no. 36*). None of these works seems to be of sufficient quality or immediacy to guarantee Bishan Dās's actual authorship; neither the figures nor the landscape in *no. 36*, shows the vitality and aliveness that distinguishes *The Birth of Jahāngīr* (*no. 15*), one of the artist's greatest works. Certainly, many copies of this Iranian subject matter would have been made at the emperor's behest to distribute in celebration of the success of the embassy.

An inscription in the borders of the *Muraqqaʿ-e-Gulshan* tells us that Bishan Dās was a nephew of the painter Nānhā,[4] whose work is also included here (*nos. 50* and *51*). His earliest known commissions were included in two imperial manuscripts of the 1590s, and by the first decade of the seventeenth century he had attained sufficient eminence to be included among the portraits of painters found in the margins of the *Gulshan Album* (*fig. 8*). There is really only one painting presently known that can explain the basis for this reputation at such an early date, however. This is *The House of Sheikh Phūl*, a signed work that in gentleness of color, simplicity of composition, and intensity, relates to other paintings of about 1605.[5] Together with his relatively modest contribution to the 1604–10 *Anwār-i-Suhailī*, this is the basis for understanding Bishan Dās's style, for there are few other major signed works. His style is sufficiently recognizable and consistent, however, to assure confidence in further attributions.

Such an attributed page from the *Jahāngīr-nāma* showing *The Birth of Jahāngīr*, is seen here (*no. 15*). The painter used a palette of dark earth colors, and draws with a free and seemingly unself-conscious line (unlike Mansūr or Hāshim) that gives his figures warmth and animation. The variety of personalities he depicts is extraordinary, confirming Jahāngīr's praise of his portraits. This is particularly notable among the harem women in the top half, for stock formulas were more customary when showing groups of female figures. Court ladies were in rigid seclusion (purdah) and visible only to members of their immediate families, and consequently there was little chance for true portraiture—compare the difference in treatment of the women here and in *no. 26*, by an anonymous artist, for example.

Bishan Dās is also far less concerned with the use of space generally, or shading to give physical bulk to his forms, than Abūʿl Hasan, for example, or Govardhan. It is characterization and gesture, not modelling, that give his figures life. The painter's works—especially his later illustrations—are occasionally even spatially inconsistent, as can be seen in another *Jahāngīr-nāma* page, a *Processional Scene* which exhibits Bishan Dās's characteristic color, brushwork, and character types. Here, however, his tendency to cluster figures is more pronounced, and the line work is harder. The extreme contrasts in the proportions of

FIG. 8. Portrait of Bishan Dās. By Daulat, ca. 1605–9. From the *Muraqqaʿ-e-Gulshan*. Imperial Library, Tehran. After Y. Godard, "Marges," fig. 13.

figures—both front to back and left to right across the surface of the scene—have no rational basis, and the very oddness of the effect is sufficiently distinctive to allow us to attribute other works to his hand, as well as to be confident that this is a development of the artist's later years. The *Processional Scene* finds exact counterparts in pages from the Windsor *Padshāh-nāma*, and a subimperial *Mathnavī* made for Zafar Khān probably in the 1640s. It may be that the quirks of Bishan Dās's last paintings were not appreciated by the emperor, and he had to seek patronage elsewhere.

Literature: Das, "Bishan Das"; Coomaraswamy, "Notes," pp. 283–94.

36

THE MEETING OF SHĀH ᶜABBĀS AND KHĀN ᶜĀLAM

From the *Late Shāh Jahān Album*
Inscribed: *amal-i-Bishan Dās* ("work of Bishan Dās")
Circa 1650
37 × 25.2 cm.
Provenance: Goloubev Collection
Lent by the Museum of Fine Arts, Boston: Francis Bartlett Donation of 1912 and Picture Fund (14.665)
Bibliography: *Coomaraswamy Boston*, no. LXXV, Pl. XXXV; *Coomaraswamy Goloubev*, no. 123, Pl. LXXIII; Schulz, *Miniaturmalerei*, vol. II, Pl. 179; Gangoly, "Historical Miniature," *Rupam* 4 (1920)

A. K. Coomaraswamy has noted that the object held by Khān ᶜĀlam's Indian servant (upper left) is a *huqqa* ("water pipe"),[6] and Jahāngīr's memoirs alert us to its appropriateness in this instance:

In consequence of the disturbance that tobacco brings about in most temperaments and constitutions, I had ordered that no one should smoke. My brother Shah ᶜAbbas had also become aware of the mischief arising from it, and had ordered that in Iran no one should venture to smoke. As Khan ᶜAlam was without control in continual smoking of tobacco, he frequently practiced it. Yadgar ᶜAli Sultan, ambassador of the ruler of Iran, represented to Shah ᶜAbbas that Khan ᶜAlam could never be a moment without tobacco, and he wrote this couplet in answer—

"The friend's envoy wishes to exhibit tobacco;
With fidelity's lamp I light up the tobacco-market"

Khan ᶜAlam in answer wrote and sent this verse—

"I, poor wretch, was miserable at the tobacco notice;
By the just Shah's favour the tobacco-market became brisk."[7]

The similarities in treatment of border figures and the portraits in the central scene suggest that the painting was

36

copied from an original work by Bishan Dās about 1650, when the *Late Shāh Jahān Album* was formed. For a discussion of the artistic impact of the embassy on both India and Iran, and a list of related works, see especially B. W. Robinson, "Shah ᶜAbbas and the Mughal Ambassador."

Further Major Attributions to Bishan Dās

Bābur-nāma Manuscript (fol. no. unknown)
Inscribed to Bishan Dās and Nānhā
Circa 1590
Victoria and Albert Museum, London
Bibliography: Binyon and Arnold, *Court Painters*, Pl. IV

Anwār-i-Suhailī Manuscript (fol. no. unknown)
Inscribed to Bishan Dās
Dated 1596–97
Bharat Kala Bhavan, Benares

Muraqqaᶜ-e-Gulshan (fol. 64r)

  Inscribed to Bishan Dās
  Circa 1605
  Imperial Library, Tehran
  Bibliography: Wilkinson and Gray, "Indian Paintings,"
  Pl. IIB

The House of Sheikh Phūl

  Inscribed: "work of Bishan Dās"
  Circa 1605
  Bharat Kala Bhavan, Benares
  Bibliography: Mehta, *Studies*, Pl. 37 (color); Mehta, "New
  Picture"; Smith, *History*, Pl. 8 (color); Das, "Bishan Das,"
  Pl. 18 (color)

Anwār-i-Suhailī Manuscript (fol. 320a)

  Inscribed to Bishan Dās
  Dated 1604–10
  British Library (Add. 18579)
  Bibliography: Wilkinson, *Lights*, Pl. XXVIII; Das, "Bishan
  Das," fig. 353

Rājā Surāj Singh

  From the *Berlin Album* (p. 22b)
  Inscribed to Bishan Dās
  Dated 1608
  Staatsbibliothek, Berlin
  Bibliography: Kühnel and Goetz, *Indian Book Painting*, Pl. 35;
  Das, "Bishan Das," fig. 358

Bahādur Khān Uzbeq

  From the *Berlin Album* (p. 22b)
  Inscribed to Bishan Dās
  Circa 1610
  Staatsbibliothek, Berlin
  Bibliography: Kühnel and Goetz, *Indian Book Painting*, Pl. 35

Shāh-nāma Manuscript (fol. no. unknown)

  Inscribed to Bishan Dās and ᶜInāyat
  Circa 1610
  Los Angeles County Museum of Art
  Bibliography: Strzygowski et al., *Miniaturmalerei*, T. 84,
  Abb. 225

Two further pages probably also from this otherwise unknown
manuscript were formerly in the Rothschild Collection. See
Colnaghi, *Persian and Mughal Art*, no. 88.

Rāī Bharah and Jassa Jām

  From the *Wantage Album*
  Inscribed to Bishan Dās
  Circa 1618
  Victoria and Albert Museum, London
  Bibliography: *Welch AMI*, no. 34; Coomaraswamy, "Notes,"
  fig. 21

See *Tūzuk*, vol. II, p. 19, dated 1618, where both men are
mentioned.

Bustān of Saᶜdī Manuscript (fol. 116r)

  Attributed to Bishan Dās
  Circa 1620
  Collection of Philip Hofer
  Bibliography: *Welch AMI*, no. 23; Grube, *Classical Style*,
  no. 97

The manuscript was prepared at Bukhara for Sultān ᶜAbd-al-
ᶜAzīz (r. 1540–50), but notes in the book refer to its acquisition
by Jahāngīr. Two of the three paintings seem to have been
executed at Bukhara; the third has been attributed to Bishan Dās
by S. C. Welch. It seems possible, however, that the Mughal
artist added figures to an already existing, although perhaps
unfinished, composition. Aśok Das has properly noted the
frequency with which an identical architectural composition
has appeared in other Iranian books. See Das, "Bishan Das,"
pp. 184–91.

Processional Scene

  From a *Jahāngīr-nāma* manuscript
  Attributed here to Bishan Dās
  Circa 1620–25
  Rampur State Library
  Bibliography: *Brown*, Pl. XXXI (color)

The page has a later inscription of attribution to Manōhar.

Padshāh-nāma Manuscript (fols. 119v, 120r)

  Attributed here to Bishan Dās
  Circa 1633
  Royal Library, Windsor

A double page miniature, this depicts the wedding procession of
Dārā Shikōh. In addition to the traits noted above, Bishan Dās
has a curious habit when showing the farther arms of figures
seen in three-quarter view; as in the man at the bottom center
here, or at the bottom right of *The Birth of Jahāngīr* (no. 15), the
sleeves have no substance and appear as if pinned to the body.

Mathnavī of Zafar Khān Manuscript

  Attributed here to Bishan Dās
  Circa 1640–45
  Royal Asiatic Society, London (No. 203)
  Bibliography: Pinder-Wilson, *Three Illustrated Manuscripts*,
  pp. 418–22, figs. 13–22

The manuscript was completed at Lahore in 1663 by Zafar Khān,
but the illustrations seem earlier. Folios 11v and 12r are organized
identically to the *Padshāh-nāma* processional scene noted immediately above, and the background figures in each are identical
to those in the *Jahāngīr-nāma Processional Scene*. All are drawn
with very fluid lines, and betray an identical choice of figures:
acrobats and buffoons, including, in two cases, a man with his
pants falling off. Pinder-Wilson has noted that two of the folios
of the *Mathnavī*, originally composed as a double page illustration, have been bound separately; that the events shown are
datable to the early 1640s on the basis of the ages of men depicted;
and that fols. 11v and 12r seem to be modelled on Akbari prototypes. As with the Windsor *Padshāh-nāma*, it seems that paintings
were later added to a book for which they were not originally

intended. The portrait of the painter at work, on fol. 19v, may therefore be the elderly Bishan Dās.

Other Attributions

Rāj Kunvār Manuscript (fols. 15b, 69b, 106a, 122a)
Dated 1603
A. Chester Beatty Library, Dublin
Bibliography: Das, "Bishan Das," figs. 354–55

The attributions, made by Aśok Das, are not accepted here.

Jog Bashisht Manuscript (fol. 249)
A. Chester Beatty Library, Dublin
Literature: Robinson, "Shah ᶜAbbas," n. 4, which records an attribution by Robert Skelton.

Jahāngīr with a Falcon
Present location unknown
Bibliography: Sotheby 10 July 1973, Lot 37

Bābur, Miranshah, and Humāyūn
From the *Nāsir-ud-dīn Album*
Imperial Library, Tehran
Bibliography: Godard, "Album," fig. 63

A Courtier
Present location unknown
Bibliography: Sotheby 10 July 1973, Lot 23

Rājā Surāj Singh
From the *Kevorkian Album*
Metropolitan Museum of Art, New York

A Horse
British Museum (Stowe Or. 16)
Bibliography: Binyon and Arnold, *Court Painters*, Pl. XXXVIII

Shāh ᶜAbbās and Khān ᶜĀlam
Victoria and Albert Museum, London
Bibliography: Robinson, "Shah ᶜAbbas," fig. 7

Shāh ᶜAbbās
British Museum (1920-9-17-013/2)
Bibliography: *BM*, no. 115; W. Blunt, *Isfahan* (New York, 1966), fig. 79

Shāh ᶜAbbās
Present location uncertain (ex-Rothschild Collection)
Bibliography: Colnaghi, *Persian and Mughal Art*, no. 112

Shāh ᶜAbbās with a Long Gun
From the *Nāsir-ud-dīn Album*

Imperial Library, Tehran
Bibliography: Godard, "Album," fig. 68; Das, "Bishan Das," fig. 360

Shāh ᶜAbbās Riding
From the *Leningrad Album*
Academy of Sciences, Leningrad
Bibliography: Ivanova et al., *Albom Indiyskikh*, Pl. 16

Shāh ᶜAbbās Enthroned
From the *Leningrad Album*
Academy of Sciences, Leningrad
Bibliography: Ivanova et al., *Albom Indiyskikh*, Pl. 15

Khodabande Mīrzā
From the *Nāsir-ud-dīn Album*
Imperial Library, Tehran
Bibliography: Godard, "Album," fig. 98; Das, "Bishan Das," fig. 362

Khodabande Mīrzā
British Museum (1920-9-17-013/24)

Rānā Amar Singh of Udaipur
From the *Wantage Album*
Victoria and Albert Museum, London
Bibliography: *Wantage Bequest*, no. 28, Pl. 19

While bearing an inscribed date of 1615, this seems a later work of about 1800.

Prince and Companions Listen to a Singer
Victoria and Albert Museum, London (9-1965)
Bibliography: *BM*, p. 120; Gray et al., *R.A. Arts of India and Pakistan*, no. 758, Pl. H

Chitarman

Few illustrations by Chitarman have been identified, but he was clearly a skilled portraitist, working in a highly—and occasionally overly—refined style that isolated figures against plain backgrounds devoid of narrative or spatial interest. His earliest works (the portrait of *Dārā Shikōh, no. 37*, is an example) are so carefully and smoothly modelled that they seem unnatural, and there is often a seeming lack of skill in the drawing of proportions, or in such details as hands. Nonetheless, the illustrations are often effective in ways unknown to more orthodox painters. The depiction of Shāh Jahān's eldest son, the only

37

To show a Mughal prince aureoled is unusual, unless, as in the *Jahāngīr-nāma* (*no. 15*) or *Padshāh-nāma*, it is a retrospective reference to the emperor's life preaccession. There are, however, several examples relating to Dārā, whose position as heir apparent was publicly proclaimed and accepted. The earliest is the probable wedding picture once in the Museum of Fine Arts, Boston (*Coomaraswamy Boston*, no. LXXVI, Pl. XXXVI); another example, attributed here to Chitarman, is in the Keir Collection (*Robinson ed., Keir*, V.71). A third such work is the small medallion portrait included in this exhibition (*no. 64*).

The artist placed the term *khākipā* ("dust under the feet") in reference to himself, literally under where the prince is standing, as a sign of his own humility and unworthiness.

Further Major Attributions to Chitarman

Equestrian Portrait of Dārā Shikōh

> Circa 1639–40
> Keir Collection
> Bibliography: *Robinson ed., Keir*, V.71

Unsigned, this can be attributed to Chitarman on the basis of its stylistic identity to *no. 37*.

Dārā Shikōh

> From the *Minto Album*
> Inscribed: "A good likeness of Bābā Dārā Shikōh, painted by Chitarman"
> Circa 1645
> Victoria and Albert Museum, London (19-1925 I.M.)
> Literature: *BM*, no. 158

Portrait of a Nobleman

> Inscribed: "work of Chitarman"
> Circa 1650
> Fondation Custodia, Paris
> Bibliography: Fondation Custodia, no. 174, Pl. 73

Portrait of ᶜAlā al-Mulk Tunī, Fazīl Khān

> Inscribed: "work of Chitarman"
> Circa 1650–60
> British Library (Add. 18801)
> Bibliography: Martin, *Miniature Paintings*, Pl. 187A; Binyon and Arnold, *Court Painters*, Pl. XXVI

Portrait of Jaᶜfar Khān

> Inscribed: "work of Chitarman"
> Circa 1650–60
> British Library (Add. 18801)
> Bibliography: Martin, *Miniature Paintings*, Pl. 187B

This portrait, and the one listed immediately above, come from an album dedicated in 1661–62. In these works, the taste shown

known work by Chitarman in the United States, is a powerful image, enhanced by the oval aureole which surrounds the doomed prince. Paintings made by the artist after 1645, and his last known portraits, all of which are drawings, are sensitive, highly controlled, and more technically traditional studies.

37
DĀRĀ SHIKŌH

> Inscribed: *khākipā* ("dust under the feet") *Chitarman*
> Dated A.H. 1049 = A.D. 1639–40
> 25.8 × 15.5 cm.
> Lent by the Pierpont Morgan Library, New York (M. 458, fol. 9)

for highly finished drawings concentrating on the facial characteristics of the subjects was shared by such other artists as Hāshim, Anupchatar, and Muhammad Nādir of Samarqand.

Portrait of Islam Khān Rumī
Inscribed to Chitarman
Circa 1670
Bibliography: Hambly and Swaan, *Cities*, p. 132, fig. 17

Islam Khān fled to India from Turkey in 1669 and entered Aurangzēb's service; he died in 1676. An accurate date for the work can be thus established.

Shāh Jahān and Dārā Shikōh
From the *Nāsir-ud-dīn Album*
Inscribed to Chitarman
Imperial Library, Tehran
Bibliography: Godard, "Album," fig. 74

Shāh Jahān
From the *Kevorkian Album*
Inscribed to Chitarman
Metropolitan Museum of Art, New York
Bibliography: R. Craven, *Miniatures and Small Sculptures from India* (Gainesville, Florida, 1966), no. 82

The work bears an inscription naming the painter and giving a date = A.D. 1628–29. Clearly later, it may be based on a lost work by the artist.

Daulat

On a marginal figure in the *Muraqqaᶜ-e-Gulshan*, Daulat wrote: "Made by the least of the servants, Daulat, of Jahāngīr Shah. . . ." But besides being a name, Daulat means "empire," and the inscription had a double meaning: "Made by the least of the servants of the empire of Jahāngīr Shah. . . ."[1] Such verbal plays, often refined to extreme subtlety,[2] were frequent among Muslim artists, however. Daulat was particularly insistent on using them to proclaim his humility, for elsewhere he signed himself "the *faqīr* ('poor') Daulat" (*no. 38*), and even "the poor, miserable Daulat."[3] These tiny phrases, actual signatures, are usually all but invisible—in *no. 38*, they are found on a rock beneath the dervish's feet; in *no. 17* [below], at the waterline of the boat—and they contrast with the strong, vibrant, and innovative personality that comes across in his work, or through the two self-portraits we have of him (one is reproduced here as *fig. 9*).[4]

Daulat was a *khānazād*, a "house-born" artist, meaning that his father—whose identity we do not know—was in imperial service (presumably as a painter) at Daulat's birth. This is information inscribed on the earliest of Daulat's known works, a page of the Delhi *Bābur-nāma* of circa 1597. Further pages in the *Nafahāt-al-Uns* of 1603–4 and the *Akbar-nāma* of 1604—both major imperial manuscripts—show us a style uncommonly dependent on areas of pure, bright color, at a time when muted, dark tones were more prevalent. Additionally, Daulat invented an easily recognizable, rather heavy featured figure type, to which he reverted throughout his career when commissioned to paint crowd scenes; for it was in small scale works, portraits (*no. 38*) and marginalia (*figs. 4* and *8–10*), or books such as the superb small *Gulistān* of Saᶜdī (*no. 17* [below]), that his work is finest.

Besides his distinctive figure types, which must be visually learned rather than verbally described,[5] Daulat is recognizable, even in his early works, by his arrangement of groups of figures in densely packed clusters, but with intense concern for describing spatial relationships within these masses. Avoiding the even distribution of figures over the surface of the painting, as we see in extreme form in *no. 14*, Daulat's style prepares the way for such compositions as we find in *no. 25*, from the *Padshāh-nāma*, where figures lose individual distinctness to an overwhelming sense of mass.

By 1609, the date inscribed on a *Gulshan Album* border figure, Daulat had already clearly become an extremely skilled portraitist. Among his greatest and most interesting studies are the marginal portraits he painted of his fellow artists (*figs. 4* and *8–10*), which help compensate for our lack of contemporary verbal references to these men. Here Daulat has painted not

FIG. 9. Portraits of Daulat (left) and Govardhan (right). By Daulat, ca. 1605–9. From the *Muraqqaᶜ-e-Gulshan*. Imperial Library, Tehran. After Y. Godard, "Marges," fig. 14.

by the manipulation of predetermined figural formulae, but by direct and penetrating observation of each subject. This is true, as well, of the marvelous small portrait of *A Dervish and a Musician* (*no. 38*), in which, moreover, he has contrasted the extravagance of the religious sentiments of the two men with the small deer at the lower left—all innocence and trust.

In his later works—the Sa'di page (*no. 17* [below]), and an unsigned *Jahāngīr-nāma* page in Berlin, attributed here to Daulat—the painter used more orthodox color, and his technique is even further refined. The man at the bow of the boat in *no. 17* [below], for example, is presented in a way that makes us as appreciative of the artist's ability to paint the thin muslin shirt and the body beneath, as of his focussed and intense sense of drama. This work is a perfect balance of Daulat's narrative and technical skills.

The last works definitely attributable to Daulat are of very different character, for these are album pages with purely floral marginalia; there is little way to link them visually with Daulat's earlier works. They date from the early years of Shāh Jahān's reign, and it may well be that the painter ended his career

executing marginalia of this newly fashionable type.

Several further works are known, including an illustration bound into the Windsor *Padshāh-nāma*, that have been attributed to Daulat.[6] In style, they are quite distinct from the illustrations discussed above; and all are signed with a name that can be read as either Daula or Daulat, but written in Arabic rather than Persian. As they do not follow the style or spelling of Daulat's signatures (which we find on his *Shāh Jahān Album* borders, as well as on his earliest works), it would seem best for the present to consider Daula a separate personality.

38

A DERVISH AND A MUSICIAN

Inscribed: *Amal-i-faqīr Daulat* ("work of the poor Daulat")
Circa 1610
13.3 × 9 cm.
Anonymous Loan
Bibliography: Welch and Beach, *Gods*, no. 8

This is certainly a portrait of specific men, and one should note that the arms of the figure on the left are scarred, probably through self-mutilations inflicted by religious ecstasy.

There are two later works known based on this composition: one, in the British Museum and the other, in the Musée Guimet, Paris. A drawing of the musician is in the Fondation Custodia, Paris.

Further Major Attributions to Daulat

Bābur-nāma Manuscript (fols. 137r, 226r, 247r)
    Inscribed to Khānazāda Daulat
    Circa 1597
    National Museum of India, New Delhi

Nafahāt-al-Uns Manuscript (fol. 135v)
    Inscribed: "Daulat"
    Dated A.H. 1012 = A.D. 1603–4
    British Library (Or. 1362)
    Bibliography: Wellesz, *Akbar's Religious Thought*, fig. 35

Folio 142r from this manuscript can be attributed to Daulat as well (see Barrett and Gray, *Painting*, p. 87).

Akbar-nāma Manuscript (fols. 168v–169r)
    Inscribed: "Daulat"
    Dated A.D. 1604
    A. Chester Beatty Library, Dublin (Ms. 3)
    Bibliography: *Beatty Library*, vol. III, Pls. 27–28

38 (detail)

Būstān of Saʿdī Manuscript (fol. 92)

Inscribed: "The humble work of the khānazāda Daulat Muhammad"
Dated A.H. 1014 = A.D. 1605–6
Private Collection (ex-Rothschild Collection)
Bibliography: Stchoukine, "Un Bustan de Saʿdi," fig. 2

Muraqqaʿ-e-Gulshan

Imperial Library, Gulistan Palace, Tehran

There are several folios of marginal decoration signed by Daulat, one of which is dated A.H. 1018 = A.D. 1609–10. See especially Godard, "Marges," pp. 18–33 and figs. 9–23; and Wilkinson and Gray, "Indian Paintings," Pls. Ia and IIa. On the basis of the latter of these, it might be possible to attribute to Daulat the margins on an album page in the Freer Gallery of Art (54.116v). See also *figs. 4* and *8–10*.

Khamsa of Nizāmī Manuscript (fol. 325b)

Inscribed to Daulat
Circa 1605–10
British Library (Or. 12208)
Bibliography: *Brown*, Pl. XVIII; *Welch IMP*, Pl. 19 (color)

This is the closing author page, added during Jahāngīr's reign to a manuscript otherwise dated 1595. It shows Daulat with the scribe ʿAbd-al-Rahīm, ʿAmbarīn Qalam, with whom he worked on several occasions (e.g., the *Nafahāt-al-Uns* listed above).

Jahāngīr in the Shrine at Ajmer

Probably from a *Jahāngīr-nāma* manuscript
Attributed here to Daulat
Circa 1615
Staatliche Museen, Berlin
Bibliography: Anand and Goetz, *Miniaturen*, Pl. 6 (color)

ʿIyār-i-Dānish, fols. 2 and 3

Inscribed to Daulat
Dated (?) 1606
A. Chester Beatty Library, Dublin (Ms. 4)

Minto Album: marginalia

Inscribed to Daulat
Circa 1630
Victoria and Albert Museum, London
Bibliography: Skelton, "Motif," Pl. LXXXVIIIa

For reference to a second such page see *BM*, no. 143; other signed marginalia are in the *Kevorkian Album*.

Shāh Jahān Album: marginalia

Inscribed: "work of the least, Daulat"
Circa 1630
Present location uncertain
Bibliography: Colnaghi, *Persian and Mughal Art*, no. 101

Other Attributions

Portrait of ʿInāyat Khān

From the *Wantage Album*
Inscribed to Daulat Kalan ("Daulat the Elder")
Victoria and Albert Museum, London
Bibliography: *Wantage Bequest*, no. 26, Pl. 17

Portrait of a Nobleman

Inscribed to Daulat
Present location unknown
Bibliography: Sotheby 10 July 1973, Lot 9

A later work, the calligraphy on the reverse has been attributed to ʿAbd-al-Rahīm.

Ghulām (or Mīrzā Ghulām)

Two signed works are known by a painter who terms himself *Ghulām* ("the slave"): *Portrait of a Courtier* (*no. 39*), and a *Madonna and Child*, in the British Museum. They are stylistically identical, with an interchangeable, impersonal formula used for the faces, both of which are very smooth and oval. Even a heavy modelling of the forms through highlights and shadow gives no individuality or physical immediacy to the figures—the reason such techniques were adopted by most Mughal painters. The end result seems personally eccentric, and eccentricity is a distinguishing characteristic of the artist's work.

Like *no. 30* by Āqā Rizā whose style is discussed elsewhere, the composition of the *Portrait of a Courtier* is derived from Iranian sources, and any indication of specific identity would have been given by inscription, rather than physiognomy. This combination of Iranian motif and figural generalization with new Mughal techniques of shading produced a work that is really in neither tradition—and this is equally true of the Āqā Rizā portrait. A further correspondence is found in the inscriptions. Both artists express their dependence on their patron, Prince Salīm, by the terms they use for themselves (*murīd* ["disciple"] for Āqā Rizā, and *ghulām* for the present painter), and by the presence of the name Shāh Salīm, independently placed on the surface of the works (in *no. 39* just above the turban). Abūʾl Hasan, Āqā Rizā's son, placed similar inscriptions on several early works, including his drawing of *St. John*,[1] which is otherwise notable for an interest in shading similar, if more skillful and restrained, to that of Ghulām. There are, therefore, several reasons for seeing Ghulām as a painter closely related to the circle of Āqā Rizā, but with a distinct identity.

Since the name Shāh Salīm is found on inscribed works by Āqā Rizā dated 1599 and 1604,[2] and on the Abūʿl Hasan *St. John* of 1600–1601, it seems to refer to the title (*Shāh*, or "King") which Salīm assumed for himself after 1599, when he rebelled and set up his own court at Allahabad. There is no reason to believe that any of the works inscribed with the name date after 1605, when Salīm became Jahāngīr and a *Padshāh* ("Great King"), although the Italian traveller Pietro della Valle wrote in 1623:

the Name *Sciah Selim* [Shāh Salīm], tenaciously inhering in the memory of people, remains still to him [Jahāngīr], and in common discourse he is more frequently call'd by this than any other Name.[3]

Common usage would not be proper justification for an inscription meant for the emperor's eyes, however, and after 1605 he was referred to (on paintings) by his rightful titles.

The dating of the Ghulām *Portrait of a Courtier* to Jahāngīr's patronage as a prince is strengthened by a glance at the *Dīwān* of Amīr Hasan Dihlavī manuscript, copied at Allahabad in 1602 (*no. 1*). Several pages (e.g., fols. 15r, 32v, 84v, 127r, and 157r) seem, for visual reasons, to be by Ghulām. They show, in particular, the swarthy modelling of figures seen also in *no. 39*, a trait—when in so excessive a form—evidently unique to the artist. Furthermore, the standing man at the upper right of fol. 127 is simply the courtier of *no. 39* in a different posture. Like Āqā Rizā's pages of 1604 in the British Library *Anwār-i-Suhailī*,[4] the compositions are organized in an Iranian manner. The intention is clear, for example, that the figures be carefully placed in, or framed by, architectural or landscape forms (compare fol. 15 with fol. 109, a more typically Mughal composition, where space is free and open). Yet while landscapes are fanciful and decorative, they are, as well, flat and insubstantial. And while Āqā Rizā's figures are graceful and lively, those of Ghulām are heavy and overly serious. He lacks the precision of line or touch of the older Iranian master, as well as the effortless naturalism of Abūʿl Hasan. Nonetheless, it is to their works that he is best compared.

Three of the Hasan Dihlavī manuscript folios (15r,

84v, and 157r) give us a further clue about the artist. More complex and sophisticated—but not necessarily more successful—than fols. 32v and 127r, and consistent in figure type and technique, the paintings have a greater precision and richness of effect, as can be seen from the arrangement of the tree in fol. 15r, or the birds in fol. 157r. The illustrations are virtually identical in style to paintings inscribed to Mīrzā Ghulām in the *Anwār-i-Suhailī* manuscript, where the distinctive use of a flat gold background, enlivened by highly stylized clumps of grass, is also found. It seems, therefore, that Ghulām and Mīrzā Ghulām are the same man.

The work of Mīrzā Ghulām (which is evident also in *no. 12*) is strange and idiosyncratic when compared to paintings by other artists discussed here. The prevailing trend of the time was for ever greater naturalism, combined with increasing formal perfection of line and color, yet Mīrzā Ghulām manipulates landscape into forms that respond to him rather than to nature, and presents us with figures that scowl and appear angry, as if immersed in a private world. Too, he negates natural space by the use of the decorative gold background. Beginning as a very heavy handed artist, he created, in the *Anwār-i-Suhailī*, a recognizable, highly personal style of considerable expressiveness. The *Portrait of a Courtier*, together with the *Dīwān* of Amīr Hasan Dihlavī, charts this development. Unfortunately, nothing yet seems attributable to him after 1610.

39

PORTRAIT OF A COURTIER

Inscribed: *amal-i-Ghulām* and *Shāh Salīm* ("work of Ghulām" or "work of the slave of Shāh Salīm")
Circa 1600–1605
9.8 × 5.4 cm.
Provenance: Heeramaneck Collection
Lent by the Los Angeles County Museum: Nasli and Alice Heeramaneck Collection (L.69.24.259)
Bibliography: Strzygowski et al., *Miniaturmalerei*, Abb. 208; *Beach Heeramaneck*, no. 210

Ghulām is a word meaning

in Arabic a young man or boy; . . . then, by extension, either a servant, sometimes elderly . . . and very often, but not necessarily, a slave-servant; or a bodyguard, slave or freedman, bound to his master by personal ties, or finally sometimes an artisan working in the workshops of a master, whose name he used along with his own as his signature.[5]

39

اے یحیٰ پنبر زلذت شریب مدام ما

ما در پیالہ عکس رخ یار دیدہ ایم

British Museum
Bibliography: Bussagli and Sivaramamurti, *5000 Years*, fig. 372 (color); *BM*, no. 88

Bussagli notes that the source is a print by Bernart van Orley, but cites no evidence.

A Youth

Attributed here to Mīrzā Ghulām
Circa 1600–5
Private Collection
Bibliography: Sotheby 7 April 1975, Lot 111

Būstān of Saʿdī Manuscript (fol. 89)

Attributed here to Mīrzā Ghulām
Dated A.H. 1014 = A.D. 1605–6
Private Collection (formerly Rothschild and Goelet Collections)
Bibliography: Stchoukine, "Un Bustan de Saʿdi," fig. 5

The style is exactly that of the British Library *Anwār-i-Suhailī* pages by Mīrzā Ghulām (Wilkinson, *Lights*, Pls. VIII, XXVII), and further suggests that the bulk of that manuscript may have been contemporary with the Āqā Riẓā pages of 1604.

Anwār-i-Suhailī Manuscript (fols. 64b, 311b, 396a)

Inscribed to Mīrzā Ghulām
Dated 1604–10
British Library (Add. 18579)
Bibliography: Wilkinson, *Lights*, Pls. IX, XXVII, XXXVI; see also Pl. VIII

Shāh-nāma Manuscript

Inscribed as painted by Daʿud, corrected by Mīrzā Ghulām
Circa 1610
Present location unknown
Literature: Sotheby 7 December 1971, Lot 55

That this artist took Ghulām as a name, however, is evidenced by his later use of the preceding honorific *Mīrzā*. There is no reason to think that the presence of the name Shāh Salīm indicates that the work is meant to be an idealized portrait of the prince. As discussed by Anthony Welch, it is clear that such studies were often metaphoric statements comparing Muslim ideals of physical attractiveness with divine beauty.[6]

Further Major Attributions to Mīrzā Ghulām

Madonna and Child

Inscribed: *raqam-i-Ghulām* and *Shāh Salīm* ("work of the slave [of] Shāh Salīm")
Circa 1600–5

Govardhan

That so many of Govardhan's paintings are portraits of holy men and other characters considered eccentric even by Mughal standards is important to our understanding of the painter. No other Mughal artist of the period celebrates, with such sympathy and insight, the variety of humanity found in India. In this exhibition, for example, we find portraits by Govardhan of princes, nobles, servants, musicians, *mullās* or "religious teachers," and naked ascetics, including a man whose fingernails have grown so long that they curl like claws (*no. 41*). Govardhan constantly makes these portraits the center of our attention;

they are not subservient to an abstract patterning of the surface or to a showy display of technical brilliance. Furthermore, Govardhan, unlike Hāshim or Bichitr, is not a detached observer. His personal involvement with his subjects is evident, as is their rapport with each other. Indeed, most of his works show people conversing, or otherwise interacting. In *no. 5* verso, for example, one of the artist's greatest works, there is an intense, even if unspoken, communication among the grouped figures, whether those of the upper or lower margin; and, in *no. 41*, the ascetic at the left stares directly out at us, forcing even our direct participation in that scene. A quick comparison of *nos. 41* and *62* both showing groups of naked mendicants, alerts us to the sense of seriousness, even profundity, that further defines Govardhan's style. His figures have a solidity and power—due as much to his knowledge of modelling and shading to give substance, as to his insights into character—that is not found in the other work.

The marginal figures mentioned above (*no. 5* verso) are datable to about 1609, for a page in the Berlin volume of Jahāngīr's albums—identical in style—is dated in that year. The Berlin page also informs us that Govardhan was a *khānazād*, or "house-born" painter, and that his father was Bhavānī Dās, a minor Akbar period artist.[1] Earlier works by Govardhan (all in manuscripts, as listed below) are in a less developed style, for figures are not as convincingly portraitlike, and tend to repeat, instead, a limited repertoire of figure types. The freshness and enthusiasm of perception which is so evident in the border portraits, therefore, must be a result of the artist's own delight at his achievements.

A broad framework for the further evolution of Govardhan's style can be suggested, based on a small number of reliably dated works. This is more than usually tentative, however. The figures in many of Govardhan's paintings remain unsatisfactorily identified, a puzzling situation for such a skillful portraitist; and consequently, lacking this historical information, dating must often be made on less reliable (e.g., purely visual) grounds.

A portrait of Rāo Bharah, signed and dated 1617, is also found in the *Berlin Album*. In comparison to the 1609 borders, it is denser; colors are rich and heavy, the modelling so extreme that the figure seems almost released from the page. A brilliant portrait, and one of the most vivid and immediate in the entire Mughal tradition, it nonetheless lacks the simplicity and freshness that—coupled with the even then no less superb technique—makes the artist's marginal figures so extraordinary.

This direction seems to continue. Paintings by Govardhan that are datable to after 1620 are even more highly worked; *no. 22*, for example, is drawn with a thinner line and more detailed shading than we find in *no. 5* verso. On occasion, the modelling is so careful and elaborate that figures seem unnatural; at other times, the line is so thin, hard and controlled that little warmth or animation is felt. But the best works simply show an intense refinement and very humane sensibility. A well-known portrait of *Shāh Jahān Riding with Prince Dārā Shikōh*, from the *Minto Album*, must be dated to about 1638, to judge by the age of the prince. Both men cross a landscape the color and texture of gold dust and pearls; it is similar in palette to *A Falconer (no. 42)*, or to the *Ascetics (no. 41)*. These are among the most elegant of Mughal works, technically faultless, emotionally restrained, and yet observed with great care.

The development of Govardhan's style follows the general trend of painting at the time. Yet, more than any of his compatriots, Govardhan, in his later illustrations, seems to work at an extreme of refinement that, on occasion, passes into the effete, and this is true of subject as well as style. It also seems evident that Govardhan's manner of painting was unusually responsive to his own enthusiasms and sensibilities, a claim that could not be made for such diverse other artists as Manōhar, Hāshim, or Mansūr, among others. He needs a study of far greater length than can be provided here.

See also fig. 9 (p. 113).

40

TWO COURTIERS AND A HOLY MAN

From an Album of Jahāngīr
Inscribed: *amal-i-Govardhan* ("work of Govardhan")
Circa 1610–15
6.9 × 5.2 cm. and 13.9 × 9 cm.
Provenance: Sevadjian and Welch Collections
Lent by the Williams College Museum of Art (76.3)

The figures are fragments of the borders of a Jahāngīrī *muraqqaᶜ* folio. Other than the *Berlin Album* borders of 1609 and possibly the *Gulistān* of Saᶜdī manuscript listed below, this seems to be the only work known inscribed to Govardhan by an actual signature. The style is almost

40

identical to that of *no. 5* verso, although each of the faces has been slightly reworked.

41

ASCETICS

Attributed to Govardhan
Circa 1625
24.1 × 15.2 cm.
Lent Anonymously
Bibliography: *Welch FEM*, no. 63 (color)

An eighteenth-century copy of this work with a marginal attribution to Govardhan is in West Berlin.

42

A FALCONER

Attributed to Govardhan
Circa 1630
15.9 × 9.5 cm.
Provenance: Cartier Collection
Anonymous Loan
Bibliography: *Brown*, Pl. XVII, fig. 2

Hunting with falcons was a major imperial pastime, and for a period, Khān ᶜĀlam, Jahāngīr's ambassador to Iran, served also as the *qushbegī* ("chief falconer"). It has been suggested by Stuart C. Welch that this portrait, which he attributes to Govardhan, is of the *Khān*.

41

43

FOUR *MULLĀS*

Attributed to Govardhan
Circa 1630
20.6 × 13.3 cm.
Provenance: Demotte and Heeramaneck Collections
Lent by the Los Angeles County Museum of Art: Nasli and
Alice Heeramaneck Collection (L.69.24.287)
Bibliography: *Brown*, Pl. LXVII; *Beach Heeramaneck*, no. 212;
Welch AMI, no. 46

The painting, which had been extended in size at all four
margins, was inserted into borders from a Shāh Jahān
album by the French dealer Demotte. Confirmation of
the attribution to Govardhan, first proposed by Stuart C.
Welch, is given by the stylistic similarity of these figures
with those in the signed fragment of marginal decoration
(*no. 40*).

Further Major Attributions to Govardhan

Akbar-nāma Manuscript (fols. 49b, 176b, 201)
Inscribed to Govardhan
Dated 1604
A. Chester Beatty Library, Dublin
Bibliography: *Beatty Library*, vol. II, Pls. 16, 31, and frontis-
piece

Akbar-nāma Manuscript (fol. 17a)
Inscribed to Govardhan
Dated 1604
British Library (Or. 12988)

Būstān of Saᶜdī Manuscript (fol. 44v)
Attributed here to Govardhan
Dated 1605
Private Collection (formerly Rothschild and Goelet Collec-
tions)

Khamsa of Mīr ᶜAlī Shīr Navāᵓī
Inscribed to Govardhan
Circa 1605
Royal Library, Windsor
Literature: *BM*, no. 94

Berlin Album: marginalia (fol. 25b)
Inscribed: "work of the meanest of those born in the house,
Govardhan, the servant of Jahāngīr, the son of Bhavanī Dās,
finished in the year A.H. 1018 = A.D. 1609–10"
Staatsbibliothek, Berlin
Bibliography: Kühnel and Goetz, *Indian Book Painting*, p. 9
and Pl. 38

Bearded Ascetic
From an Album of Jahāngīr
Attributed to Govardhan
Circa 1610–15
Keir Collection
Bibliography: *Robinson ed., Keir*, V.68

Rāo Bharah
From the *Berlin Album* (fol. 23a)
Inscribed to Govardhan
Dated 1617
Staatsbibliothek, West Berlin
Bibliography: Kühnel and Goetz, *Indian Book Painting*, Pl. 36

Sheikh Husain Jāmiᶜ and Attendant
Inscribed to Govardhan
Circa 1615–25
Musée Guimet, Paris
Bibliography: *Stchoukine Louvre*, Pl. XI; Marteau and
Vever, *Miniatures Persanes*, vol. II, Pl. CLXVI

43

Prince and Consort on a Terrace
   From the *Minto Album*
   Inscribed to Govardhan
   Circa 1615–25
   A. Chester Beatty Library, Dublin (Ms. 7, No. 2)
   Bibliography: *Beatty Library*, vol. III, Pl. 54; Goetz, *The Art of India*, p. 222 (color)

A Young Prince with Friends
   From the *Minto Album*
   Inscribed to Govardhan
   Circa 1630
   A. Chester Beatty Library (Ms. 7, No. 8)
   Bibliography: *Beatty Library*, vol. III, Pl. 59

The usual identification of the prince here, and in the work immediately above, as Parviz is not convincing; for portraits of the latter see *BM*, nos. 109 and 111. A closely related work, also attributable to Govardhan, is illustrated in Binyon and Arnold, *Court Painters*, Pl. XXIII.

An Ascetic
   From the *Leningrad Album*
   Inscribed to Govardhan
   Circa 1630
   Academy of Sciences, Leningrad
   Bibliography: Ivanova et al., *Albom Indiyskikh*, Pl. 12

Visit to a Sage
   From the *Leningrad Album*
   Inscribed to Govardhan
   Circa 1630
   Academy of Sciences, Leningrad
   Bibliography: Ivanova et al., *Albom Indiyskikh*, Pl. 13

A Group of Servants
   From the *Minto Album*
   Inscribed to Govardhan
   Circa 1630
   A. Chester Beatty Library, Dublin (Ms. 7, No. 11)
   Bibliography: *Beatty Library*, vol. III, frontispiece (color); *Welch IMP*, Pl. 28 (color)

Holy Men
   Attributed to Govardhan
   Circa 1630
   Musée Guimet, Paris
   Bibliography: Soustiel and David, *Miniatures de l'Inde*, p. 78

Dervish, Musician and Soldier
   Attributed here to Govardhan
   Circa 1625–30
   A. Chester Beatty Library, Dublin (Ms. 7, No. 26)
   Bibliography: *Beatty Library*, vol. III, Pl. 69

Sādiq Khān
   Inscribed to Govardhan
   Circa 1630
   British Museum (1920-9-17-013/3)
   Bibliography: Binyon and Arnold, *Court Painters*, Pl. XXVII

Mīr Muhammad Saʿīd Mīr Jumlah
   Inscribed to Govardhan
   Circa 1630–40
   British Library (Or. 18801)
   Bibliography: Martin, *Miniature Paintings*, Pl. 195

Shāh Jahān and Dārā Shikōh
   Inscribed to Govardhan
   Circa 1638
   Collection of Edwin Binney 3rd
   Bibliography: *Binney Collection*, no. 56

Shāh Jahān Riding with Prince Dārā Shikōh
   From the *Minto Album*
   Inscribed to Govardhan
   Circa 1638
   Victoria and Albert Museum, London
   Bibliography: *Welch AMI*, no. 42; Stchoukine, *Peinture Indienne*, Pl. 36

Tīmūr Riding with an Attendant
   From the *Minto Album*
   Inscribed to Govardhan
   Circa 1638
   A. Chester Beatty Library, Dublin (Ms. 7, No. 3)
   Bibliography: *Beatty Library*, vol. III, Pl. 55

The style of the painting, which was meant to form a double page composition with the work listed immediately above, is consciously archaistic and modelled on Timurid dynasty Iranian works, in deference to the subject.

Gulistān of Saʿdī (fol. 5r)
   Inscribed to Govardhan
   Circa 1640
   Private Collection (formerly Collection of the Marquess of Bute)

Majnun and Laila's Messenger
   Attributed here to Govardhan
   Circa 1640
   A. Chester Beatty Library, Dublin (Ms. 7, No. 27)
   Bibliography: *Beatty Library*, vol. III, Pl. 70

Tīmūr, Humāyūn, and Bābur
   From the *Minto Album*
   Inscribed to Govardhan
   Victoria and Albert Museum, London
   Bibliography: Welch, *Indian Drawings*, no. 17

Other Attributions

Dārā Shikōh and Sulāiman Shikōh on an Elephant
Staatliche Museen, Berlin

While this bears an inscription to Govardhan, a closely related painting, inscribed to Lālchand, is reproduced in Martin, *Miniature Paintings*, Pl. 218A.

Lovers on a Terrace
Los Angeles County Museum of Art
Bibliography: *Welch AMI*, no. 47

A Youth and an Old Man
From the *Nāsir-ud-dīn Album*
Imperial Library, Tehran
Bibliography: Godard, "Album," fig. 69

Princess and a *Mullā*
From the *Nāsir-ud-dīn Album*
Imperial Library, Tehran
Bibliography: Godard, "Album," fig. 92

Jahāngīr Playing Holī
From the *Minto Album*
A. Chester Beatty Library, Dublin
Bibliography: *Beatty Library*, vol. III, Pl. 56

Jahāngīr Celebrates the Festival of Āb-pāshī
From a *Jahāngīr-nāma* manuscript
Rampur State Library
Bibliography: *Brown*, frontispiece

While inscribed to Govardhan, the page is here attributed to Anant, and is further discussed in the list of *Jahāngīr-nāma* illustrations.

Shāh Jahān and Sons
Present location unknown
Bibliography: Sotheby 26 March 1973, Lot 22

Lion
Private Collection
Literature: *BM*, no. 123

Jahāngīr and a Son
Present location unknown
Bibliography: Sotheby 26 March 1973, Lot 7

Old Man and a Youth
Present location unknown
Bibliography: Sotheby 26 March 1973, Lot 31

Rūp Singh, Sar Rāī Chanda
From the *Kevorkian Album*
Metropolitan Museum of Art, New York
Bibliography: *Dimand Bulletin*, p. 97

ʿĀlamgīr I
Present location unknown
Bibliography: Sotheby 15 July 1970, Lot 16

A *Mullā*
Present location unknown
Bibliography: Sotheby 10 July 1973, Lot 18

Holy Man and a Prince
Present location unknown
Bibliography: Sotheby 26 March 1973, Lot 28

Shāh Jahān Riding
From the *Kevorkian Album*
Metropolitan Museum of Art, New York

Jahāngīr Embracing Nūr Jahān
Los Angeles County Museum of Art
Bibliography: *Welch AMI*, no. 32; Stchoukine, "Portraits II," pp. 168–76 and Pl. 56; *Beach Heeramaneck*, no. 212; Khandalavala, "Some Problems," pp. 8–13

Man with a Bear
From the *Kevorkian Album*
Metropolitan Museum of Art, New York
Bibliography: *Dimand Bulletin*, p. 101

Man with a Bear
From the *Kevorkian Album*
Metropolitan Museum of Art, New York

Lovers
From the *Kevorkian Album*
Metropolitan Museum of Art, New York

Akbar with a Lion and a Heifer
From the *Kevorkian Album*
Metropolitan Museum of Art, New York

A second, superior version of this composition, in grisaille, is in the Cleveland Museum of Art.

محمد هاشم

44

Mīr Hāshim

All the works ascribable to Hāshim are portraits, and the vast majority are single figures, placed against a plain background. Only one work is inscriptionally dated, but it seems generally reliable to date acceptable paintings on the basis of the age of the subject, which is the initial framework used below. What results from this is an indication that Hāshim's style, not surprisingly, became more and more technically secure; the extraordinary portraits of *Shāh Jahān* (*no. 45*), *Dārā Shikōh* (*no. 64*), and the unknown *Abyssinian* (*no. 44*) are executed with breath-taking control, but with little warmth. As his style evolved, and unlike a painter such as Govardhan, Hāshim shows increasingly less involvement or sympathy with his subjects. More even than Bichitr, he is a detached, highly objective observer, constantly concerned with refining and perfecting his materials and technique.

Many works have inscriptions naming Hāshim, for he was evidently a prestigious and popular portraitist; yet several of these are certainly late copies. It is not always a clear decision, however, for Hāshim's range is so severely restricted that it is no easy task to distinguish authentic works of less than the highest quality from faithful later copies.

44

AN ABYSSINIAN

> From an Album of Shāh Jahān
> Inscribed: *amal-i-Hāshim* ("work of Hāshim")
> Circa 1633
> 15 × 8.1 cm. (33.5 × 21 cm.)
> Provenance: Rothschild Collection
> Anonymous Loan
> Bibliography: Colnaghi, *Persian and Mughal Art*, no. 117; *Welch IMP*, Pl. 34 (color); Stchoukine, "Portraits IV," no. 11, fig. 5; Khandalavala, "Identification," fig. 4

Several Mughal and Deccani portraits of Abyssinians are known. The most famous may depict the great general Malik ᶜAmbar, who came to notice when he was purchased in the slave bazaars of Baghdad, and eventually rose to become virtual ruler of the Deccani kingdom of Ahmadnagar. The identity of the man shown here is not given, but Stuart C. Welch has suggested that it is Fath Khān, Malik ᶜAmbar's son, whose presence at the Mughal court in 1633 may be responsible for the extraordinary immediacy and power of this portrait.

45

Literature: Coomaraswamy, "Notes," pp. 8–9; *Stchoukine Louvre*, no. XXIX.

45

SHĀH JAHĀN IN OLD AGE

> From the *Late Shāh Jahān Album*
> Inscribed: *amal-i-Hāshim* ("work of Hāshim")
> Circa 1650–55
> 21.5 × 13.0 cm. (36.4 × 24.7 cm.)
> Provenance: Cartier Collection
> Anonymous Loan
> Bibliography: Welch, "Mughal and Deccani Miniature Paintings," no. 18, fig. 18

The men along the right margin are portraits of specific imperial servants, the canopy at the top is a regal insignia, and the contented companionship of lion and goat (or lamb, etc.) recurs frequently as a metaphor of beneficent rule. Unlike Jahāngīrī album pages, here the borders relate to, and comment upon, the central panel. A careful examination of the turban of the emperor reveals Hāshim's ability to seemingly transmute paint and line into the substances they describe.

Further Major Attributions to Hāshim

Jahāngīr
From the *Minto Album*
Inscribed to Hāshim
Circa 1620
A. Chester Beatty Library, Dublin (Ms. 7, No. 12)
Bibliography: Gascoigne, *Great Moghuls*, p. 114 (color)

Jahāngīr
From the *Minto Album*
Inscribed to Hāshim
Circa 1620
A. Chester Beatty Library, Dublin (Ms. 7, No. 13)
Bibliography: *Beatty Library*, vol. III, Pl. 61

The two works listed above are facing pages in the *Minto Album*, and both show Jahāngīr with a globe; the second is among the most powerful characterizations of the emperor.

Sultān Muhammad Qutb Shāh
From the *Minto Album*
Inscribed to Hāshim
Circa 1625
Victoria and Albert Museum, London
Bibliography: *BM*, no. 131; Stchoukine, *Peinture Indienne*, Pl. XXX

Muhammad, nephew of Muhammad Qulī Qutb Shāh, ruled from 1611 to 1626.

Khwāja Abūʿl Hasan
Inscribed to Hāshim
Circa 1625–30
Musée Guimet, Paris
Bibliography: Stchoukine, *Peinture Indienne*, Pl. XXXI; Bussagli, *Indian Miniatures*, fig. 66 (color)

ʿAbd-al-Rahīm, Khān-i-Khānān
From the *Kevorkian Album*
Inscribed to Hāshim
Circa 1625
Freer Gallery of Art, Washington, D.C.

Portrait of an Abyssinian
Inscribed: "work of Hāshim"
Circa 1625–30
Musée Guimet, Paris
Bibliography: Stchoukine, *Peinture Indienne*, Pl. XXIX

A second portrait of the same man is in the Museum of Fine Arts, Boston (*Coomaraswamy Boston*, no. LXXVII, Pl. XXXVIIA). See also *no. 44*.

Muhammad ʿAlī Beg
From the *Minto Album*
Inscribed: "work of Hāshim"
Circa 1630–31
Victoria and Albert Museum, London (IM 25-1925)

Muhammad ʿAlī Beg was sent from Iran to Shāh Jahān's court as Ambassador in 1630, and arrived just after the Mughal defeat of the Iranian fortress of Qandahar. The inscription on this work has been attributed to Jahāngīr (see *BM*, no. 130)—a historical impossibility.

Shāhnawāz Khān
From the *Minto Album*
Inscribed to Hashim
A. Chester Beatty Library (Ms. 7, No. 6)

Khān Daurān, *Nasrat-i-Jang*
Inscribed: "work of Hāshim"
Circa 1635–40
A. Chester Beatty Library (Ms. 7, No. 36)
Bibliography: *Beatty Library*, vol. III, Pl. 72

Khān Daurān was particularly active in the Deccan in the 1630s, and is the major figure in several Windsor *Padshāh-nāma* pages.

A Nobleman
Inscribed: "work of Hāshim"
Circa 1640–50
Present location unknown (ex-Demotte Collection)
Bibliography: *Brown*, Pl. XXVIII

Young Prince
Inscribed: "work of Hāshim"
Present location unknown
Bibliography: Sotheby 26 March 1973, Lot 2

Prince Sulāiman Shikōh and Tutor
Inscribed: "work of Mīr Hāshim"
Circa 1645
Bristol City Art Gallery
Bibliography: Welch, *Indian Drawings*, no. 20

The same prince is evidently seen in Martin, *Miniature Paintings*, Pl. 199.

Two Musicians
Inscribed to Mīr Hāshim
Staatliche Museen, Berlin

Tīmūr, Bābur, and Humāyūn
Inscribed: "work of Hāshim"

21

45 (detail)

Dated: 1653–54
Present location unknown (ex-de Béarn and Demotte Collections)
Bibliography: Martin, *Miniature Paintings*, Pl. 214; Marteau and Vever, *Miniatures Persanes*, vol. II, no. 226, Pl. CLVIII

Such illustrations, usually accompanied by facing pages showing Akbar, Jahāngīr, and Shāh Jahān (e.g., Marteau and Vever, *Miniatures Persanes*, vol. II, no. 227, Pl. CLIX) were executed by many leading artists. This scene relates closely to the listing immediately below.

Tīmūr and Four Mughal Emperors

Inscribed to Hāshim
Circa 1650–55
India Office Library, London (Johnson Album 64-38)
Bibliography: *BM*, no. 138

Mīrzā Nauzar (d. 1664)

Inscribed: "work of Mīr Hāshim"
Circa 1650–60
British Library (Add. 18801)
Bibliography: Martin, *Miniature Paintings*, Pl. 185A

Hakīm Sadrā (d. 1650)

Inscribed: "work of Mīr Hāshim"
Bibliography: Martin, *Miniature Paintings*, Pl. 185B

Further Attributions

A Shrike

Present location unknown
Literature: Gray et al., *R.A. Arts of India and Pakistan*, no. 741

Saʿād Allāh Khān

A. Chester Beatty Library, Dublin (Ms. 62, No. 5)

Shāh Jahān with a Courtier

A. Chester Beatty Library, Dublin (Ms. 62, No. 4)

Mīrzā ʿAbd-al-Rahīm, Khān-i-Khānān

Present location uncertain (formerly: Museum of Archaeology, Delhi)
Bibliography: Delhi, Museum of Archaeology, *Loan Exhibition of Antiquities: Coronation Darbar 1911*, C104, Pl. XL

An Archer

Present location uncertain
Bibliography: Sarre and Martin, *Ausstellung*, no. 992, T.37

Sheikh Saʿīd-ud-dīn Hamunī and Sheikh Āʿīn-al-Zamand

Museum für Völkerkunde, Berlin
Bibliography: Sarre and Martin, *Ausstellung*, no. 923, I.38

Mir Rustam of Qandahar

Los Angeles County Museum of Art
Bibliography: *Beach Heeramaneck*, no. 217; *Welch AMI*, no. 45

Blind Pilgrim at Ajmer

From the *Wantage Album*
Victoria and Albert Museum, London
Bibliography: *Wantage Bequest*, no. 29

Prince and Princess in Hermitage at Night

Present location unknown
Bibliography: Sotheby 26 March 1973, Lot 21

Fireworks

Present location unknown
Bibliography: Sotheby 26 March 1973, Lot 32

The two works listed above are of eighteenth-century date.

Amīr Khusrau Dihlavī Manuscript

Staatsbibliothek, Berlin (Or. 1278)
Bibliography: Arnold and Grohmann, *Islamic Book*, Pl. 86

The signature, published as Hāshim, should be read Qasim, a painter whose work is known in several popular Mughal manuscripts.

Manōhar

Manōhar was a subtle and extremely gifted painter, whose primary interest was a depiction of the majesty and decorum of the imperial Mughal court. Although many of his paintings lack a sense of dramatic encounter, the serpentine rhythms and brilliant patterns of his finest compositions are as visually exciting as the most emotionally charged Mughal paintings.

Manōhar was the son of Basāwan, one of the foremost artists of the late sixteenth century. Based on the evidence of two known portraits of the painter, Manōhar must have been born in the late 1560s. The first work, a self-portrait in a manuscript of the *Gulistān* of Saʿdī dated 1581–82, shows a twelve or thirteen year old boy, while the second, a portrait by Daulat from the *Gulshan Album* (*fig. 10*), circa 1605–9, was painted roughly twenty-five years later and shows Manōhar that much older.

Manōhar's career spans at least four decades, from the early 1580s to the 1620s. During this time he developed from a rather typical Akbari artist into a painter whose most memorable works, the portraits and intimate court scenes that he painted for Jahāngīr, are among the greatest Mughal paintings.

Any attempt to study the artist's work must begin with a careful examination of its relationship to the style of Basāwan. Not only was the latter probably Manōhar's first teacher—a relationship common among Mughal painters of the same family—but both artists worked together on several paintings during the 1580s and 1590s. Manōhar's interests, however, were distinct from those of his father. Basāwan was particularly intrigued by the exploration of spatial effects. His compositions frequently make use of a deep space, and a glance at any of his paintings reveals his ability to suggest recession and roundness of form.[1] His details are modelled in high relief, enhancing our sense of volume, while his figures lead us back and away from the surface of the painting.

If we look for these qualities in Manōhar's paintings, however, we are at once struck by their absence. Where Basāwan is interested in space and volume, Manōhar seems concerned with line and surface pattern. These differences can be easily seen if we examine the small painting of *Two Students* (*no. 46*). The two male figures—one nude save for a loin cloth, the other fully robed—in the center of this simple composition, are both well drawn and delicately modelled. But by avoiding deep shadows, and by working only in subdued tones of color, Manōhar has not imparted as great a sense of weight or volume to his figures as his father might have done. For instead of strong colors and incisive modelling, the younger man prefers to focus our attention on the linear interplay of the various forms on the surface of the painting. The attendant in the lower right, for instance, which Basāwan would have made into a full-bodied form and then used as a means to give an illusion of depth to the composition, has been presented by Manōhar as a thin figure that moves across, but not into, the painting.

While Manōhar does not fully incorporate Basāwan's use of space and modelling, he has nevertheless absorbed his father's sense of rhythm and color, major expressive elements in all of Basāwan's paintings. For the older artist, color was a means of balancing compositions, of building internal rhythms (and, therefore, visual interest), and of emphasizing major figures or events. And while he never tries to merely imitate the dramatic effects that are so typical of his father, Manōhar does adapt Basāwan's carefully bal-

Fig. 10. Portrait of Manōhar. By Daulat, ca. 1605–9. From the *Muraqqaʿ-e-Gulshan*. Imperial Library, Tehran. After Y. Godard, "Marges," fig. 12.

anced tonal arrangements to his own needs. An early example of this is an illustration (known as "The Garden of the Fairies") from a *Khamsa* of Amīr Khusrau Dihlavī, dated 1597–98 and now in the Metropolitan Museum of Art, New York.[2] Here a royal couple, attended by winged musicians and tray-bearing servants, is seated in a garden pavilion. This evening tryst, bathed in an eerie blue light, seems very tranquil. Manōhar has, however, undermined this tranquility, as his father would have done, by vivid touches of strategically placed color. The orange drapery around the pavilion contrasted against the dark green background, for example, both draws our attention to the two lovers and adds a vibrant charge to the atmosphere of the scene. This excitement is echoed in a manner worthy of Basāwan by contrasting the coolness of the prince's white and blue-tinged robes with the warm red of the princess's costume.

Although Manōhar has created an uncharacteristically deep and complicated space here, the strong tones of the figures, compared to the softer, more subtle tones of the architecture and background, indicate that he is concerned mainly with the play of these colors on the surface of the painting. In fact, Manōhar actually denies us the possibility of exploring the background space, for he lets the building behind the pavilion be cut off by the flat rectangular area of the script. The result of this is that despite some well-modelled figures in the lower foreground, and the suggested recession in the upper left-hand corner of the painting, the figures do not seem to be integrated into a consistent spatial framework. This conflict between surface tension and spatial recession is so unresolved that it destroys the unity of the composition.

Manōhar eventually solves this problem in many of his mature works by creating shallow spaces emphasized by oblique parallel lines that skim across, but never lead into, the painting. For instance, in a superb portrait of *Akbar Listening to a Courtier*, circa 1602, reproduced here as *fig. 11*, the background has become a thick tangle of dark green trees that form a virtual wall against which the action takes place; and the attendant's angled arms are paired with the guardsman's rifle to form the oblique parallel lines. One might even notice that the diagonal lines of the pavilion are so sharply slanted that instead of leading us back into space, as they easily could, they only accentuate the shallowness of the composition. Linear rhythms abound, as well. We need only trace the sinuous line of the dog's neck in *Akbar Listening to a Courtier* (*fig. 11*) as it leads to the attendant's feet, and beyond, to see this. And accentuating this movement is a progression from the somber colors of the dog's back to the intense orange of the robe of Prince Khurram, standing behind the Emperor. Similar interests are found in the *Gulistān* of Saʿdī page (*no. 19* [above]).

Our understanding of Manōhar's style would be incomplete if we did not look at his human figures and particularly his portraits. It is here that we see the full development of his line and modelling as well as his artistic intentions. The majority of his figures, whether they are actual portraits or not, are easily recognized by a distinctive modelling technique, for Manōhar usually concentrates the modelling along his subjects' contours, leaving the rest in neutral tones. Although as a general trait this is common to many late sixteenth and early seventeenth-century Mughal artists, the extent to which Manōhar emphasizes outlines and avoids shading within them helps identify his work.

This kind of modelling has the effect of suggesting a sense of volume, while not making the figures conflict with a shallow compositional space. The effect is particularly convincing in such paintings as *Akbar Listening to a Courtier* (*fig. 11*) and the *Two Students* (*no. 46*), for the major figures are given just enough presence to seem substantial without disturbing the decorative strength of the surface.

Manōhar's finest portraits (many are found in the great *Darbār of Jahāngīr, no. 14*) are works of extraordinary draughtsmanship. But no matter how precisely he depicts his subjects and their surrounding details, his view of mankind is always one of courtly elegance. Whereas Abūʿl Hasan (e.g., *no. 27*) and Govardhan (e.g., *no. 5* verso) were interested in every aspect of a figure's personality, Manōhar is concerned with formal appearance. He is, consequently, more adept at accurately describing textures of cloth and opulent jewels than in penetrating personalities. This is evident whether we are looking at a portrait such as *Akbar Listening to a Courtier* (*fig. 11*) or at *The Undoing of an Ill-Natured Wazīr* (*no. 19* [above]), a narrative scene; on the other hand, if we try to get a sense of the aged Akbar's feelings as he consults with his courtier, or of the tension between the wazīr and his captors, we meet an emotional vacuum.

If Manōhar has not fully explored the depth of his subjects' personalities in these, his most successful, works, he has more than made up for it by the sheer beauty of his painting. Moreover, the scenes of carefully orchestrated royal splendor provide a unique insight into the courts of Akbar and Jahāngīr. By guiding our attention only to those details that reflect the imperial majesty of Mughal court life, and by emphasizing these through his use of line and color, Manōhar has given us the vision of a world that—as Akbar and Jahāngīr would have wished—is unmarred by imperfections of character or appearance.

Glenn D. Lowry

FIG. 11. Akbar in Old Age. By Manōhar, ca. 1604.
The Cincinnati Art Museum—Gift of John J. Emery.

46

46

TWO STUDENTS

Attributed to Manōhar
Circa 1600–1605
10 × 10.5 cm.
Provenance: Heeramaneck Collection
Lent by the Los Angeles County Museum of Art: Nasli and
Alice Heeramaneck Collection (L.69.24.251)
Bibliography: *Beach Heeramaneck*, no. 204

Pages from the following manuscripts bear
contemporary inscriptions to Manōhar:

Gulistān of Saʿdī (fol. no. unknown)
  Inscribed to "Manōhar son of Basāwan"
  Dated A.H. 990 = A.D. 1581
  Royal Asiatic Society, London
  Bibliography: Gray et al., *R.A. Arts of India and Pakistan*,
  no. 642, Pl. 121; Wellesz, *Akbar's Religious Thought*, fig. 11

The colophon page, which bears a self-portrait by Manōhar at
the age of twelve or thirteen, is dated 1581. It has been suggested
that the illustration is of Jahāngīrī date (see Barrett and Gray,
Painting, p. 82). While it does seem extraordinarily mature for so
young a painter, a more convincing explanation is that Manōhar
was "helped" by his father, Basāwan.

Tīmūr-nāma (fol. no. unknown)
  Circa 1584
  Khuda Bakhsh Public Library, Patna

An incomplete marginal inscription seems to record Manōhar's
name.

Khamsa of Nizāmī (fol. 195b)
  Circa 1585
  Keir Collection
  Bibliography: *Robinson ed., Keir*, V.26, Pl. 115

Akbar-nāma (fol. no. unknown)
  Circa 1590
  Victoria and Albert Museum, London

Bābur-nāma (fol. 283b)
  Circa 1590
  British Library (Or. 3714)
  Bibliography: H. Suleiman, *Miniatures of Babur-nāma* (Tash-
  kent, 1970), Pl. 42

Dīwān of Hafīz (fol. no. unknown)
  Circa 1590–95
  Rampur State Library

Khamsa of Nizāmī (fols. 13v, 72r, 132r)
  Dated 1595
  British Library (Or. 12208)
  Bibliography: Martin, *Miniature Paintings*, Pl. 178 (fol. 132r)

Jāmiʿ-al-Tawārīkh (fol. no. unknown)
  Dated 1596
  Gulishan Library, Tehran
  Bibliography: Marek and Knizkova, *The Jenghiz Khan Mini-
  atures* (London, 1963), Pl. 3

Anwār-i-Suhailī (fol. no. unknown)
  Dated 1596
  Bharat Kala Bhavan, Benares

Khamsa of Amīr Khusrau Dihlavī (fol. no. unknown)
  Dated 1597–98
  Metropolitan Museum of Art, New York
  Bibliography: Gray et al., *R.A. Arts of India and Pakistan*,
  no. 652, Pl. 124; Grube, *Classical Style*, Pl. 94; *Islamic Art*,
  Metropolitan Museum of Art, New York, n.d., no page or
  plate number given

Gulistān of Saʿdī (fol. no. unknown)
  Circa 1595–1600
  Cincinnati Art Museum

Akbar-nāma (fols. 34a, 138a)
  Dated 1604
  British Library (Or. 12988)

Akbar-nāma (fols. 32b, 57a, 212a, 212b)
  Dated 1604
  A. Chester Beatty Library, Dublin (Ms. 3)
  Bibliography: *Beatty Library*, vol. II, Pls. 15 and 18

The two manuscripts listed immediately above are sections of one work. Two additional pages, attributed here to Manōhar, are in the Metropolitan Museum of Art, New York.

Khamsa of Mīr Alī Shīr Navāʿī (fol. 5v)

Circa 1605
The Royal Library, Windsor Castle
Bibliography: *BM*, no. 94a

Further Major Attributions to Manōhar

A Lady Playing a Lyre

From the *Muraqqaʿ-e-Gulshan*
Inscribed to Manōhar
Circa 1600
Imperial Library, Tehran
Bibliography: Wilkinson and Gray, "Indian Paintings,"
Pl. 3a

Layla Visiting Majnun in the Desert

From the *Muraqqaʿ-e-Gulshan*
Inscribed to Manōhar
Circa 1600
Imperial Library, Tehran
Bibliography: Wilkinson and Gray, "Indian Paintings,"
Pl. 3b

A second version of this painting, also inscribed to Manōhar, is in the *Nāsir-ud-dīn Album* (see Godard, "Album," no. 44).

Sultān Murād and Sultān Daniyāl in a Garden Pavilion

Inscribed to Manōhar
Circa 1600
Present location unknown
Bibliography: Sotheby 10 July 1973, Lot 131

Picnic Scene

From the *Nāsir-ud-dīn Album*
Inscribed to Manōhar
Circa 1600
Imperial Library, Tehran
Bibliography: Godard, "Album," fig. 92

A Man with a Staff

From the *Berlin Album* (fol. 18b)
Inscribed to Manōhar
Circa 1600–1602
Staatsbibliothek, Berlin
Bibliography: Kühnel and Goetz, *Indian Book Painting*, Pl. 37

A Courtier

From the *Berlin Album* (fol. 18b)
Inscribed to Manōhar
Circa 1600–1602
Staatsbibliothek, Berlin
Bibliography: Kühnel and Goetz, *Indian Book Painting*, Pl. 37

The inscribed attributions on the two paintings listed above have been incorrectly published as Minushir.

A second version of *A Man with a Staff*, also inscribed to Manōhar, but identified by an inscription as Madhu Singh, is in the Walters Art Gallery, Baltimore (W. 668, fol. 29).

Prince Daniyāl

From the *Kevorkian Album*
Inscribed to Manōhar
Circa 1600–1605
Metropolitan Museum of Art, New York
Bibliography: Skelton, "Two Mughal Lion Hunts," fig. 6

Prince Daniyāl

Inscribed to Manōhar
Circa 1600–1605
Walters Art Gallery, Baltimore (W. 668, fol. 28)

Akbar Listening to a Courtier

Inscribed to Manōhar
Circa 1602–4
Cincinnati Art Museum (1950.289)
Bibliography: *Welch IMP*, Pl. 15

Reproduced here as fig. 10 (color).

Prince Khurram

From the *Muraqqaʿ-e-Gulshan*
Inscribed to Manōhar
Circa 1603–5
Imperial Library, Tehran
Bibliography: Godard, "Marges," fig. 26

This painting is inscribed, "My portrait done during my childhood, written by Shāh Jahān."

Battle Procession

Attributed here to Manōhar
Circa 1605
Freer Gallery of Art, Washington, D.C. (59.30)

Jahāngīr Drinking Wine under a Canopy

Inscribed to Manōhar
Circa 1605
British Museum
Bibliography: Binyon and Arnold, *Court Painters*, frontispiece; *BM*, no. 109

A second version of this painting, also inscribed to Manōhar, is in the *Leningrad Album* (Ivanova et al., *Albom Indiyskikh*, Pl. 19).

Standing Portrait

Inscribed to Manōhar
Circa 1610
Rothenstein Collection
Bibliography: Lionel Heath, *Examples of Indian Art at the British Empire Exhibition, 1924* (London, 1925), Pl. 1

Jahāngīr

From the *Leningrad Album*
Inscribed to Manōhar and Mansūr
Circa 1610
Academy of Sciences, Leningrad
Bibliography: Ivanova et al., *Albom Indiyskikh*, Pl. 17

Prince Parvīz Received by Jahāngīr

From the *Minto Album*
Attributed to Manōhar
Circa 1614
Victoria and Albert Museum, London (IM 9-1925)
Bibliography: *BM*, no. 111; Stchoukine, *Peinture Indienne*,
Pl. 28; Stchoukine, "Portraits I," p. 215ff

Sheikhs Waiting to Greet Jahāngīr at Ajmer

From a *Jahāngīr-nāma* manuscript
Inscribed to Manōhar
Circa 1616
Prince of Wales Museum, Bombay (15.280)
Bibliography: Gascoigne, *Great Moghuls*, p. 111

ᶜAbd-al-Rahīm, Khān-i-Khānān

From the *Berlin Album* (fol. 23a)
Inscribed to Manōhar
Dated 1618
Staatsbibliothek, Berlin
Bibliography: Kühnel and Goetz, *Indian Book Painting*, Pl. 36

Another portrait of the Khān-i-Khānān, also inscribed to Manōhar, is in the *Nāsir-ud-dīn Album* (Godard, "Album," Pl. 100).

Other Attributions

An Elephant Tamer

From the *Berlin Album* (fol. 24b)
Staatsbibliothek, Berlin
Bibliography: Kühnel and Goetz, *Indian Book Painting*, Pl. 34

Presentation Scene

Private Collection
Bibliography: Welch, "Mughal and Deccani Miniature
Paintings," no. 11, fig. 11

While attributed to Manōhar by S. C. Welch, this seems
more akin to works by Kesu Khurd (see Beach, "Kesu Das,"
pp. 42–52).

The Emperor Akbar on a Verandah with Musicians

Inscribed to Manōhar
Mahboubian Collection
Bibliography: Sotheby 10 July 1973, Lot 22

Hunting Scene

Kraus Collection
Bibliography: Grube, *Kraus Collection*, Pl. 243

Amīr Mīrzā Ghazī Beg

From the *Wantage Album*
Inscribed to Manōhar
Victoria and Albert Museum, London
Bibliography: *Wantage Bequest*, Pl. 12

Jahāngīr Receiving Qutb-ud-dīn Khān Koka
at Lahore in 1605

From the *Wantage Album*
Inscribed to Manōhar
Victoria and Albert Museum, London
Bibliography: *Wantage Bequest*, Pl. 7

Śiva

Inscribed to Manōhar
Present location unknown
Bibliography: Sotheby 7 April 1975, Lot 102

Jahāngīr Enthroned in a Pavilion

Attributed to Manōhar
Collection of the Maharaja of Jaipur
Bibliography: Gray et al., *R.A. Arts of India and Pakistan*,
no. 680

Portrait of a Bearded Man

From the *Nāsir-ud-dīn Album*
Inscribed to Manōhar
Imperial Library, Tehran
Literature: Godard, "Album," no. 71

A Small Falcon on a Perch

Inscribed to Manōhar
Collection of Geoffrey C. N. Sturt
Literature: Gray et al., *R.A. Arts of India and Pakistan*, no. 620

Layla and Majnun in the Wilderness

Inscribed to Manōhar
A. Chester Beatty Library, Dublin (Ms. 11a, No. 12)
Literature: *Beatty Library*, vol. I, pp. 45–46

A Black Buck

Inscribed to Manōhar
British Museum
Bibliography: Havell, *Sculpture*, Pl. 60

Processional Scene at the Court of Jahāngīr

From a *Jahāngīr-nāma* manuscript
Inscribed to Manōhar
Rampur State Library
Bibliography: *Brown*, Pl. XXXI (color)

This painting, attributed here to Bishan Dās, is discussed elsewhere in the catalogue with that painter's work.

Akbar Receiving Two Mansabdars in a Palace Garden

From the *Wantage Album*

Inscribed to Manōhar
Victoria and Albert Museum, London
Bibliography: *Wantage Bequest*, Pl. 6

Bābūr Kneeling on a Carpet

Inscribed to Manōhar
Present location unknown
Bibliography: Sotheby 7 April 1975, Lot 105

Portrait of a Man

From the *Nāsir-ud-dīn Album*
Inscribed to Manōhar
Imperial Library, Tehran
Literature: Godard, "Album," no. 53

Murtaza Khān

From the *Wantage Album*
Inscribed to Manōhar
Victoria and Albert Museum, London
Bibliography: *Wantage Bequest*, Pl. 11

Shāh Jahān Riding with his son Dārā Shikōh

From the *Minto Album*
Inscribed to Manōhar
Victoria and Albert Museum, London
Bibliography: Archer, *Indische Miniaturen*, Pl. 5 (color);
Stchoukine, *Peinture Indienne*, Pl. 33

Hakīm ᶜAlī

From the *Nāsir-ud-dīn Album*
Inscribed to Manōhar
Imperial Library, Tehran
Bibliography: Godard, "Album," Pl. 106

Jahāngīr Killing a Lion

From the *Leningrad Album*
Inscribed to Manōhar
Academy of Sciences, Leningrad
Bibliography: Ivanova et al., *Albom Indiyskikh*, Pl. 13

Jahāngīr in Darbār with his Courtiers and a Young Prince

From a *Jahāngīr-nāma* manuscript
Inscribed to Manōhar
Keir Collection
Bibliography: *Robinson ed., Keir*, V.70, Pl. 127 and Color
Plate 37

Āsaf Khān

From the *Nāsir-ud-dīn Album*
Inscribed to Manōhar
Imperial Library, Tehran
Bibliography: Godard, "Album," Pl. 80

Jahāngīr Embracing Prince Khurram

Inscribed to Rājā Manōhar Singh (?)

India Office Library, London
Bibliography: Coomaraswamy, *Indian Drawings*, Pl. 11;
Brown, Pl. LVIII; Welch, *Indian Drawings*, no. 18; Wilkinson,
Mughal Painting, Pl. 7; Gray et al., *R.A. Arts of India and
Pakistan*, no. 732

This drawing does not appear to be in the style of Manōhar, and
the name as published, Rājā Manōhar Singh, is both inappropriate and otherwise unknown.

A Horse

Inscribed to Manōhar
India Office Library, London
Bibliography: Lionel Heath, *Examples of Indian Art at the
British Empire Exhibition, 1924* (London, 1925), Pl. 2

Portrait of a Dark Brown Horse

Inscribed to Manōhar
Private Collection
Bibliography: Sotheby 1 December 1969, Lot 153

The two paintings listed above are stylistically attributable to
about 1640. Although there is no firm evidence that Manōhar
was active after about 1620, a painting in the Bibliothèque
Nationale is inscribed to "Manōhar Dārā Shikōhī" and it has
been suggested that Manōhar ended his career in Dārā Shikōh's
employ (see Godard, "Album," p. 183). This work in Paris,
however, is a late copy.

Ustād Mansūr, *Nādir-al-ᶜAsr*

The following references to Mansūr appear in
Jahāngīr's memoirs:

Ustad Mansur has become such a master in painting that
he has the title of Nadiru-l-ᶜAsr, and in the art of drawing
is unique in his generation. In the time of my father's
reign and my own, these two [Abuᶜl Hasan is included
here, as well] have no third.[1]

What can I write of the beauty and colour of this falcon?
... As it was something out of the common, I ordered
Ustad Mansur, who has the title of Nadiru-l-ᶜAsr (wonder
of the age) to paint and preserve its likeness.[2]

[The emperor describes the flowers of Kashmir, and then
states] ... those that Nadiruᶜl-ᶜAsr Ustad Mansur has
painted are more than 100.[3]

In this stream I saw a bird like a *saj*. A *saj* is of black color
and has white spots, while this bird is of the same colour
as the *bulbul* with white spots, and it dives and remains for
a long time underneath, and then comes up from a different place. ... I ordered Nadiru-l-ᶜAsr Ustad Mansur
to draw its likeness.[4]

With these few phrases, the emperor elevated Mansūr well above the artist's peers, for no other painter received even this much attention—and most were not mentioned at all. An understanding of Mansūr's style, therefore, must provide an important glimpse of Jahāngīr's interests and standards. Yet such an understanding is not easy, for Mansūr's evident productivity would certainly have resulted in some works of less than highest quality, and his fame encouraged both contemporary and later copies. The *Kevorkian* and *Wantage Albums* (discussed on pp. 74–76 in this catalogue), for example, each contain several works datable to circa 1800, but with elaborate inscriptions nonetheless attesting to Mansūr's authorship. These are easily recognizable by their soft, imprecise brushwork, and by the often overmodelled, amorphous character of figural and landscape forms —traits typical of painting especially in Delhi early in the nineteenth century.[5] Such works were probably faithful copies of illustrations in the imperial albums, perhaps made for British purchasers who accepted on trust that they were acquiring royal treasures. Since Mughal libraries were not otherwise accessible, there would have been no reason for doubts of authenticity.

The problem of Mansūr articulates, in extreme form, the problem of attributing Mughal painting generally. For in addition to authentic works by Mansūr, and recognizably late copies, there are contemporary seventeenth-century duplicates as well, perhaps made for use by different members of the royal household, or as presentation gifts. An example is the marvellous *Cheer Pheasant* (*no. 70*). Such copies were not necessarily made by the original painter, but sometimes included original inscriptions. With the popular and prolific Mansūr, this produced a situation in which the major portion of attributions can only be defended by visual judgments of quality and style. These judgments, however, must use irrefutably authentic works to establish their criteria, and this forces us to put extraordinary importance on the context in which the paintings are, or were, found. The *Zebra* of the *Minto Album*, for example, is initially more trustworthy than any painting in the *Kevorkian Album*, because by methodical examination of each page, it seems that the *Minto Album* paintings are actually by the artists to whom they are ascribed. Contrariwise, the *Kevorkian Album* is so filled with later copies that we must argue particularly strongly in order to defend an early date for any folio. Manuscripts with marginal attributions to Mansūr are also generally acceptable, for only the exceptional imperial manuscript marginal notations are untrustworthy. However, it is only Mansūr's earliest work that is found in manuscripts. The majority of paintings attributed to him are on loose sheets, independent of any context, and they are the real problem.

Many of Mansūr's early manuscript illustrations are painted, but not designed, by him, meaning that he was not immediately recognized as a major artist. It may have been routine assignments for the Victoria and Albert Museum *Akbar-nāma* and *Bābur-nāma* manuscripts that brought his talent for animal illustration to imperial notice. A *Bābur-nāma* page of about 1590–95 (*fig. 12*) in the Freer Gallery of Art, designed by Kanha, but painted by Mansūr, shows the basic elements of his style fully formed. The importance and unquestioned authenticity of the page justify its publication here. It is essentially a colored drawing, rather than a full painting, for the pigment is thin, the lines evident, and empty uncolored paper serves as a background. The animals are carefully observed and drawn with slow, scientific precision that never allows the line or color to become purely decorative or independently expressive. This is really natural history drawing at its best, and the style continues throughout Mansūr's career, for it is seen still in the *Zebra* of the *Minto Album* of 1621. There is a minimum of personal expressiveness in Mansūr's paintings, and this makes a chronology of his works hard (and, to a degree, unnecessary) to establish.

The superb painting of *Peafowl* in this exhibition (*no. 47*), however, must be an example of the artist's later work, and the differences between it and the *Bābur-nāma* page are important, if subtle. In the *Peafowl*, color is far more brilliant, not only in intensity (on the blue neck of the cock, for example), but in range and variation (most remarkable on the chest and neck of the hen). Furthermore, Mansūr makes minute distinctions in the texture and patterning of the different parts of the birds' bodies; he has become even more detailed and precise in his observations. The overall composition, too, is highly controlled. The flowers at the bottom are beginning to take on the formality which we have noted as dominating works made for Shāh Jahān. The contrast of the peacock's tail, the willowy shrub, and the green tree (at the top) is very conspicuously "arranged," as is the placement of the various plants' leaves, for they are animated as if blown by a wind. The direction of their movements is determined by compositional effec-

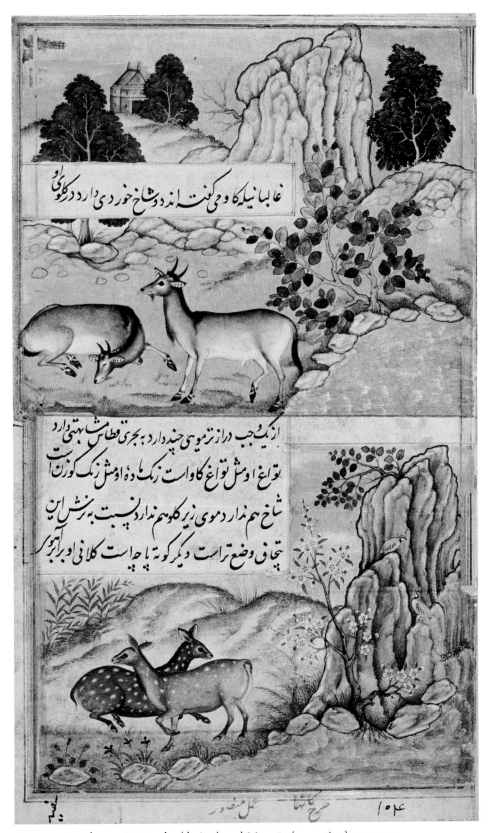

FIG. 12. Antelopes. By Kanha (design) and Mansūr (execution), ca. 1590.
From a *Bābur-nāma* ms. Courtesy of the Smithsonian Institution,
Freer Gallery of Art, Washington, D.C.

tiveness, however, not by any natural consistency of wind source. So while the painting seems initially identical in style to one of Mansūr's earliest works, the *Bābur-nāma* page, we find that sophistication has replaced simplicity. Clearly, as Mansūr's style develops, it simply becomes more refined; there is no radical shift of intent, as with a painter such as Payāg. The increased surface and technical brilliance of the later works, however, enrich the basic descriptiveness, and also adapt the painter's style to the taste of the 1620s.

It has been plausibly suggested that the artist may have been responsible for many of the floral borders found on Shāh Jahān album pages.[6] His work as an illuminator is known at an early date, for there is a signed frontispiece in the Walters Art Gallery *Khamsa* of Amīr Khusrau Dihlavī of 1597.

Literature: Aśok Kumar Das, "Ustad Mansur"; Tasneem Ahmad, "Nadiruᶜl-ᶜAsr Mansur."

47
PEAFOWL

From an Album of Shāh Jahān
Attributed to Mansūr
Circa 1620
19.1 × 10.8 cm. (36.8 × 25.1 cm.)
Provenance: Rothschild Collection
Anonymous Loan
Bibliography: *Brown*, Pl. XXIII; Colnaghi, *Persian and Mughal Art*, no. 99 (color); *Welch IMP*, Pl. 26 (color)

The illustration is presently set within superb Shāh Jahān album borders, although it is not certain that this was its original mount. There are strong visual similarities between this work and certain early Ming dynasty imperial paintings.[7] The Mughal Empire was in contact with China, and Chinese porcelains were imported in some quantity,[8] but whether correspondences are actually due to contact has yet to be satisfactorily determined.

Further Major Attributions to Ustād Mansūr

Akbar-nāma Manuscript (fols. 56, 112)
> Both inscribed as painted, but not designed, by Mansūr
> Circa 1590
> Victoria and Albert Museum, London

Bābur-nāma Manuscript (fol. no. unknown)
> Inscribed: "design by Kanha, painted by Mansūr"

Circa 1590–95
Freer Gallery of Art, Washington, D.C. (54.29)
Reproduced here as *fig. 11*

Bābur-nāma Manuscript (fols. 387r, 387v, 388r, 388v, 389r)
> Inscribed to Mansūr
> Circa 1595
> British Library (Or. 3714)

Bābur-nāma Manuscript (fol. 8v)
> Inscribed to Mansūr
> Circa 1598
> National Museum of India, New Delhi
> Bibliography: Das, "Mansur," Pl. XIII, fig. 3

Jāmiᶜ al-Tawārīkh Manuscript (fol. no. unknown)
> Inscribed: "design by Nānhā, painted by Mansūr"
> Dated 1596–97
> Imperial Library, Tehran

Khamsa of Amīr Khusrau Dihlavī Manuscript (fol. 1v)
> Inscribed to Mansūr Naqqash
> Dated 1597–98
> Walters Art Gallery, Baltimore

Two Magpies
> From the *Berlin Album* (p. 17b)
> Attributed here to Mansūr
> Circa 1595–1600
> Staatsbibliothek, West Berlin
> Bibliography: Kühnel and Goetz, *Indian Book Painting*, Pl. 10 (color); Dimand, *Indian Miniature Painting*, frontispiece (color)

While the painting is on cloth, which gives it a somewhat different texture, it is precisely in the style of the Freer *Bābur-nāma* illustrations listed above.

Hen and Chicks
> Inscribed to Mansūr, *Nādir-al-ᶜAsr*
> Circa 1595–1600
> British Museum (1953-2-104-02)
> Bibliography: *BM*, no. 99 (color)

Like the work immediately above, this is also on cloth.

Akbar-nāma Manuscript (fols. 35b, 110a and b, 112a)
> Inscribed to Mansūr
> Dated 1604
> British Library (Or. 12988)

Flower
> From the *Muraqqaᶜ-e-Gulshan* (fol. 53r)
> Imperial Library, Tehran
> Literature: Wilkinson and Gray, "Indian Paintings," p. 177

47

Vina Player

Inscribed to Mansūr
Circa 1600
Collection of Edward Croft Murray, London
Bibliography: *Welch AMI*, no. 18

Chameleon

Inscribed: "Ustād Mansūr"
Circa 1600
The Royal Library, Windsor Castle
Bibliography: Welch, *Indian Drawing*, no. 15; Gray et al., *R.A. Arts of India and Pakistan*, no. 724, Pl. 135

Jahāngīr

From the *Leningrad Album* (fol. 3)
Inscribed to Manōhar and Mansūr
Circa 1605
Academy of Sciences, Leningrad
Bibliography: Ivanova et al., *Albom Indiyskikh*, Pl. 17

West Asiatic Tulip and Butterfly

Inscribed to Mansūr
Circa 1620–25
Habib Ganj Library, Aligarh Distt.
Bibliography: Mehta, "'Red Lilies,'" pp. 117–19; Mehta, *Studies*, Pl. 31 (color); Skelton, "Motif," fig. XCa

A discussion of the role of European herbals in Mughal floral paintings is found in Skelton, "Motif."

Iris and Bird

From the *Nāsir-ud-dīn Album*
Inscribed to Mansūr
Imperial Library, Tehran
Bibliography: Godard, "Album," no. 81 and fig. 113

Narcissus

From the *Nāsir-ud-dīn Album*
Inscribed to Mansūr
Imperial Library, Tehran
Bibliography: Godard, "Album," no. 80

Zebra

From the *Minto Album*
Inscribed to Mansūr
Dated 1621
Victoria and Albert Museum, London
Bibliography: *Welch IMP*, Pl. 27 (color); Archer, *Indian Miniatures*, Pl. 26

A second, extremely close but slightly less sensitive, version of this work is in the Museum of Fine Arts, Boston; its relation to Mansūr was noted by A. K. Coomaraswamy in *Coomaraswamy Boston*, no. LXXXV, Pl. XLII.

Other Attributions

Many of the works listed here were brought to my notice through the article by Aśok Kumar Das, mentioned above, to whom I am very grateful.

Turkey

From the *Wantage Album*
Inscribed: "work of Ustād Mansūr, Nādir-al-ᶜAsr"
Victoria and Albert Museum, London
Bibliography: Gascoigne, *Great Moghuls*, p. 132; *Wantage Bequest*, no. 23, Pl. 15

This evidently is the animal referred to by the emperor as coming from Goa in 1612 (*Tūzuk*, vol. I, pp. 215–16). An unsigned, almost identical alternate version of this page is reproduced in *Brown*, Pl. LIII and H. Mode, *Calcutta* (London, 1973), Pl. 39 (color).

Cheer Pheasant

From the *Wantage Album*
Inscribed: "work of Ustād Mansūr"
Victoria and Albert Museum, London
Bibliography: Welch, *Indian Drawing*, no. 14; *Wantage Bequest*, no. 24, Pl. 16

At least two other major versions of this composition exist, neither of which is signed. One, formerly in the Rothschild Collection, is exhibited here (*no. 70*). The second is reproduced in Martin, *Miniature Paintings*, Pl. 220.

Himalayan Blue-Throated Barbet

From the *Wantage Album*
Inscribed: "work of Nādir-al-ᶜAsr, Ustād Mansūr"
Victoria and Albert Museum, London
Bibliography: Gascoigne, *Great Moghuls*, p. 62 (color); *Wantage Bequest*, no. 22, Pl. 15

The three paintings listed above have the best claim, on qualitative grounds, as works actually by Mansūr. Those from the *Wantage Album* listed below, although inscribed to Mansūr, are probably of about 1800.

Wazīr Khwāja Kalān Beg

From the *Wantage Album*
Victoria and Albert Museum, London
Bibliography: *Wantage Bequest*, no. 25, Pl. 17

Saras Cranes

From the *Wantage Album*
Victoria and Albert Museum, London
Bibliography: *Wantage Bequest*, no. 20, Pl. 14; Gray et al., *R.A. Arts of India and Pakistan*, no. 714, Pl. G (color)

Red-Wattled Lapwing

From the *Wantage Album*
Victoria and Albert Museum, London
Bibliography: *Wantage Bequest*, no. 21, Pl. 14

Black and White Hornbill

From the *Kevorkian Album*
Inscribed to Ustād Mansūr
Metropolitan Museum of Art, New York
Bibliography: *Welch AMI*, no. 37; *Dimand Bulletin*, p. 100

A later, identical copy of this page is reproduced in Sotheby
26 March 1973, Lot 36.

Nilgae

From the *Kevorkian Album*
Inscribed to Ustād Mansūr
Metropolitan Museum of Art, New York

A second, unsigned study of a Nilgae, now in the British
Museum, was once attributed to Mansūr (Gray et al., *R.A. Arts
of India and Pakistan*, no. 719, Pl. 139).

Water Birds

From the *Kevorkian Album*
Inscribed to Mansūr
Metropolitan Museum of Art, New York

The three paintings listed above are of *Kevorkian Album* pages
closest in style to undoubted works by Mansūr. Other paintings
inscribed to Mansūr in the album seem to have been added about
1800.

Wounded Buck

Private Collection
Bibliography: Welch and Beach, *Gods*, no. 10; Welch,
Mughal and Deccani Miniature Paintings, no. 14, fig. 15

This work is attributed to Mansūr by S. C. Welch, but it has
recently been suggested that this is by Abūᶜl Hasan (*Welch FEM*,
no. 61).

Salt Water Fish

Red Fort Museum, Delhi
Bibliography: Das, "Mansur," fig. 1

Falcon

Museum of Fine Arts, Boston (14.683)
Bibliography: Marteau and Vever, *Miniatures Persanes*, vol. II,
no. 255, Pl. CLXXVI; *Coomaraswamy Boston*, no. LXXXIV,
Pl. XLI; *Coomaraswamy Goloubev*, no. 132, Pl. LXXVIII;
Gascoigne, *Great Moghuls*, p. 133

Falcon on a Perch

Prince of Wales Museum, Bombay
Bibliography: Krishnadasa, *Mughal Miniatures*, Pl. 4

Partridge

Present location unknown
Bibliography: Martin, *Miniature Paintings*, Pl. 219

Hen Pheasant

Vever Collection
Bibliography: Marteau and Vever, *Miniatures Persanes*, vol. II,
no. 259, Pl. CLXXVIII

Two Birds

Vever Collection
Bibliography: Marteau and Vever, *Miniatures Persanes*, vol. II,
no. 257, Pl. CLXXVII

White Eye

Eckstein Collection
Fitzwilliam Museum, Cambridge

Siberian Crane

Indian Museum, Calcutta

Blackbird

Present location unknown
Bibliography: Christie's 21 June 1971, Lot 155

Bengal Florican

Indian Museum, Calcutta
Bibliography: Das, "Mansur," fig. 2

Goldfinch

National Museum of India, New Delhi
Bibliography: Alvi and Rahman, *Jahangir*, Pl. XVIIA

Flamingoes

Cowasjee Jahangir Collection, Bombay
Bibliography: Khandalavala and Chandra, *Jahangir Collection*, no. 20, fig. 20; Alvi and Rahman, *Jahangir*, Pl. XV
(color)

Flower

Collection of Geoffrey Sturt
Literature: Gray et al., *R.A. Arts of India and Pakistan*, no. 696

Muhammad ʿAlī

Muhammad ʿAlī is a painter whose existence has only recently been widely accepted. Two works inscribed to his authorship had long been known, although one was attributed instead to Farrukh Beg by Robert Skelton.[1] The recent discovery of two further paintings by the artist, one of which is lengthily inscribed, makes it clear that he is a distinct personality, albeit working in a style close to that of Farrukh Beg (see *no. 59*). Both painters exhibit an extreme refinement of technique and sensibility, although Muhammad ʿAlī seems to be free of the bizarre and unorthodox elements often found in the other master. Since the four known works all seem to be from the same period, however, we have little idea of the variations, or even the development, of his style. Nonetheless, the two painters must have worked closely together. Both show a general disinterest in Mughal trends towards naturalism; they use similar brilliant, strongly contrasting colors, ornamentally arranged floral forms, and flat backgrounds. Works by both men have strong affinities with paintings made at the Muslim courts in the Deccan, but whether this is due to similarity of temperament and interest, or actual contact, has not been firmly established. The relationship of Muhammad ʿAlī and Farrukh Beg makes very evident the problems encountered when trying to establish artistic identities by purely visual criteria.

48

A THOUGHTFUL MAN

> From an Album of Shāh Jahān
> Inscribed: *amal-i-Muhammad ʿAlī* ("work of Muhammad ʿAlī")
> Circa 1610–15
> 12.2 × 10.3 cm.
> Provenance: Goloubev Collection
> Lent by the Museum of Fine Arts, Boston: Francis Bartlett Donation of 1912 and Picture Fund (14.663)
> Bibliography: *Coomaraswamy Boston*, no. LVI, Pl. XXV; *Coomaraswamy Goloubev*, no. 119, Pl. LXX; Marteau and Vever, *Miniatures Persanes*, vol. II, Pl. XIX (color); Schulz, *Miniaturmalerei*, Pl. 138; Barrett and Gray, *Painting*, p. 125 (color); *Welch IMP*, Pl. 20 (color)

This work has had a particularly adventurous art historical career. When published by Schulz in 1914, it was attributed to Tranoxiana and the early sixteenth century; subsequently, in the publications listed above, it has been called Mughal, early seventeenth century (by Coomaraswamy); Deccani, attributed to Farrukh Beg at Bijapur, circa 1608 (by Skelton); and Deccani, at Golconda, circa 1605 (by Barrett). S. C. Welch has recently returned it again to Mughal India.

The painting is set within a fragmentary border from one of Shāh Jahān's albums, and the inscription, as is customary, is in the lower margin.

49

PORTRAIT OF A YOUNG GIRL

> Inscribed: "work of Muhammad ʿAlī Jahāngīr-shāhī, done as a memento for Amīr Wajih-ud-dīn Muhammad"
> Circa 1610
> 14.6 × 7 cm.
> Provenance: Dent Collection
> Lent by Edwin Binney 3rd
> Bibliography: *Binney Collection*, no. 123

The important inscription on this drawing establishes that Muhammad ʿAlī was in Jahāngīr's employ; unfortunately, the identity of the recipient of the work is unknown. The style of the drawing immediately allows the further attribution to Muhammad ʿAlī of *A Prince Riding*, formerly in the Rothschild Collection (see below). For a useful discussion of these works, see *Binney Collection*, p. 144; and Colnaghi, *Persian and Mughal Art*, p. 178.

Further Major Attributions to Muhammad ʿAlī

Youth Reading

> Inscribed: "work of Muhammad ʿAlī"
> Circa 1610
> Freer Gallery of Art, Washington, D.C.
> Bibliography: Ettinghausen, *Sultans*, Pl. 9 (color)

A Prince on Horseback

> Attributed to Muhammad ʿAlī
> Circa 1610
> Collection of Prince Sadruddin Agha Khan, Geneva (formerly Rothschild Collection)
> Bibliography: Colnaghi, *Persian and Mughal Art*, no. 92; Skelton, "Farrokh," fig. 9; Stchoukine, "Portraits IV," pp. 202–3, Pl. LXIX

The attribution of this portrait to Muhammad ʿAlī was first suggested by Richard Ettinghausen (Ettinghausen, *Sultans*, text for Plate 9).

48

49

Nānhā

That Mughal painters had specialties (in terms of subjects) is continually evident. Three of Nānhā's greatest Jahāngīr period works, for example, show lions in combat with humans: fol. 280b of the 1604–10 *Anwār-i-Suhailī*, the attributed *Jahāngīr-nāma* page, and *Lion Attacking a Man* (*no. 50*). In all three, the narrative is of greatest importance, and if we compare *no. 50* with the study of *Peafowl* by Mansūr (*no. 47*), we can discover other of Nānhā's traits. The *Lion Attacking a Man*—very typical of his illustrations of the period—is painted in earth tones, especially brown and green, and there is a wide variety of brush stroke shapes to define the shrubs and grasses. There is little layering and building-up of pigment; Nānhā's touch is light, and the total effect is quiet and controlled. The Mansūr painting, on the other hand, makes us immediately aware of the brilliance of the color (in flowers as well as birds), and there is a highly conscious arrangement of surface pattern. The flowers are minutely outlined and colored, and set on the surface like gems. The birds are so precisely described that they lack the warmth and sympathy resulting from Nānhā's freer brushwork (and this is true when comparing Nānhā to earlier works by Mansūr, as well). There is nothing spontaneous about the Mansūr picture, just as there is nothing consciously elegant about the *Lion Attacking a Man*.

Nānhā was a nephew of the painter Bishan Dās,[1] whose works are also seen and discussed here, but both men must have been about the same age, for they were active during the same years. Nānhā began painting by at least the mid-1580s, and his paintings are found in almost all the major Akbarī manuscripts; yet, he was not among the painters listed in the *Aᶜīn-i-Akbarī*, the contemporary chronicle of Akbar's court.[2] This is understandable, for his early manuscript paintings seldom rise above generally expected levels of competence; figures are often lumpy, and faces too crudely shaded, or insufficiently individualized. As with many Mughal painters, Nānhā was usually at his best when working in a small format, as in the two superb paintings exhibited here (*nos. 50* and *51*).

It is possible that Nānhā joined Jahāngīr at Allahabad during the Prince's rebellion, for he did not make a major contribution to the great imperial manuscript of the early 1600s, the *Akbar-nāma* of 1604, now divided between the A. Chester Beatty Library and the British Library (*nos. 3* and *4*). Instead, his work is found in the 1604–10 *Anwār-i-Suhailī*, definitely begun for Jahāngīr before his accession; and he may have executed a page found in the *Dīwān* of Amīr Hasan Dihlavī, made at Allahabad in 1602. The final author page of that manuscript (*no. 1, fol. 127*) has been attributed to Nānhā by Stuart C. Welch, and seems a more controlled version of Nānhā's Akbarī style. The man at the bottom right, shown burnishing paper, for example, is drawn with amorphously bulky shoulders, a trait that was characteristic of Nānhā in the 1580s and 1590s.[3] The quiet mood, strong character studies, clean composition, and evident delight in such details as the flowering tree, make this scene—in comparison to Nānhā's earlier and later works—a perfect transition between the taste of Akbar, and that of Jahāngīr.

A *Jahāngīr-nāma* page in the Indian Museum, Calcutta, depicting an event of 1615, is Nānhā's most complex composition among the works he is known to have made for Jahāngīr. It is identical in style to the *Lion Attacking a Man* (*no. 50*), and both are developments from the 1604–10 *Anwār-i-Suhailī*. All three episodes are placed in landscapes similar in color, types of vegetation, and the immediacy with which the paint is applied. If, in the *Anwār-i-Suhailī*, the figures are less well integrated into the setting, this is understandable, for it is Nānhā's first work of this type.

A series of portraits, found on Shāh Jahān album pages, suggests that Nānhā worked for that emperor, as well. The *Portrait of Zāhid Khān* (*no. 51*), however, is likely to be a work of the late Jahāngīr period, when the subject was an important member of that emperor's court. Quite different from the *Lion Attacking a Man*, it shows an interest in richness of material textures and in physical substantiality that alerts us to Nānhā's adaptability. The painter's latest works are technically superb, intense characterizations, set, in some cases, within the highly artificial landscape and floral references that became typical of Shāh Jahān period paintings.

Throughout Nānhā's long career, his paintings always followed prevailing stylistic patterns, and he became an increasingly skillful artist. There is no indication, among his known works, however, that he was an innovator. Unlike Payāg or Abūᶜl Hasan, for example, Nānhā neither predicted nor provided new directions for the tradition.

50

148   NĀNHĀ

50

LION ATTACKING A MAN

Inscribed: *amal-i-Nānhā* ("work of Nānhā")
Circa 1615
19 × 29 cm.
On cloth
Provenance: John Frederick Lewis Collection (from Sotheby,
12–13 June 1922)
Lent by the Free Library of Philadelphia (M. 36)
Bibliography: Coomaraswamy, "Notes," pp. 5–11, fig. 20

It cannot easily be established whether this records an
actual incident; in any case, such maulings were frequent
occurrences, given the Mughal passion for hunting.

The painting is, uncharacteristically, on cloth, as are
two animal studies given in the check list of works by
Mansūr. Early Akbarī paintings on cloth, such as the
Hamza-nāma manuscript,[4] were known in some quantity,
and may have been inspired by Hindu village banners, or
Tibetan temple paintings. Here the use of cloth for an
intimate work, as well as Nānhā's evident delight in the
clarity and variety of brush strokes, suggests that an awareness of the Chinese tradition should be investigated.

51

PORTRAIT OF ZĀHID KHĀN

From an Album of Jahāngīr
Inscribed: *amal-i-Nānhā shabeh Zāhid Khān* ("work of Nānhā,
portrait of Zāhid Khān")
Circa 1620
15 × 7.4 cm. (33.1 × 21.1 cm.)
Provenance: Rothschild Collection
Lent by Axel Röhm
Bibliography: Colnaghi, *Persian and Mughal Art*, no. 114

Zāhid Khān is an honorific title, rather than the name of a
specific person. The likeliest candidate for this portrait is
the son of Sādiq Khān of Herat, who received the title
from Akbar in the forty-ninth regnal year (= A.D. 1605),
and later served under Jahāngīr.[5]

While placed within superb Shāh Jahān album borders,
it is likely that this is a portrait of about 1620, the time of
the subject's political prominence.

Pages from the following manuscripts bear
contemporary inscriptions to Nānhā:

Razm-nāma (fol. 115)
  Circa 1584
  Collection Maharaja of Jaipur

51

Timūr-nāma (fols. 30r, 55v, 56r)
  Circa 1584
  Khuda Baksh Public Library, Patna

Dārab-nāma (fol. no. unknown)
  Circa 1585
  British Library (Or. 4615)

Khamsa of Nizāmī (fols. 152, 186b, 227a, 230a)
  Circa 1585–90
  Keir Collection
  Bibliography: *Robinson ed., Keir*, V.7, V.25, V.33, V.34

Akbar-nāma (fols. 23, 57)
  Circa 1590
  Victoria and Albert Museum, London

Bābur-nāma (fol. no. unknown)

Circa 1590
Victoria and Albert Museum, London
Bibliography: Binyon and Arnold, *Court Painters*, Pl. IV

Khamsa of Nizāmī (fols. 63v, 159, 305)

Dated 1595–96
British Library (Or. 12208)

Khamsa of Nizāmī (fol. 16b)

Dated 1595
Walters Art Gallery, Baltimore (W. 613)
Bibliography: S. C. Welch, "The Emperor Akbar's *Khamsa* of Nizāmī," *Journal of the Walters Art Gallery* XXIII (1960): 87–96

Jāmiᶜ al-Tawārīkh (fol. no. unknown)

Dated 1596
Imperial Library, Tehran
Bibliography: Marek and Knizkova, *The Jenghiz Khan Miniatures* (London, 1963), Pl. 8

Akbar-nāma (fol. 25a)

Dated 1604
British Library (Or. 12988)

Khamsa of Mīr ᶜAlī Shīr Nawāᶜī (fol. no. unknown)

Circa 1605
Royal Library, Windsor Castle
Bibliography: *BM*, no. 94a

ᶜIyār-i-Dānish (no. 6)

Dated (?) 1606
A. Chester Beatty Library, Dublin (Ms. 4)

Anwār-i-Suhailī (fol. 280b)

Dated 1604–10
British Library (Or. 18679)
Bibliography: Wilkinson, *Lights*, Pl. XXV; Coomaraswamy, "Notes," p. 208, fig. 15

A page from the following manuscript has been attributed to Nānhā:

Dīwān of Anwarī

Dated 1588
Fogg Art Museum, Cambridge, Massachusetts
Bibliography: *Welch AMI*, no. 4C (where the attribution is given)

Further major attributions to Nānhā

Camel Fight

From the *Muraqqaᶜ-e-Gulshan*
Inscribed to Nānhā
Dated A.H. 1017 = A.D. 1608–9
Imperial Library, Tehran
Bibliography: *BWG*, no. 133, Pl. LXXXVIIB

The inscription has been published as reading: "Allah is the greatest. This work of the master Bihzad was seen and copied by Nanha, the painter, to my orders. Written by Jahangir son of Akbar, Padshah, Ghazi. A.H. 1017" (*BWG*, p. 131). The presumed original painting by Bihzad, the most famous of fifteenth-century Iranian artists, is reproduced in *BWG*, Pl. LXXXVIIA.

Jahāngīr Shoots a Lioness

From a *Jahāngīr-nāma* manuscript
Attributed here to Nānhā
Circa 1615
Indian Museum, Calcutta
Bibliography: *Brown*, Pl. XLII; Das, "Mughal Royal Hunt," pp. 1–5

While attributed to Manōhar by Aśok Das, this seems clearly a work by Nānhā, probably executed soon after the incident in 1615.

Two Men Conversing

From the *Leningrad Album*
Inscribed: "work of Nānhā"
Circa 1620
Academy of Sciences, Leningrad
Bibliography: Ivanova, *Albom Indiyskikh*, Pl. 12

Rājā Bhim Singh

From the *Kevorkian Album*
Inscribed: "work of Nānhā"
Metropolitan Museum of Art, New York (55.121.10.2)

A second version of this portrait is in the Museum of Fine Arts, Boston (60.172). Less vital in execution and presumably later in date, it is a page from the *Late Shāh Jahān Album*.

Zulfiqār Khān

From the *Minto Album*
Inscribed: "work of Nānhā"
Circa 1635
Victoria and Albert Museum, London
Bibliography: Skelton, "Motif," Pl. LXXXVIII

Zulfiqār Khān, when known as Khanlar, had fled from the court of Shāh ᶜAbbās to India and entered Jahāngīr's service at the end of the reign. In the sixth year of Shāh Jahān's rule, he received his ancestral title of Zulfiqār Khān, and by the end of the reign was in retirement at Patna (Khan, *Maasir-ul Umara*, vol. II, 1045ff.). He died in 1660. Because of these circumstances, this portrait seems evidence that Nānhā remained active into the Shāh Jahān period.

Payāg

Whereas the majority of Mughal painters worked in styles that were consistent throughout their careers, Payāg, in his earliest paintings, does not prepare us for his mature and most famous works. His illustrations are included in several manuscripts of the 1590s, although not the great Akbarī productions, and this indicates that his talent was not considered to be of imperial caliber. Indeed, these early works do not show the keen interest in portraiture, the complexity of composition, or the technical mastery that Akbar was then eliciting from his best painters. And after this initial spurt of activity, we have no knowledge of Payāg's career until the reign of Shāh Jahān, when he painted several of the most brilliant and innovative pages in the Windsor *Padshāh-nāma*. A self-portrait on fol. 194 verso of that manuscript (*fig. 11*), showing us a foppish courtier attending a darbār, indicates that the flamboyance of Payāg's style of painting extended to his personal life. It is also inscribed with the information that Payāg was the brother of Bālchand, the painter to whom his later style is most closely related.

The *Battle Scene* (*no. 25*) is from the *Padshāh-nāma*, and is both Payāg's masterpiece and one of the most superb Shāh Jahān period paintings. No signature has been found on it, although current practice was often to hide an inscription (in vegetation, for example), and it may yet appear. That it is by Payāg is certain, for his later style is very idiosyncratic, and paintings of the same character, signed by the artist, are found in the Windsor manuscript and in a *Gulistān* of Saʿdī, formerly in the collection of the Marquess of Bute.[1]

Payāg's works are sombre in palette, but against the predominant dark tones gold and color appear with increased intensity. We see this as well in *Officers and Wise Men* (*no. 52*), a night scene, like several other Payāg illustrations. This latter work also reveals an inspiration for the artist's style. The men are seated around a centrally placed candle, the only source of illumination for the figures, and this novel device is clearly derived from European chiaroscuro techniques, as is the glowing sky.[2] Both of the works mentioned contain superb character studies, for Payāg's interest in modelling was combined with extreme perceptiveness regarding human personality. This is shown also in the extraordinary border figures found on a *Late Shāh Jahān Album* page, showing a prince

FIG. 13. Portrait of Payāg. By Payāg, ca. 1635–40. From the Windsor *Padshāh-nāma* ms. (fol. 194v, detail). The Royal Library, Windsor.

and various holy men (*no. 22* recto). This may have been painted as late as 1650, when the album is thought to have been formed. Payāg, thus, had a long career, and the brilliance of its conclusion makes one wish its development could be more easily charted.

52

OFFICERS AND WISE MEN

Attributed here to Payāg
Circa 1655
10.5 × 17.1 cm. (55.6 × 34.9 cm.)
Provenance: A. C. Ardeshir Collection
Lent by Edwin Binney 3rd
Bibliography: *Binney Collection*, no. 59

The seated officer has been identified as ʿIzzat Khān, Governor of Bhakkar, who died in 1633, but the identification is questionable.[3] Other comparable night scenes are known, one of which, *A Gathering of Mystics* (listed below), is signed by Payāg. Robert Skelton believes the group to represent the late style of the artist, but none of the works are dated, and an exact identification of the subjects is lacking. In any case, the style is broader, less detailed and miniaturistic than the *Padshāh-nāma Battle Scene* (*no. 25*).

Like several other works formerly in the Ardeshir Collection, this bears an unreliable inscription, in this case to Bichitr.

52

52 (detail)

Further Major Attributions to Payāg

Bābur-nāma Manuscript (fol. 334v)
Inscribed to Payāg
British Library (Or. 3714)
Bibliography: H. Suleiman, *Miniatures of Babur-nama* (Tashkent, 1970), Pl. 49

Bābur-nāma Manuscript (fols. 131v, 203r, 274r)
Inscribed to Payāg
National Museum of India, New Delhi

Razm-nāma Manuscript (fol. no. unknown)
Inscribed to Payāg
Dated 1598
State Museum, Baroda
Bibliography: Wellesz, "Mughal Paintings," fig. 23; Wellesz, *Akbar's Religious Thought*, Pl. 31

ʿIyār-i-Dānish Manuscript (no. 50)
Inscribed to Payāg
Dated (?) 1606
A. Chester Beatty Library, Dublin (Ms. 4)

Man Singh of Amber
Inscribed: "the work of Payāg"
Circa 1615 (?)
A. Chester Beatty Library, Dublin (Ms. 11A, No. 1)
Bibliography: *Beatty Library*, vol. III, Pl. 76

Shāh Jahān on a Globe
Inscribed to Payāg
Circa 1635
A. Chester Beatty Library, Dublin (Ms. 7B, No. 28)

Gulistān of Saʿdī Manuscript (fol. 59v)
Inscribed: "the work of Payāg"
Circa 1640
Private Collection (formerly Collection of the Marquess of Bute)

This is one of the most important Shāh Jahān period manuscripts, with signed paintings by Govardhan, Lālchand, Murād, and Bālchand. Fol. 59v seems transitional between the technical finesse of the *Battle Scene* (*no. 25*), and the looser brush work of *Officers and Wise Men* (*no. 52*).

Padshāh-nāma Manuscript (fols. 101v, 194v, 213v)
Inscribed to Payāg
Circa 1635–40
Royal Library, Windsor Castle

Fol. 101v, depicting the siege of the Deccani fortress of Qandahar in 1630, is immediately comparable in style to the *Battle Scene* (*no. 25*), while fol. 213v seems contemporary with *Shāh Jahān on a Globe*, listed above. Robert Skelton has attributed fol. 175v, as well, to Payāg (*Robinson ed., Keir*, V.72).

A Persian Embassy
Probably from the Windsor *Padshāh-nāma* manuscript
Attributed here to Payāg
Circa 1640
Bodleian Library, Oxford (Ouseley Add. 173, No. 13)
Bibliography: Binyon and Arnold, *Court Painters*, Pl. XXXVI; *Brown*, Pl. XXIV

A Nobleman
From the *Late Shāh Jahān Album*
Inscribed: "the work of Payāg"
Circa 1650
Metropolitan Museum of Art, New York

Holy Men
From the *Leningrad Album*
Inscribed: "the work of Payāg"
Circa 1650
Academy of Sciences, Leningrad
Bibliography: Ivanova et al., *Albom Indiyskikh*, Pl. 13

A Holy Man
From the *Leningrad Album*
Inscribed to Payāg
Circa 1650
Academy of Sciences, Leningrad
Bibliography: Ivanova et al., *Albom Indiyskikh*, Pl. 12

A Gathering of Mystics
Inscribed: "work of Payāg"
Circa 1650–55
Keir Collection
Bibliography: *Robinson ed., Keir*, V.72

Night Scene
Attributed here to Payāg
Circa 1650–55
Indian Museum, Calcutta
Bibliography: *Brown*, Pl. LI (color)

Other Attributions

Shāh Jahān Riding
From the *Kevorkian Album*
Inscribed to Payāg
Bibliography: *Dimand Bulletin*, cover (color); Dimand, *Indian Miniature Painting*, cover (color)

Nobleman with Attendants
A. Chester Beatty Library, Dublin (Ms. 7, No. 20)
Bibliography: *Beatty Library*, vol. III, Pl. 66

Certainly by a major Mughal artist. Several of the same men are seen in *Officers and Wise Men* (*no. 52*), and the painting may represent a yet unknown phase of Payāg's work.

European Subjects

Throughout the discussions of which we have spoken, the King [Jahāngīr] always showed his deep regard for Christ our Lord. He also spoke very strongly in favour of the use of pictures, which, amongst the Moors, are regarded with abhorrence; and on coming from Lahor, and finding his palaces at Agra very beautifully decorated and adorned both inside and outside with many pictures which had already been completed, and others that were being painted, in a balcony where he sits daily to be seen by the people: nearly all these pictures were of a sacred character, for in the middle of the ceiling there was a painting of Christ our Lord, very perfectly finished, with an aureola, and surrounded by angels; and on the walls were some small pictures of the Saints, including John the Baptist, St. Anthony, St. Bernadine of Sena, and some female Saints. In another part were some Portuguese figures of large size, also very beautifully painted.[1]

This contemporary account of the presence of European subjects in the decoration of Jahāngīr's palace is visually illustrated for us by the small head of the Virgin above the emperor's throne in *no. 14*.

Christian missionary activity in India began soon after Vasco da Gama's arrival in 1498. By 1510, territory for a colony had been seized at Goa, although serious access to a Mughal emperor was not granted until 1580, when Akbar invited a group of Jesuits to come to the court to explain Christianity and the Bible to him.

The Fathers took with them and presented to him all the volumes of the Royal Bible, in four languages, sumptuously bound, and clasped with gold. The King received these holy books with great reverence, taking each into his hand one after the other and kissing it, after which he placed it on his head, which, amongst these people, signifies honour and respect. . . . The Fathers also presented to him two beautiful portraits, one representing the Saviour of the world, and the other the glorious Virgin Mary, his Holy Mother. The latter was a copy of that in the church of Notre Dame la Maieur, in Rome.[2]

While several Mughal copies of the Sta. Maria Maggiore *Madonna* are known to us,[3] these were not the first European works available to Akbar, or at least to his artists, for European influences are clearly discernible in manuscripts of the 1560s and 1570s.[4]

The European illustrations that travelled to India follow a definite pattern. According to their own dates, the first works that were influential were German, by Albrecht Dürer and his circle (including the

Beham brothers and Georg Pencz—see *nos. 10* and *10A*); these must have come through Antwerp, the major embarkation point for voyages to the East until at least 1585. Dürer himself visited the city in the early 1520s and the appearance of his prints in India may be a result of the known dispersal of his "stock," by gift and sale, at that time.[5]

A second major group of European prints found in India includes the work of the Antwerp printmakers of the later sixteenth century (e.g., Jan, Raphael, and Aegidius Sadeler, Jerome Wierix, and Cornelis Cort —see *no. 54A*—among many others). These were probably prints sent out specifically in response to the increased activity of the various missionaries at the Mughal court after 1580; and, in addition to loose illustrations, shipments included bound books. Chris-

53

topher Plantin's *Royal Polyglot Bible* of 1568–73, referred to in the passage quoted above, the *Thesaurus Sacrarum Historiarum Veteris Testamenti* of 1585, and the *Evangelicae Historiae Imagines* of 1593, all printed in Antwerp, were among the books known in India.[6]

The next impact came from England in 1615, when Sir Thomas Roe arrived at the court as ambassador, and brought with him various English "miniatures" of his family and friends. Some of these works the emperor saw and coveted. Roe related one famous episode as follows:

Asaph chan asked mee for my little Picture, and presented it to the King. He took extreame Content, showeing it to euerie man neare him; at last sent for his Cheefe Paynter, demanding his opinion. The foole answered he could make as good. Whereat the King turned to mee, saying: my man sayeth he can do the like and as well as this: what say yow? I replyed: I knew the Contrarie.[7]

Jahāngīr then proceeded to have copies made, which he showed Roe, intending him to be uncertain as to which was his own. The ambassador recounted that he

was by candle-light troubled to discerne which was which; I confesse beyond all expectation; yet I shewed myne owne and the differences, which were in arte apparent, not to be iudged by a Common eye.[8]

The picture thus discussed is said to have been by Isaac Oliver,[9] and while none of the copies are presently known, an adaptation of a portrait of James I by his Sargeant Painter John de Critz is found in a celebrated allegorical portrait of Jahāngīr.[10] The concept behind such symbolic works (for example, paintings of the emperor standing on, or holding, a globe, particularly popular after 1615) must be a direct result too of English examples introduced at the time of Roe's visit.

During this entire period, occasional Dutch, Italian, and French prints appear, but not in major quantity.[11] Dutch influence seems to increase after about 1620; the landscape background in *no. 43* may be derived from a Dutch source, as may the clearly chiaroscuro techniques of *no. 52*. The Dutch in India were very conscious of the effect which European pictures produced; one agent wrote back in 1626, for example: "Send us two or three good battle pictures, painted by an artist with a pleasing style, for the Moslems want to see everything from close by—also some decorative pictures showing comic incidents or nude figures."[12]

After the early seventeenth century, increasing quantities of European prints from a wide variety of sources become generally available, but the situation

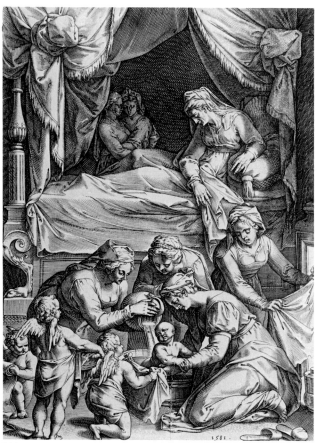

54
54A

is not unique to India. In many cases, the same prints and books were sent to the Far East, but the effect there was very different. Artists in India were receptive to the techniques and attitudes of the new works they saw, for Akbar and Jahāngīr were demanding close observation, and a virtually scientific attitude to the physical world; this was not the case in China or Japan, where the European tradition was too alien to be so seriously influential.[13]

In addition to prints and paintings, a few European artists and amateurs were known to the court (see *no. 9*).

Literature: Maclagan, *The Jesuits*; Du Jarric, *Akbar*; Guerreiro, *Jahangir*; Ettinghausen, "New Pictorial Evidence"; Wilkinson and Gray, "Indian Paintings"; Beach, "The Gulshan Album"; Kühnel and Goetz, *Indian Book Painting*.

53

SYMBOLIC FIGURE

Circa 1590–1600
11.6 × 8.1 cm.
Provenance: Heeramaneck Collection
Lent by the Los Angeles County Museum of Art: Nasli and Alice Heeramaneck Collection (L.69.24.255)
Bibliography: *Beach Heeramaneck*, no. 205

The closest iconographic source for this drawing seems to be a print by Binck, after H. S. Beham, entitled *Eve*.[14] A group of works roughly similar in style and subject is known; several are signed by Basāwan or Manōhar, although neither artist seems indisputably responsible for this example (see also *no. 8*).

54

THE BIRTH OF THE VIRGIN

Circa 1610
21 × 14 cm.
Provenance: John Frederick Lewis Collection
Lent by the Free Library of Philadelphia (M. 93)

The painting is an exact copy of an engraving by Cornelis Cort dated 1581 (*no. 54A*), an identification made by Glenn D. Lowry. The Indian artist has changed the surface effect to accord with Mughal taste, however, adding gold, and creating patterns (on the bed covers, or the shawl of the kneeling figure at the lower right) where the surfaces of the source are plain. A second version of this composition is also known,[15] but such literal and entire reproduction of a European print is less common than the use of a single motif.

55

54A

THE BIRTH OF THE VIRGIN

By Cornelis Cort, after Taddeo Zuccaro
Dated 1581
Engraving
Lent by the Metropolitan Museum of Art, New York: The Elisha Whittelsey Fund, 1951 (51.501.3285)

55

THE ENTOMBMENT OF CHRIST

Circa 1610
16.5 × 11.2 cm.
Provenance: John Frederick Lewis Collection
Lent by the Free Library of Philadelphia (M.92)

The European source for this Mughal work has not yet been identified.

Miscellaneous Portraits

56

A COURTIER

Circa 1610
11.9 × 6.8 cm.
Lent by the Fogg Art Museum, Harvard University: Purchase—Grace Nichols Strong Fund, Francis H. Burr Fund, and Friends of the Fogg Art Museum Fund (1950.133)
Bibliography: Welch and Beach, *Gods*, no. 9

Portraits of single figures set against a plain green background became the norm in India during the later Akbar period—and was probably the formula used in the portrait album formed by the emperor.[1] While this was an accepted format in Iran even earlier,[2] the degree of realism and individuality in characterization here is quite different.

56

57

LADY HOLDING A PORTRAIT OF JAHĀNGĪR

Circa 1605–10
14.1 × 6.6 cm. (30.2 × 22.2 cm.)
Lent by Ralph Benkaim

Women of the imperial family were formally secluded in the harem, or in purdah, and inaccessible to any men beyond the immediate family circle. Nonetheless, and surprisingly, a number of remarkable studies of court ladies exist, often so individualized that they seem taken from life (e.g., *no. 15*). The present important work shows a woman holding a portrait of the emperor, and this implies that she is a lady of status; her identity, however, eludes us.

58

JAHĀNGĪR

Circa 1615
10.8 × 5.4 cm.
Provenance: Heeramaneck Collection
Lent by the Los Angeles County Museum of Art: Nasli and Alice Heeramaneck Collection (L.69.24.272)
Bibliography: *Beach Heeramaneck*, no. 214

Late in the ninth regnal year (= A.D. 1614–15), Jahāngīr recorded in the *Tūzuk*:

During my illness it had occurred to me that when I had completely recovered, inasmuch as I was inwardly an ear-bored slave of the Khwaja (Muᶜinu-d-din) and was indebted to him for my existence, I should openly make holes in my ears and be enrolled among his earmarked slaves. On Thursday, 12 Shahriwar . . . I made holes in my ears and drew into each a shining pearl.[3]

This, naturally, produced an instant fashion, but it allows us an added tool in dating imperial portraits. Here Jahāngīr is wearing earrings, but he appears markedly younger than in the darbār scene of circa 1619 included in the exhibition (*no. 14*). The portrait is similar in interpretation, if not finesse, to the figure of the emperor in a superb audience scene by Manōhar, datable as an event to 1605–6.[4]

59

YOUTH HOLDING A NARCISSUS

Inscribed: *amal-i-Farrukh Beg* ("work of Farrukh Beg")
Circa 1610
15.9 × 8.3 cm. (36.8 × 23.5 cm.)
Lent by Edwin Binney 3rd
Bibliography: *Binney Collection*, no. 122

57

MISCELLANEOUS PORTRAITS 159

58

59

60

The reliable identification of works by Farrukh Beg is extremely difficult, as at least one other painter, Muhammad ʿAlī, was working in an identical style. Furthermore, there have been both suggestions and strong denials that Farrukh Beg and a known Deccani artist, Farrukh Husain, are the same man; various arguments are explained in the references listed below.

In any case, this portrait—which represents a type rather than a specific individual—is closely related to a signed portrait by Muhammad ʿAlī,[5] as well as to the *Portrait of a Courtier* by Ghulām (*no. 39*). Certainly, in the earliest years of Jahāngīr's reign, several artists worked in an Iranian-oriented, and possibly Deccani-influenced, style that had little relation to current naturalistic attitudes.

Literature: Skelton, "Farrokh"; Nazir Ahmed, "Farrukh Husain, the Royal Artist at the Court of Ibrahim ʿAdil Shah II," *Islamic Culture*, XXX, no. 1 (1956); Ahmed, "Farrukh Beg"; Ettinghausen, *Sultans*, text for Pl. 9.

60

THE DYING ʿINĀYAT KHĀN

Circa 1618–19
9.5 × 13.3 cm.
Provenance: Goloubev Collection
Lent by the Museum of Fine Arts, Boston: Francis Bartlett Donation of 1912 and Picture Fund (14.679)
Bibliography: *Coomaraswamy Boston*, no. LXX, Pl. XXXII; *Coomaraswamy Goloubev*, no. 124, Pl. LXXI; Marteau and Vever, *Miniatures Persanes*, vol. II, Pl. 173; Martin, *Miniature Paintings*, Pl. 200; Welch, *Indian Drawings*, no. 16

The occasion for this extraordinary drawing is well documented in the *Tūzuk-i-Jahāngīrī* during the thirteenth regnal year (= A.D. 1618–19):

On this day news came of the death of ʿInayat Khan. He was one of my intimate attendants. As he was addicted to opium, and when he had the chance, to drinking as well, by degrees he became maddened with wine. As he was weakly built, he took more than he could digest, and was attacked with the disease of diarrhoea, and in this weak state he two or three times fainted. By my order Hakim Rukna applied remedies, but whatever methods were resorted to gave no profit. At the same time a strange hunger came over him. . . . He also would throw himself like a madman on water and fire until he fell into a bad state of body. At last he became dropsical, and exceeding low and weak. Some days before this he petitioned that he might go to Agra. I ordered him to come into my presence and obtain leave. They put him into a palanquin and brought him. He appeared so low and weak I was astonished. . . . As it was a very extraordinary case I directed painters to take his portrait. . . . Next day he travelled the road of non-existence.[6]

The finished painting, for which this is a preparatory study, is in the Bodleian Library, Oxford.[7] A superb portrait, it has nonetheless lost elements of immediacy which this drawing so powerfully holds. A published attribution to Bishan Dās[8] should be discounted, as that painter, who is discussed elsewhere, was in Iran during these years.

61

PRINCE VISITING AN ASCETIC

Circa 1610
22.9 × 15 cm.
Provenance: Spencer-Churchill Collection
Anonymous Loan
Bibliography: Binyon and Arnold, *Court Painters*, Pl. VI (color)

The identities of the prince who is dressed according to Persian fashion, and the ascetic are not known. While the surface is worn, the work need not necessarily be accepted as late eighteenth-century, as has been suggested;[9] in its directness, this seems to be one of the earliest full-scale treatments of the theme. *No. 62* provides an excellent comparison.

62

HOLY MEN

From an Album of Shāh Jahān
Circa 1630
16.5 × 11.3 cm. (36.1 × 24.3 cm.)
Provenance: Rothschild Collection
Anonymous Loan
Bibliography: *Brown*, Pl. LII; Colnaghi, *Persian and Mughal Art*, no. 103 (color)

The greater richness, even ripeness, of line and modelling, and the embellishment of the surface with gold, are indications of a date later than that of *no. 61*; and the comparison is an excellent guide to changes of Mughal style during this period. The lowering of the horizon line here and the addition of a distant town so that the landscape becomes free space rather than a backdrop, are also important. The major difference, however, is mood. In *no. 61*, the figures are simple and sincere, whereas here nudity seems an indulgence. The turbanned *faqīr*, with his *huqqa* and attendant, has the air of a rājā; his chains are worn with such chic that only with effort do we realize that they are intended to mortify the flesh.

61

62

63

64

63

DĀRĀ SHIKŌH WITH SAGES

Circa 1630
20.3 × 9.8 cm.
Lent by the Fogg Art Museum, Harvard University: Gift—
Eric Schroeder in honor of John Coolidge (1968.47)

Almost nothing is known of Dārā Shikōh's early education. It is only about 1630, at the time his marriage was initially planned (it was postponed for two and a half years when his mother, Mumtāz Mahal, died in 1631), that he first emerges as a public figure. Always the favorite of the emperor, he was spared the physical exertions, military experience, decision making, and absences from court that would have been proper preparation for a ruler. Instead, he spent his time in religious discussions, for example, and the translation of Hindu texts. From his frequent appearances in paintings, it can be assumed that he was himself a patron of the arts, and by his free access to his father's painters, he probably was a determining factor in the development of the contemporary Mughal style. Shāh Jahān, after all, never mentions painting or painters in his memoirs, and seems to have been enthusiastic only about architecture.

Several closely related paintings are known, including a late eighteenth-century composition using several of the same figures.[10]

Literature: Hasrat, *Dara Shikoh*; Qanungo, *Dara Shikuh*.

64

DĀRĀ SHIKŌH

Inscribed: *amal-i-Muhammad Hāshim* ("work of Muhammad Hāshim")
Circa 1650
5.1 × 3.6 cm.
Lent by the Cleveland Museum of Art: Gift of J. H. Wade (20.1969)

The small, oval medallion portrait, usually placed in a jewelled mount and often worn in a turban or around the neck, may have been a favorite format for portraits of Dārā Shikōh; at least three other examples by major court painters are known, including *no. 32*, attributed to Bālchand.[11] The inspiration for the shape must certainly have come with English works of the type brought by Sir Thomas Roe in 1615.

65

THE BATTLE OF SAMUGARH

Circa 1658
22.6 × 32.7 cm. (sight)
Lent Anonymously
Bibliography: Welch, *Indian Drawings*, no. 21

Shāh Jahān's rule did not end with his death, but rather with the seizure of the throne by Aurangzēb, his third son, in 1658. The overindulged Dārā Shikōh led the imperialists against his brother, once the younger prince's rebellious motives were clear. The extraordinary Venetian traveller Niccolo Manucci, then nineteen, has left us an eyewitness account of the battle. He wrote that Dārā was persuaded by a traitor to dismount from his elephant, and attack Aurangzēb on horseback.

Poor Dara! without fully understanding what he was doing, and what would follow when he was no longer to be seen on his elephant, towards which all turned their gaze . . . alighted . . . and this was as if he had quitted victory; for the soldiers and commanders, who in the midst of the battle kept an eye on Dara, not seeing him on his elephant, assumed that he must already be dead. . . . I myself was in astonishment and in great dismay . . . meanwhile the whole army was fleeing to the rear, like dark clouds blown by a high wind.[12]

The drawing is a superb, if unintentional, illustration of Manucci's observations. Dārā dismounts, at the left, while Aurangzēb, to the right, observes. And the figures are formed into dynamic and massive grey shapes, the "dark clouds" of the Italian's report.

65

66

A SCRIBE

Circa 1625
10.5 × 7.1 cm. (31.9 × 32.1 cm.)
Provenance: Rothschild Collection
Lent Anonymously
Bibliography: *Brown*, Pl. XLVIII, fig. 2; Colnaghi, *Persian and Mughal Art*, no. 118; *Welch IMP*, Pl. 29 (color)

The subject of this intense and powerful study has not been identified. While stylistically it seems Jahāngīrī in date, Robert Skelton has pointed out that the floral motifs in the architecture and in the sash (*patkā*) are otherwise known only in the mid-Shāh Jahān period.[13]

66

66 (detail)

67

67

DARBĀR OF AURANGZĒB

Circa 1660
19.1 × 21.4 cm.
Provenance: Cartier Collection
Lent Anonymously
Bibliography: Marteau and Vever, *Miniatures Persanes*, vol. II,
Pl. 20 (color); Welch, "Miniature Paintings," no. 16, fig. 19;
Welch IMP, Pl. 37 (color); *Welch AMI*, no. 59

The figures in front of the emperor include Sultān Āᶜzam
(b. 1653) and his guardian Shāyistah Khān. Stuart C.
Welch attributes the painting to Bichitr.

Calligraphy

68

CALLIGRAPHY

Inscribed by Dārā Shikōh
Circa 1630
17.5 × 11.1 cm.
Lent Anonymously

An album of calligraphies by the prince is known (see
BM, no. 140).

68

Animal Studies

69

TIBETAN YAK

Circa 1610
8.3 × 15.9 cm.
Provenance: Sevadjian Collection
Anonymous Loan
Bibliography: Welch, "Mughal and Deccani Miniature
Paintings," no. 14, fig. 15; *Welch FEM*, no. 61

This is one of a series of fragments mounted together on
an album page, probably early in this century. The smaller
animals were presumably from the margins of a muraqqaᶜ
folio. Robert Skelton has suggested an attribution to
Abūᶜl Hasan.[1] Only one other major animal painting by
that artist is known, although it is the greatest of all

Mughal nature studies (see *Squirrels in a Plane Tree*, listed
on p. 90 with the discussion of Abūᶜl Hasan).

70

A CHEER PHEASANT

From an Album of Shāh Jahān
Circa 1630–40
20.6 × 13.4 cm. (32.9 × 20.3 cm.)
Provenance: Rothschild Collection
Lent by Edwin Binney 3rd
Bibliography: Colnaghi, *Persian and Mughal Art*, no. 100;
Brown, Pl. LIV

Of the two further versions of this work, one is inscribed
with an attribution to Mansūr and may be the original
illustration.[2] This painting, clearly not by Mansūr, seems
to be a contemporary copy; Edwin Binney 3rd has sug-

gested that it might be by Payāg. It was common practice for Mughal artists to adapt single figures and even whole compositions from the work of their compatriots.

71

A NILGAE

Circa 1630–40
20 × 27.1 cm.
Lent by Mr. and Mrs. John Gilmore Ford

The *nilgae*, or blue deer, was a favorite target for the Mughal hunter. Jahāngīr records, for example:

On this day was killed a nilgaw. . . . In the two past years, during which I had come to this place to wander about and hunt I had shot at him each time with a gun. As the wounds were not in a fatal place, he had not fallen, but gone off. . . . This time I again saw that nilgaw in the hunting-ground. . . . I fired at him again three times on that day. It was in vain. I pursued him rapidly on foot for three kos, but however much I exerted myself I could not catch him. At last I made a vow that if this nilgaw fell I would have his flesh cooked, and . . . would give it to eat to poor people. . . . Soon after this the nilgaw became worn out with moving, and I ran to his head and ordered them to make it lawful (cut its throat in the name of Allah) on the spot, and having brought it to the camp I fulfilled my vow as I had proposed.[3]

This particular painting seems later in date than Jahāngīr's reign. In decorative strength, it is most comparable to works made after 1630; while such motifs as the grasses are found in certain folios of the Windsor *Padshāh-nāma*. A second, contemporary and closely related illustration was formerly in the collection of P. C. Manuk.[4]

69

71

70

POSTLUDE

33

Mughal Painting:
A Personal View

MOST OF THE PICTURES assembled here are hushed —not dumbly silent, for they tease our ears with whispered innuendoes, calls of a peahen or even distant booming and whirring of cannon and rockets— but quiet through self-imposed restraint. Their weather, too, is evenly agreeable, never perspiringly warm or shiveringly cool, with few storms, ideally suited to a land whose emperor, Shāh Jahān, could inscribe his palace walls with the claim that "If there be Paradise on Earth, it is here, it is here, it is here." Although close inspection reveals these paintings to be tactile, with rounded pillows and palpably full-bodied figures, they are no more the sort of art that reaches out and seizes you than shouts. Their people and animals are mostly grave and dignified, well-mannered to the nth degree. Humor is usually in the form of wit, touching off occasional smiles but no guffaws. The few instances of sexuality are equally low-keyed: an elegant courtier casting a side glance at a dancing girl, or the merest hint of a voluptuous bosom or well-turned ankle. Compared to most paintings, they are also excessively small (and some of the more moving ones are scarcely larger than a few postage stamps); but their littleness is that of diamonds, a Chopin étude, or Buddhist *mantras*— great power compacted.

To whet one's appetite for this visual chamber music, it is necessary to scrutinize these miniatures and note how accurately yet sensitively Mughal artists studied such subjects as the emperor's albino elephant, with his light-susceptible pink eye, jewel-studded caparison, and blunted tusks (*no. 33*).

Such open-eyed appreciation of their world had been a Mughal characteristic since the beginning. Although Jahāngīr and his son Shāh Jahān were the fourth and fifth Mughal emperors, Bābur, the founder, who invaded India in 1526, had already revealed this in his *Memoirs* (the *Bābur-nāma*), which are among the liveliest and most informative in Eastern literature and which already set the tone for Mughal thought and art. Descended from both Genghiz Khān and Tīmūr, he possessed their physical energy and military genius, and like most of his family, he had a marked penchant for literature and art. While no paintings made for him have survived from his brief reign, he wrote about painting in his auto-biography, which contains lovingly accurate descriptions of all nature: of birds, animals, trees, fruit, and flowers; of landscapes, weather and its changes; and above all of mankind. Bābur's incisive, trenchant, at times embarrassingly candid accounts of people (including himself) are verbal equivalents of later Mughal portraiture, perhaps the most movingly original contributions of the school.

Like the later artists at their peaks, Bābur was incapable of trite, second-hand responses. Although he saw through the eyes of a poet, he was an unflinching realist whose true expression, like that of Mughal painters, was in prose. He was an unflinching realist who did not turn away from the unpleasant or even disgusting, a characteristic that brings to mind the upsetting but transcendental portrait of the dying ʿInāyat Khān (*no. 60*). Drawn in "prose" as bereft of furbelows and graces as Bābur's, this magnificent depiction of terminal illness was commissioned by Bābur's great-grandson, Jahāngīr. It proves that he had inherited his ancestor's buoyantly hardheaded view of life (and death), a family trait that maintained the dynasty through very trying times until 1858, when the last emperor was exiled to Burma by the British in the aftermath of the Mutiny.

Both in Bābur's memoirs and in Mughal painting, accurate description extends to current events which were recorded with the immediacy of newsreel photography. The founder's exhaustive accounts of his arduous, often unsuccessful campaigns in Central Asia and India are as lively as his descendants' historical manuscripts, with their scores of detailed battle scenes, receptions, and other newsworthy episodes (e.g., *nos. 3, 4, 13–15,* and *24–26*).

While Bābur's writings are the precursors of Mughal pictures, the first miniatures known to us were painted for his son and successor, Humāyūn (r. 1530–56). He gave the school a brilliant beginning by hiring outstanding Safavī painters from the court of Shāh Tahmāsp during his years of exile from India. Luckily for Mughal art, the Iranian shāh had not only given sanctuary to the Mughal emperor when he was forced out of India by Sher Shāh Afghan, but he had also lessened his interest in the patronage of painting. This made it possible for Humāyūn to invite Mīr Sayyid ʿAlī and ʿAbd-as-Samad to join his court. Trained in the shāh's unrivalled ateliers at Tabriz, these artists brought the most sophisticated technical skills and artistic mastery to the newly formed workshops. It can hardly have been coincidental, moreover, that Mīr Sayyid ʿAlī was the sharpest-eyed observer in the shāh's school, a painter who doted on recording each feather of a bird or tuft of fur on a kitten.

Humāyūn died soon after reconquering northern India, and he was followed by the mighty Akbar, then a mere boy (r. 1556–1605). Charismatic and dynamic, Akbar not only enlarged, enriched, and stabilized the empire, but also inspired architects, musicians, poets, and artists assembled from many disparate traditions to create vigorous new Mughal idioms. Directed by inherited ex-Safavī masters, a virtual army of freshly recruited painters was set to work carrying out Akbar's ambitious artistic programs. Always reflections of the emperor's fertile imagination and insatiable curiosity, most of these were intended to further his imperial aims. Inasmuch as the empire's unity was threatened by India's two major religious groups (Muslims and Hindus), Akbar commissioned illustrated translations of Hindu epics and ordered Muslims to read them. To record the noble deeds of his and his ancestors' reigns, lavishly illustrated histories were composed. His library contained thousands of volumes on topics ranging alphabetically from astrology to zoology, and many of them were illustrated by his large corps of painters.

Stylistically, Akbar's pictures reflect his emotional development. During the early years of his aggressive military forays, his almost explosive power led artists to compose highly charged, dynamic designs, in vividly raw colors. Gradually, as the empire gained solidity and the emperor's furious energies calmed, his artists designed less agitated pictures. Arrangements of figures in landscape or architectural settings took on greater logic and subtlety, portraits assumed increasing psychological depth, and coloring became more harmonious. Although such a refined artist as Mīr Sayyid ʿAlī must have been discouraged in the 1560s by his patron's preference for earthy gusto to elegance in art, he would have been well pleased by the gains in subtlety had he survived until the end of Akbar's reign.

From the point of view of many of Akbar's painters, the period of this exhibition began with a crisis. For Jahāngīr, the "World-Seizer" (r. 1605–27), was a very different patron from his father. The vast, protean scenes of illustrated manuscripts requiring countless painters to complete were no longer in demand. An eager aesthete and connoisseur, Jahāngīr commissioned paintings as personal pleasures, not

state documents; and he soon released most of the court painters whose work failed to meet his standards. Before his father's death, while still governor of Allahabad, he had encouraged his artists in new directions, with emphasis on increased sensitivity to nature and closer observation than had been the wont of his father's painters. In effect, his artists concentrated longer and more intensively on fewer miniatures. The taste for large, crowded, busy hunting and battle scenes gave way to a preference for calmer subjects, minutely analyzed and intricately detailed, more often intended for albums than as manuscript illustrations. Under Jahāngīr's inspired guidance, artists such as Abūʾl Hasan and Mansūr often isolated a few figures, a single animal or flower, and recorded outer shapes, textures, and colors as well as inner essences, seemingly oblivious to the number of days or weeks required for such detailed accuracy. Although Akbar's innovative portraitists had caught overall spirits and gestures, Jahāngīr's probed more deeply, with a psychiatrist's concern for human motives and emotions, often seizing fleetingly characteristic moods.

As the first Mughal emperor to have inherited a well-ordered, vastly rich empire, Jahāngīr could spend much of his time with artists. For him, painting was as important as statecraft had been to his father. Through the continuing dialogues between the dedicated patron and his virtual alter egos, the artists, exciting progress was made. Limited color harmonies were developed, occasionally resembling the warm hues of old ivory or Whistler Nocturnes. A small number of carefully screened, devotedly nurtured master artists vied with one another to delight imperial eyes. Those who succeeded were generously rewarded with bonuses of money, robes of honor, elephants, horses, and impressive titles, such as "The Wonder of the Age." Imperial displeasure probably doomed the less fortunate to the oblivion of seeking work elsewhere. Fortunately, this was not difficult, as busy workshops welcomed them at the courts of Muslim and Hindu (Rājput) noblemen as well as in commercial centers, such as Agra, where ex-imperial talent supplied a large, if unexhilarating, market.

Imperial artists, on the whole, occupied enviable positions under Jahāngīr and Shāh Jahān. Portraits of them tell us that they were men of substance, well clothed and looked after (figs. 4–10 and 13); and their surviving works proclaim not only that they worked very hard but that they enjoyed doing so. Although no school of painting ever turned on inspiration like water from a tap, the Mughal partnership between patrons and artists frequently produced arousing work. This suggests that the artists felt the freedom to create, despite the emperor's total control.

Ideas for pictures usually came from the emperor himself, excited upon seeing a flower, witnessing an historical event or a notable kill while hunting. Jahāngīr went so far as to commission artists to paint his dreams and fantasies. These subjects usually prompted the choice of a suitable painter, one apt to share the emperor's pictorial thought. If it was in the area of natural history, Mansūr, a specialist in the field, might have been summoned; and he probably set to work immediately. Seated on the ground, surrounded by little shells containing pigments, binding medium (gum arabic or glue), a water pot, and brushes, with a drawing board propped up on one knee, he sketched the design. Some artists, including Mansūr, seem to have made their pictures directly from nature, building them up from outlines and washes to full body color on the same piece of paper. Others also sketched from life, but transferred these preparatory drawings by tracing or pouncing to the commissioned painting. Presumably, the patron observed the artist's step-by-step progress; and he must have relished the frequent discussions with his artists about such matters as the shading of a torso, an elephant's stance, or highlighting emeralds.

Once finished, pictures were burnished by being placed upside down on a hard, smooth surface and gently but firmly stroked from the back with a polished agate, a process comparable to varnishing oil paintings, that gave them evenness and unity. When the emperor had decided a picture's destination—for an album, manuscript, or more rarely to be attached unframed to a wall—it was turned over to a specially trained craftsman for mounting. Ordinarily, he attached it to a card made from layers of paper glued together, and an appropriate border was created for it. As can be seen from examples shown here (e.g., *nos 5–12* and *21–23*), these infinitely varied borders were enriched by drawings or paintings in line, gold, or full color. Although they seldom outdo the pictures, calligraphies, Persian miniatures, or European prints they surround, Jahāngīr's and Shāh Jahān's borders were usually of compelling beauty.

Next, the mounted miniature, sometimes composed with others within the same border, was allotted its precise place within an album or manu-script. If for the former, its position was thoughtfully planned to relate effectively to the facing page. Binding followed, again by specialized craftsmen, either in lacquered papier maché or leather boards stamped in arabesque designs of various tones of gold. The artists themselves were sometimes assigned to lacquer especially sumptuous bindings with figure compositions, flowers, or animal designs.

A delightful scene followed, when the completed work was brought to the emperor for inspection. Such moments must have been glorious to experience. From the paintings themselves as well as from visiting the surviving palaces and gardens, likely places for such presentations are easy to imagine. Especially delightful imperial picture viewings can be conjured up in gardens under the cool of the later afternoon, with Jahāngīr and his favorite wife Nūr Jahān seated beneath an awning on a carpeted platform set in the midst of a lotus pool. Wine and sweetmeats, girl pages with yak tail whisks (fly-flappers), singers and lute players, and the proud but slightly apprehensive artists and librarians offering their work would have completed the scene. Eagerly, the emperor opened the pages, seeing the lively glint of sunlight on gold and the flow of precious pigments. At such times, he liked to write comments on the edges of pictures, in his imperially self-assumed, occasionally boozy calligraphy.

Pictures comprised a greatly valued part of the Mughal treasury: but more important, many of them were intimately personal documents, revelations of the emperors' and their families' ways of life and thought. During the heyday of the empire, such bumpkins as ourselves could never have seen these treasures, which, more than any other survivals from that great age, are imbued with the imperial aura. They invite us not only into the halls of public audience to witness state occasions with all their pomp and panoply, but also into the private living quarters, where only the most trusted confidants were allowed. Through the eagerly curious eyes of the painters, we can meet the rulers and their royal households and inspect their thrones, jewels, wine cups, and matchlocks—artful wonders designed and made by the imperial craftsmen, or collected from other kingdoms as distant as Europe or China. And during the period encompassed here, each of these objects was a superb work of art, virtually on the level of the pictures themselves. However richly embroidered or gem-encrusted they were, perfect simplicity of proportion avoided fussiness. Appealingly, despite the opulence and sophistication of Mughal objects, their forms are often derived from nature. Bottles were shaped like mangoes, and plates were "translations" into jade of the leaves used to eat from by less royal Indians.

But these miniatures offer more than eye-boggling glimpses of the imperial court. They also illustrate Mughal moods and thoughts. We sense in them the emphasis placed upon human dignity; and it is clear that men were esteemed not only for their social prestige but also for accomplishment or goodness. Age, too, was revered; while raucousness or buffoonery were deemed suitable only to the young or the ill-bred.

During the reigns of Jahāngīr, Shāh Jahān, and Aurangzēb, the atmosphere at court increased in gravity, lending formal gatherings before the emperor, darbars, the semblance of gorgeously costumed ballets in slow-motion. By the mid-seventeenth century, ceremonials and rituals had taken on the flavor of religious acts, and a courtier's position and stance before the throne were as prescribed as an acolyte's at a Roman Catholic Mass. In such an atmosphere, a raised eyebrow or guarded winks were tantamount to howling brawls during the rough-and-tumble years of Akbar's reign. Shāh Jahān would never have disrupted the spit-and-polish decorum of court by summoning such an upsetting specter as the dying ʿInāyat Khān (no. 60). Nor in all likelihood would he have yielded to the temptation of commissioning a portrait of this human tragedy.

Nonetheless, deep human emotions continued to be expressed by artists, especially in the intimate family portraits as opposed to the state variety. Jahāngīr's love for Nūr Jahān and Shāh Jahān's for Mumtāz Mahal whose tomb is known as the Tāj Mahal, were reflected in such romantic wedding portraits as Bālchand's of Shāh Shujaʿ and his wife (no. 31). Although ordinarily artists dared not depict the imperial ladies familiarly (and as a result, most such portraits are icily dull), they were allowed closer access on such occasions as this, when the princess was safely involved with her husband. As a result, Bālchand could explore the couple's tenderly amorous feelings. Neither prince nor princess is prettified or sentimentalized, making the picture all the more moving, and almost photographically true to life.

Passionately concerned with human personality since the days of Bābur, Mughal portrait commissions were not limited to their nobility. Jahāngīr sent Bishan Dās to the Safavī court to bring back exact and revealing impressions of Shāh ʿAbbās, the emperor's most dangerous rival. Hāshim, who may have worked in the Deccan, made a specialty of representing Deccani rulers, who were also considered dangerous by the Mughals. More admirably motivated were the likenesses of musicians, artists, craftsmen, and holy men, whose appearance may have interested imperial patrons because they were so alive and picturesque, in contrast to the stiff immaculateness of noblemen. Usually these humbler folk were shown in characteristic surroundings, with the appurtenances of their callings. Genre miniatures of this sort stimulated the artists as well as patrons, perhaps because they sensed closer affinities and could delve even more deeply than usual into their personalities. Artists of all periods and cultures painted more excitingly when the subject was sympathetic; and one senses that Bichitr, who was best known for his grand throne scenes, outdid himself in the small study of an old scribe (no. 66), someone to whom he felt deeply attuned.

The most profound portrayals of mystics were painted by Govardhan, for whom such subjects became a specialty. Whether or not some of these were commissioned by Prince Dārā Shikōh, the eldest and favorite son of Shāh Jahān, they could serve as illustrations to some of his writings. Tragically, in mid-seventeenth century Mughal India, the religiously tolerant prince, who was as interested in Hinduism as in Islam, was pushing against the grain. Although his ancestor Akbar would have encouraged Dārā's spiritual investigations, orthodoxy was now rife. While the prince's tolerance for Hindus might have been overlooked, since he was the most privileged son of the emperor, his espousal of extremists such as Sarmad could not be. This wild, naked guru, accompanied by his beloved Hindu chela, may be represented in no. 41, a miniature which would gain in pathos from the identification. For Sarmad's fanaticism cost him his life a few years later, in the same wave of holy fervor that destroyed Dārā Shikōh. The impractically idealistic prince, foolishly or quixotically at odds with the ethos of his age, was vulnerable to his ambitiously ruthless brother, Aurangzēb, who imprisoned their father, Shāh Jahān, defeated Dārā Shikōh in a series of battles, captured him, and ordered him executed—with the full support of the Mughal religious and judiciary establishments. With such events as their background, the studies of saints become positively soul-searing.

To condemn the Mughals on the grounds of the wars of succession between the sons of Shāh Jahān would be as foolish as judging our culture on the basis of the Civil War. Most of the sixty or so years with which this exhibition is concerned were peaceful. Their most characteristic expression was not the battle scene or even the darbār but rather the gatherings of poets, princes, and musicians in gardens at dusk. Recently, at that time of day, we visited the Peri Mahal, a terraced garden with crumbling pavillions built half way up the mountains, overlooking the lakes and gardens of Kashmir. It was planned by Dārā Shikōh, for conversations with religious friends, half way between earth and sky. However stirring was the view, with its mysterious silence and seemingly endless overlapping mountains reflected in the lakes, one missed the Mughals themselves, so vividly known from their paintings. Govardhan came to mind; he must have painted there, and his long, creative, no doubt satisfying career long outlasted the far grander ones of his patrons, the emperors and princes, who sparkled like sky-rockets, then plummetted to earth. We also thought of Jahāngīr, Shāh Jahān, and Dārā Shikōh, and of their serious concern for painting; and we regretted that so often those who enjoy their miniatures emphasize Mughal worldliness, not realizing that for them this earth was the ground from which to vault heavenwards.

Stuart Cary Welch

Fogg Art Museum
Harvard University

NOTES

The Patrons

1. Zahiruᶜd-din Muhammad Bābur Padshāh, *Bābur-nāma*, trans. A. Beveridge (London, 1922), p. 518.
2. Ibid., p. 240.
3. See, however, P. Chandra, *The Tūtī-nāma of the Cleveland Museum of Art* (Graz, 1976), p. 9ff.
4. Bābur Padshāh, *Bābur-nāma*, p. 545.
5. This is discussed most fully in the book cited in n. 3.
6. Abuᶜl-Fazl, *Aᶜīn*, p. 113.
7. Ibid., p. 115.
8. *Tūzuk*, vol. I, p. 164.
9. Ibid., p. 410.
10. Ibid., pp. 96–97.
11. Foster, *Early Travels*, p. 116.

Painting under Jahāngīr

1. *Tūzuk*, vol. II, pp. 20–21.
2. Note, in particular, the *Dīwān* of Anwarī, dated 1588, in the Fogg Art Museum (*Welch AMI*, nos. 4A–D), and the *Nafahāt al-Uns*, copied at Agra in 1603, in the British Library (Or. 1362) (Barrett and Gray, *Painting*, p. 97).
3. The *Anwār-i-Suhailī* is fully published in Wilkinson, *Lights*; the *Būstān* has been discussed by Stchoukine, "Un Bustan de Saᶜdi"; and the *Kulliyāt*, unpublished and now in Iran, is referred to in *BM*, no. 72.
4. Abuᶜl-Fazl, *Aᶜīn*, p. 114.
5. Chandra, *Tūtī-nāma*, pp. 172–73 (see n. 3 to "The Patrons" given above).
6. An excellent manuscript for comparison is reproduced in L. Binyon, *The Poems of Nizami* (London, 1928).
7. See M. Sullivan, *The Meeting of Eastern and Western Art* (London, 1973); and J. McCall, "Early Jesuit Art in the Far East," *Artibus Asiae* X (1947): nos. 2–4; XI (1948): no. 1.

The Allahabad Manuscripts

1. al-Badaoni, *Muntakhabu-t-tawarikh* (Patna, 1973), vol. II, p. 390.
2. The passage is in the *Takmila-i-Akbar-nāma* of Inayat-ullah. See Elliott and Dowson, *History*, vol. VI, pp. 112–13.
3. Goetz, "Early Muraqqas," *Marg*, p. 39.
4. A few pages are reproduced. See Skelton, "Two Mughal Lion Hunts," figs. 13 and 14; and Das, "Bishan Das," figs. 354 and 355.
5. Published in Wilkinson, *Lights*.
6. Three pages, all of which show Salīm hunting, are known from this manuscript. See Sotheby 10 October 1977, Lot 28; *Binney Collection*, no. 45; Kühnel, "Indische Miniaturen," fig. 5. The illustrations, which seem to be by the painter responsible for fol. 22v of the 1602 *Dīwān* of Amīr Hasan Dihlavī (*no. 1*), use stock motifs (such as the cheetah attacking a gazelle) found in several other late Akbar period historical manuscripts.
7. Skelton, "Two Mughal Lion Hunts," p. 44.
8. The best example is the *Nafahāt-al-Uns* of 1603, in the British Library (Barrett and Gray, *Painting*, p. 97).

9. See Aziz Ahmad, *An Intellectual History of Islam in India* (Edinburgh, 1969), p. 74; and the *Encyclopedia of Islam*, 2d ed. (Leiden, 1960), vol. III, p. 249.
10. For an example see Gray et al., *R.A. Arts of India and Pakistan*, no. 642, Pl. 121. Other major pages are in the British Library *Khamsa* of Nizāmī (Or. 12208) (Martin, *Miniature Paintings*, fig. 43), and an *Anwār-i-Suhailī* at the Bharat Kala Bhavan, Benares.
11. Elliott and Dowson, *History*, vol. VII, p. 123.
12. Sotheby 11 July 1972, Lot 25.
13. Alain Daniélou, *Hindu Polytheism* (New York, 1964), pp. 298–99.

The *Akbar-nāma* of 1604

1. Several pages from this Iranian volume are in the A. Chester Beatty Library. See *Beatty Library*, vol. I, p. 50.
2. Roe, *Embassy*, p. 123.

The Albums of Jahāngīr

1. A.H. 1008 = A.D. 1599–1600 is found inscribed on a marginal figure by Āqā Rizā (Godard, "Marges," fig. 2), while the date on a border by Daulat is given as A.H. 1018 = A.D. 1609–10 (ibid., fig. 18).
2. A.H. 1018 = A.D. 1609–10 is on page 25b (Kühnel and Goetz, *Indian Book Painting*, p. 9 and Pl. 38), and A.H. 1027 = A.D. 1617 on page 23a (ibid., p. 10 and Pl. 36). Both works are by Govardhan.
3. Ibid., p. 8.
4. Only the margins of the Bodleian *Bahāristān* manuscript have been reproduced; see *Mughal Miniatures of the Earlier Periods* (Bodleian Picture Book No. 9) (Oxford, 1953), figs. 10–12. See also Martin, *Miniature Paintings*, Pls. 209–10, for related borders in the 1604 *Akbar-nāma*.
5. A Safavid example is found in A. U. Pope, *The Survey of Persian Art* (London, 1938–39), Pl. 950. For further sources, see ibid., Pl. 945C, dated 1410–11; and Basil Gray, *Persian Painting* (Lausanne, 1961), p. 49, circa 1405.
6. The signed Basāwan marginalia on fol. 84v of the *Muraqqaᶜ-e-Gulshan* are unpublished. Border figures by the other artists mentioned are listed in the discussion of each artist given here.
7. See Godard, "Marges," figs. 9 and 11–14.
8. See Kühnel and Goetz, *Indian Book Painting*, Pl. 39.
9. Bālchand is portrayed on fols. 43v and 72v; Murād on fol. 49r (Archer, *Indian Miniatures*, Pl. 28) and fol. 146v; and Payāg on fol. 194v. See also *figs. 5, 6,* and *13*.
10. *Brown*, Pl. XXXVI.
11. Acc. no. 63.4, the work is unpublished.
12. The inscription is translated as given in *Robinson ed., Keir*, p. 242.
13. His biography is given in Khan, *Maasir-ul Umara*, vol. II, nos. 816ff.
14. *Robinson ed., Keir*, V. 13, V. 21, and Pl. 113.
15. Kühnel and Goetz, *Indian Book Painting*, Pl. 38.
16. See Wilkinson, *Lights*.
17. Two drawings of elephants are in the *Muraqqaᶜ-e-Gulshan*,

one of which is published in Wilkinson and Gray, "Indian Paintings," Pl. IIIc. A third is in the Freer Gallery of Art (56.12).

18. Another strongly related page is in the *Dīwān* of Hafīz in the Rampur State Library. See Krishna, "Study," Pl. 32.
19. Ibid., pp. 353–73.
20. The *Gulshan Album* paintings, both of which are adapted from European compositions, are unpublished. The Freer page is no. 54.116.
21. For examples see Beach, "Gulshan," figs. 1–2 (by Kesu Dās); Wilkinson and Gray, "Indian Paintings," Pl. IIIa (by Manōhar); and Bussagli, *Indian Miniatures*, fig. 61 (by Basāwan). For a stylistically comparable dated page see Beach, "Kesu Das," fig. 1.
22. Roe, *Embassy*, pp. 210–11.
23. Ibid., p. 500 (see his note).
24. Du Jarric, *Akbar*, p. 67.
25. Some of these are discussed in Beach, "European Source."
26. Beach, "Kesu Das," fig. 9.

The *Jahāngīr-nāma*

1. *Tūzuk*, vol. I, p. 215.
2. Foster, *Early Travels*, pp. 115–16.
3. A particularly good discussion is found in Guerreiro, *Jahangir*, p. 63ff.
4. Abū'l-Fazl ʿAllāmi, *Akbar-nāma*, trans. H. Beveridge, 3 vols. (Calcutta, 1897–1910), vol. II, pp. 503–4.

The *Gulistān* of Saʿdī

1. For an excellent recent translation see *The Gulistan or Rose Garden of Saʿdi*, trans. E. Rehatsek (London, 1964).
2. The *Kulliyāt* is unpublished; for the *Būstan* see Stchoukine, "Un Bustan de Saʿdi," pp. 68–74.
3. See Pinder-Wilson, "Three Illustrated Manuscripts," pp. 415–22; and Wilkinson, "An Indian Manuscript," pp. 423–25.
4. The album contains seals dated A.H. 1238 = A.D. 1823. *Nos. 27* and *29* are from the same group.
5. Colnaghi, *Persian and Mughal Art*, no. 89i.
6. See n. 2.
7. The initial identification of these episodes was given by Ettinghausen, *Sultans*, text for Pl. 10. His suggestion that this shows Chapter I, Story 4, however, seems incorrect, as is his identification of the lower illustration on W. 668, fol. 36v (*no. 16*) as Story 7. For this latter correction, I am grateful to Rebecca Ruth.
8. *Welch AMI*, no. 35.
9. He is seen also just below the emperor in no. 14.
10. *Welch AMI*, no. 25 and p. 166.

The Albums of Shāh Jahān

1. Abuʿl-Fazl, *Aʿīn*, p. 115.
2. See Welch, "Miniature Paintings," no. 6, figs. 8–9; and Welch, "Mughal and Deccani Miniature Paintings," no. 1, fig. 1, and no. 6, fig. 4.
3. Compare no. 23 recto to *Beach Heeramaneck*, no. 227.
4. A particularly good example of the style when it is not consciously attempting to be archaic is in *Binney Collection*, no. 91.
5. For example, the *Berlin Album*, the *Leningrad Album*, the *Late Shāh Jahān Album*, and the *Hamza-nāma* manuscript, to name only the most notable works.

6. An example is the "Ardeshir" Album. See Sotheby 10 July 1973.
7. *Tūzuk*, vol. II, p. 105.

The *Padshāh-nāma*

1. For a discussion of these texts, and excerpts, see Elliott and Dowson, *History*, vol. VII, pp. 1–134.
2. Ibid., pp. 3–72.
3. Folio numbers of signed pages are as follows: 43v, 72v, and 134v (Bālchand); 46v (Lālchand); 48v (Rām Dās); 49r, 121v, 143r, 146v, 193v, and 216v (Murād); 50v (Bichitr); 70r (Bola); 93v (ʿĀbid); 101v, 194v, and 213v (Payāg); and 173r (Mīr Dust). In addition, other pages are attributable to various artists.
4. Colnaghi, *Persian and Mughal Art*, no. 95; two other versions of this composition are listed in the discussion of Abū'l Hasan.
5. Bernier, *Mughal Travels*, p. 268ff.
6. Tavernier, *India Travels*, vol. I, p. 303ff.
7. Elliott and Dowson, *History*, vol. VII, pp. 45–46.
8. A brief biography of Gaj Singh is given in V. S. Bhargava, *Marwar and the Mughal Emperors* (Delhi, 1966), pp. 70–79.
9. He is shown, for example, leading the siege of Qandahar (in Gujarat), an event of 1630, on fol. 101v, also by Payāg.
10. A sales catalogue in which this painting appears (*Collection Jean Pozzi*, Palais Galliéra, Paris, 5 December 1970, Lot 77) notes a marginal inscription naming six of the men as: Qulīj Khān Bahādur, Rājā Jaswant Singh Rathor, Rustam Khān, Saīd Khān, Delbar Khān Afghan, and Bahādur Khān. Since the one Rajput figure is definitely not Jaswant Singh (compare him to Hambly and Swaan, *Cities*, fig. 51), and Khān Daurān, who is included, is not mentioned, the inscription must be judged unreliable. Probably written by an eighteenth-century collector, it also states that the subject is the Siege of Qandahar.

Abū'l Hasan

1. *Tūzuk*, vol. II, p. 20.
2. See especially A. Welch, *Artists for the Shah* (London, 1976), figs. 42, 45, and 48.
3. An amusing account of this is given in Roe, *Embassy*, p. 224ff.
4. See Graham Reynolds, *Nicholas Hilliard and Isaac Oliver* (London, 1971), nos. 141–42, Pl. IV (color).
5. *Tūzuk*, vol. II, p. 152.
6. Colnaghi, *Persian and Mughal Art*, no. 111.
7. An excellent portrait of the young Murād is in Marteau and Vever, vol. II, Pl. CLXI.
8. Fol. 50v, reproduced in Gascoigne, *Great Mughals*, p. 145.

Āqā Rizā

1. *Tūzuk*, vol. II, p. 20.
2. The Abū'l Hasan inscription is on *no. 29*, while the note by ʿĀbid is on *Shāh Jahān in Darbār with Mahābat Khān and a Sheikh*, listed in the discussion of that artist's work.
3. See S. C. Welch, *Persian Painting* (New York, 1976), Pls. 34–48.
4. It may be that these references are to one man. See Coomaraswamy, "Notes," p. 205; and Qadi Ahmad, *Calligraphers and Painters*, trans. V. Minorsky (Washington, 1959), p. 166.
5. For a discussion see Schroeder, *Fogg Persian Miniatures*, p. 109ff.
6. See Rizvi, "Mughal Elite," p. 92.
7. Goetz, "Early Muraqqas," *Marg*, p. 39.

8. For Iranian examples see Martin, *Miniature Paintings*, Pl. 110; a Deccani version is in Deneck, *Indian Art*, Pl. 35; Rajasthani examples abound in works attributable to Sāwar; and an example from the Panjab Hills is in W. G. Archer, *Indian Paintings from the Panjab Hills* (London, 1973), vol. II, Kulu no. 30.

Bālchand

1. A similar object is held by the figure at the bottom right of a *Jahāngīr-nāma* page in Leningrad (see Ivanova, *Albom Indiyskikh*, Pl. 32); this work, while unsigned, is probably by Abūᶜl Hasan. It is seen as well in *Jahāngīr Preferring a Sūfī Sheikh to Kings* by Bichitr (see Ettinghausen, *Sultans*, Pl. 14), and in two additional folios of the Windsor *Padshāh-nāma* manuscript (fol. 49r by Murād and fol. 194r by Payāg). In each case, the related figure seems to be the artist's self-portrait.
2. By the late 1630s, Dārā was moustached (see *nos. 24, 32,* and *37*) and appears considerably older than in the Boston picture (*Coomaraswamy Boston*, no. LXXVI, Pl. XXXVI). The marriages of the two brothers, within days of each other, could explain the identical character of the two works.
3. Bernier, *Mughal Travels*, pp. 7–8.
4. *Coomaraswamy Boston*, no. LXXVI, Pl. XXXVI.
5. Examples abound. See R. Strong, *The Elizabethan Image* (London, 1969), nos. 72, 82, 86, 88, etc. For Roe's involvement, see Roe, *Embassy*, p. 214 and his n. 1.

Bichitr

1. See Bālchand, n. 1.
2. Biographical information is available in V. S. Bhargava, *Marwar and the Mughal Emperors* (Delhi, 1966), pp. 70–77.
3. See Bālchand, n. 4.
4. This page, for example, is closely comparable to a number of further works. See Martin, *Miniature Paintings*, Pl. 218A; an unpublished painting in the Staatliche Museen, Berlin; *Welch AMI*, no. 36; *BM*, no. 124; and Philip Rawson, *Drawing* (London, 1969), pp. 262–63. Several of these illustrations are similarly inscribed and may have come from an imperial album.
5. N. Ahmad, *The Kitāb-i-Nauras by Ibrāhīm ᶜAdīl Shāh II* (New Delhi, 1956), p. 132.
6. Van Berge et al., "Some Mughal Miniatures," no. 12, Pl. 11.
7. The standard portrait of the mature Shujāᶜ is a *Minto Album* page by Bālchand, *The Three Younger Sons of Shāh Jahān* (Deneck, *Indian Art*, Pl. 34).

Bishan Dās

1. Rahim, *Mughal Relations*, p. 28ff.
2. *Tūzuk*, vol. II, pp. 116–17.
3. Ibid., p. 117.
4. See Godard, "Marges," p. 23.
5. A good comparison is provided by the *Anwār-i-Suhailī* manuscript of 1604–10. See Wilkinson, *Lights*.
6. *Coomaraswamy Boston*, p. 47.
7. *Tūzuk*, vol. I, pp. 370–71.

Daulat

1. This was first noticed by Yedda Godard, "Marges," p. 29.
2. See also *no. 37*.

3. Ibid., p. 26.
4. See also Martin, *Miniature Paintings*, fig. 43.
5. Excellent examples of these figure types are found in the *Akbar-nāma* and *Jahāngīr-nāma* scenes noted in the check list of Daulat's work.
6. The *Padshāh-nāma* folio is 203v. See also Colnaghi, *Persian and Mughal Art*, no. 122; and *Binney Collection*, no. 60, where the figure in the bottom right corner of the margins holds an inscription to Daula(t).

Ghulām

1. See Gray et al., *R.A. Arts of India and Pakistan*, no. 665, Pl. 128.
2. These are listed with the discussion of Āqā Rizā.
3. Della Valle, *Travels in India*, vol. I, p. 52.
4. See n. 2.
5. *Encyclopedia of Islam*, new edition (Leiden, 1965), vol. II, p. 1081ff.
6. A. Welch, "Painting and Patronage under Shah ᶜAbbas I," *Journal of the Society for Iranian Studies* VII, Parts 3–4 (1974): 484ff.

Govardhan

1. He is known to have worked on the British Library *Bābur-nāma* (Or. 3714) and the 1598 *Razm-nāma*. See R. H. Pinder-Wilson, "A Persian Translation of the Mahabharata," *British Museum Quarterly* 20 no. 3 (1956): 65.

Manōhar

1. For an excellent discussion of Basāwan, see S. C. Welch, "The Paintings of Basawan," *Lalit Kala* 10, 1961.
2. The accession number is 13.288.33, and the page is reproduced in color in Metropolitan Museum of Art, *Islamic Art*, New York, n.d., no page or plate number given. See also Gray et al., *R.A. Arts of India and Pakistan*, no. 652, Pl. 124; and Grube, *Classical Style*, Pl. 94.

Mansūr

1. *Tūzuk*, vol. II, p. 20.
2. Ibid., pp. 107–8.
3. Ibid., p. 145.
4. Ibid., p. 157.
5. *Binney Collection*, no. 91, shows typical Delhi workmanship of circa 1800.
6. The suggestion has been made by Robert Skelton.
7. For example, *Bulletin of the Cleveland Museum of Art*, October 1975, cover.
8. For some references, see *Tūzuk*, vol. I, pp. 132, 206, 291, 323, and thereafter.

Muhammad ᶜAlī

1. Skelton, "Farrokh," pp. 399–400; this is *no. 48* in this exhibition.

Nānhā

1. Godard, "Marges," p. 23.

2. Abu'l-Fazl, *A'īn*, p. 114.
3. See S. C. Welch, "The Emperor Akbar's *Khamsa* of Nizami," *Journal of the Walters Art Gallery* XXIII (1960): fig. 3.
4. See G. Egger, *Hamza-nāma* (Graz, 1974).
5. A short biography is given in Khan, *Maasir-ul Umara*, vol. II, p. 1020.

Payāg

1. The manuscript, unpublished, is now in Iran. For a reference see *BM*, no. 148.
2. One of many possible comparisons would be Adam Elsheimer's *Flight into Egypt*. See *Alte Pinakothek, München: Kurzes Verzeichnis der Bilder* (Munich, 1958), fig. 94.
3. The same figure appears in Manuscript 7, No. 20 in the A. Chester Beatty Library, Dublin. The identification is made (*Beatty Library*, vol. I, pp. 33–34) on the basis of a portrait reproduced in Martin (*Miniature Paintings*, Pl. 188), which, however, bears little resemblance to this man. Martin believes his portrait to be of the governor of Bhakkar who died in 1633; it is more likely to be Saiyid 'Izzat Khān 'Abdur Razzāk Gilānī whose biography is given in Khan, *Maasir-ul Umara*, vol. II, p. 1079.

European Subjects

1. Guerreiro, *Jahangir*, p. 63.
2. Du Jarric, *Akbar*, pp. 19–20.
3. A sixteenth-century copy of the painting, of the type sent to India (and China), is reproduced in McCall, "Early Jesuit Art in the Far East," *Artibus Asiae* XI no. 1 (1948): fig. 22. A Mughal version is found in Ivanova et al., *Albom Indiyskikh*, Pl. 54; and it is informative to compare it to the Chinese copy illustrated in McCall, "Early Jesuit Art," fig. 25.
4. See Beach, "European Source," pp. 180–88.
5. Dürer's diaries are a useful source for this information. See J. A. Goris and G. Marlier, *Albrecht Dürer: Diary of his Journey to the Netherlands 1520–1521* (New York, 1971).
6. For a reference to the *Royal Polyglot Bible*, see Maclagan, *Jesuits*, p. 191. A copy from the *Thesaurus Sacrarum* is illustrated in Beach, "Gulshan," nos. 12 and 12a; and a page from the *Evangelicae Historiae Imagines*, which also reached China, is known in a private collection in Pakistan.
7. Roe, *Embassy*, pp. 213–14.
8. Ibid., p. 225.
9. Ibid., p. 214, notes.
10. The Mughal portrait is illustrated in Ettinghausen, *Sultans*, Pl. 14, while one of John de Critz' many similar portraits of James I is reproduced in R. Strong, *The Elizabethan Image* (London, 1970), no. 174.
11. For Italian contacts, see R. M. Cimino and F. Scialpi, *India and Italy* (Rome, 1974).
12. Maclagan, *Jesuits*, p. 225.
13. A good discussion and bibliography is given in M. Sullivan, *The Meeting of Eastern and Western Art* (London, 1973).
14. See F. W. H. Hollstein, *German Engravings, Etchings and Woodcuts* (Amsterdam, 1962), vol. IV, p. 12.
15. *Coomaraswamy Boston*, no. LXXXIII, Pl. XL.

Miscellaneous Portraits

1. Examples of possible dispersed pages from this album are reproduced in Welch, "Miniature Paintings," no. 6, figs. 8 and 9; and Welch, "Mughal and Deccani Miniature Paintings," no. 1, fig. 1.
2. Iranian sources are discussed in the articles listed above in n. 1; another is reproduced in *Coomaraswamy Goloubev*, no. 43, Pl. XXIII.
3. *Tūzuk*, vol. I, p. 267.
4. See *BM*, no. 109.
5. The *Youth Reading*, reproduced in Ettinghausen, *Sultans*, Pl. 9.
6. *Tūzuk*, vol. II, pp. 43–44. The Hakīm Ruknā referred to is probably the man who served as scribe for two Sa'dī manuscripts of 1629. See Pinder-Wilson, "Three Illustrated Manuscripts," pp. 415–16; and Wilkinson, "An Illustrated Manuscript," p. 423.
7. See Binyon and Arnold, *Court Painters*, Pl. XXIV; *Welch IMP*, Pl. 23.
8. Welch, *Indian Drawings*, no. 16.
9. See Christie's 25 June 1965, Lot 47.
10. See Maggs Brothers, Ltd., *Oriental Miniatures and Illumination Bulletin No. 21* (London, 1973), Lot 203.
11. See Binyon and Arnold, *Court Painters*, Pl. X (by Anupchatar); and Van Berge et al., "Some Mughal Miniatures," no. 16, Pl. 11.
12. Manucci, *Storia do Mogor*, vol. I, p. 269.
13. See also Kahlenberg, "Mughal Patka."

Animal Studies

1. See Welch, *Indian Drawings*, no. 61.
2. The inscribed painting is in the *Wantage Album* (*Wantage Bequest*, no. 24, Pl. 16). See also Martin, *Miniature Paintings*, Pl. 220.
3. *Tūzuk*, vol. I, p. 189.
4. See Gray et al., *R.A. Arts of India and Pakistan*, no. 719, Pl. 139.

ABBREVIATIONS

Beach Heeramaneck	Beach, Milo C. "Painting and the Minor Arts." In *The Arts of India and Nepal: The Nasli and Alice Heeramaneck Collection*, pp. 97–167. Boston, 1966.
Beatty Library	Arnold, Thomas W., and Wilkinson, J. V. S. *The Library of A. Chester Beatty. A Catalogue of the Indian Miniatures*. 3 vols. London, 1936.
Binney Collection	Binney, Edwin, 3rd. *Indian Miniature Painting from the Collection of Edwin Binney 3rd.* Portland, Oregon, 1973.
BM	Pinder-Wilson, R. H.; Smart, Ellen; and Barrett, Douglas. *Paintings from the Muslim Courts of India*. Exhibition catalogue, British Museum. London, 1976.
Brown	Brown, Percy. *Indian Painting under the Mughals*. Oxford, 1924.
BWG	Binyon, Laurence; Wilkinson, J. V. S.; and Gray, Basil. *Persian Miniature Painting*. London, 1933.
Coomaraswamy Boston	Coomaraswamy, A. K. *Catalogue of the Indian Collections in the Museum of Fine Arts, Boston, Vol. VI: Mughal Painting*. Cambridge, Mass., 1930.
Coomaraswamy Goloubev	Coomaraswamy, A. K. "Les Miniatures Orientales de la Collection Goloubev au Museum of Fine Arts Boston." *Ars Asiatica*, vol. 13, 1929.
Dimand Bulletin	Dimand, Maurice. "An Exhibition of Islamic and Indian Paintings." Metropolitan Museum of Art Bulletin XIV (1955):85–102.
Robinson ed., Keir	Robinson, B. W.; Grube, E.; Meredith-Owens, G. M.; and Skelton, R. W. *Islamic Painting and the Arts of the Book*. Edited by B. W. Robinson. London, 1976.
Stchoukine Louvre	Stchoukine, Ivan. *Les Miniatures Indiennes de l'Epoque des Grands Moghols au Musée du Louvre*. Paris, 1929.
Tuzuk	Jahangir. *The Tuzuk-i-Jahangiri; or Memoirs of Jahangir*. Translated by A. Rogers and edited by H. Beveridge. (2 vols. in 1). London, 1909–14.
Wantage Bequest	Clarke, S. C. *Indian Drawings: Thirty Mogul Paintings of the School of Jahangir and Four Panels of Calligraphy in the Wantage Bequest, Victoria and Albert Museum Portfolios*. London, 1922.
Welch AMI	Welch, Stuart C. *The Art of Mughal India*. New York, 1963.
Welch FEM	Welch, Stuart C. *A Flower from Every Meadow*. New York, 1973.
Welch IMP	Welch, Stuart C. *Imperial Mughal Painting*. New York, 1977.

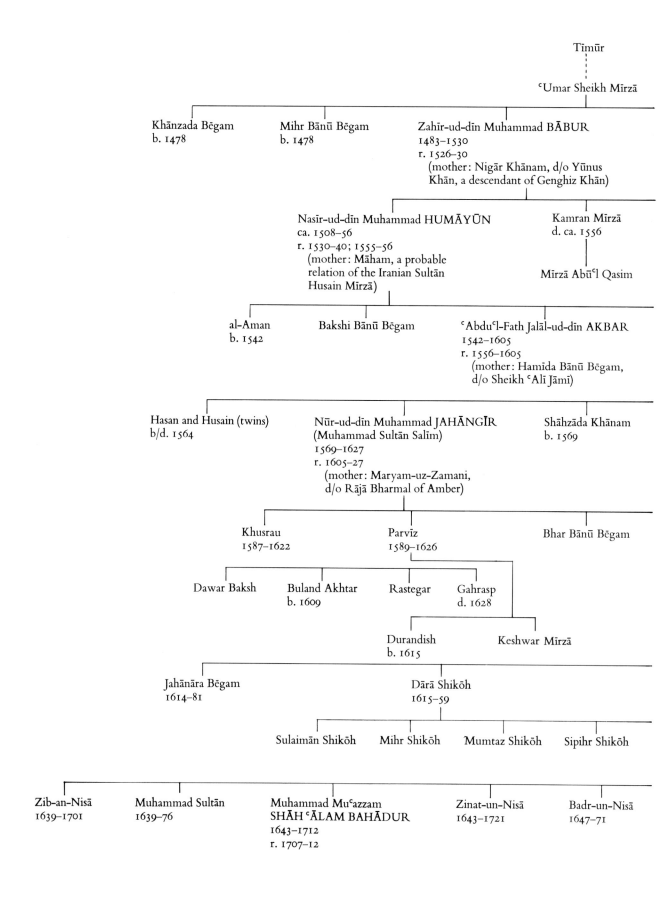

Tīmūr

ʿUmar Sheikh Mīrzā

Khānzada Bēgam
b. 1478

Mihr Bānū Bēgam
b. 1478

Zahīr-ud-dīn Muhammad BĀBUR
1483–1530
r. 1526–30
(mother: Nigār Khānam, d/o Yūnus
Khān, a descendant of Genghiz Khān)

Nasīr-ud-dīn Muhammad HUMĀYŪN
ca. 1508–56
r. 1530–40; 1555–56
(mother: Māham, a probable
relation of the Iranian Sultān
Husain Mīrzā)

Kamran Mīrzā
d. ca. 1556

Mīrzā Abūʿl Qasim

al-Aman
b. 1542

Bakshi Bānū Bēgam

ʿAbduʿl-Fath Jalāl-ud-dīn AKBAR
1542–1605
r. 1556–1605
(mother: Hamīda Bānū Bēgam,
d/o Sheikh ʿAlī Jāmī)

Hasan and Husain (twins)
b/d. 1564

Nūr-ud-dīn Muhammad JAHĀNGĪR
(Muhammad Sultān Salīm)
1569–1627
r. 1605–27
(mother: Maryam-uz-Zamani,
d/o Rājā Bharmal of Amber)

Shāhzāda Khānam
b. 1569

Khusrau
1587–1622

Parvīz
1589–1626

Bhar Bānū Bēgam

Dawar Baksh

Buland Akhtar
b. 1609

Rastegar

Gahrasp
d. 1628

Durandish
b. 1615

Keshwar Mīrzā

Jahānāra Bēgam
1614–81

Dārā Shikōh
1615–59

Sulaimān Shikōh

Mihr Shikōh

Mumtaz Shikōh

Sipihr Shikōh

Zīb-an-Nisā
1639–1701

Muhammad Sultān
1639–76

Muhammad Muʿazzam
SHĀH ʿĀLAM BAHĀDUR
1643–1712
r. 1707–12

Zinat-un-Nisā
1643–1721

Badr-un-Nisā
1647–71

GENEALOGICAL TABLE

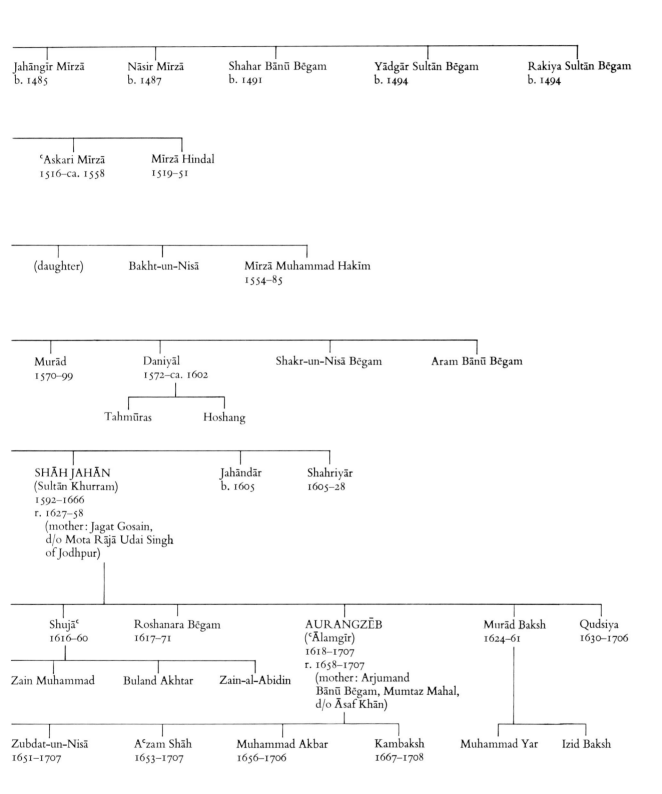

Jahāngīr Mīrzā
b. 1485

Nāsir Mīrzā
b. 1487

Shahar Bānū Bēgam
b. 1491

Yādgār Sultān Bēgam
b. 1494

Rakiya Sultān Bēgam
b. 1494

ʿAskari Mīrzā
1516–ca. 1558

Mīrzā Hindal
1519–51

(daughter)

Bakht-un-Nisā

Mīrzā Muhammad Hakīm
1554–85

Murād
1570–99

Daniyāl
1572–ca. 1602

Shakr-un-Nisā Bēgam

Aram Bānū Bēgam

Tahmūras

Hoshang

SHĀH JAHĀN
(Sultān Khurram)
1592–1666
r. 1627–58
(mother: Jagat Gosain,
d/o Mota Rājā Udai Singh
of Jodhpur)

Jahāndār
b. 1605

Shahriyār
1605–28

Shujāʿ
1616–60

Roshanara Bēgam
1617–71

AURANGZĒB
(ʿĀlamgīr)
1618–1707
r. 1658–1707
(mother: Arjumand
Bānū Bēgam, Mumtaz Mahal,
d/o Āsaf Khān)

Murād Baksh
1624–61

Qudsiya
1630–1706

Zain Muhammad

Buland Akhtar

Zain-al-Abidin

Zubdat-un-Nisā
1651–1707

Aʿzam Shāh
1653–1707

Muhammad Akbar
1656–1706

Kambaksh
1667–1708

Muhammad Yar

Izid Baksh

BIBLIOGRAPHY

Historical: Primary Sources

Abuᶜl-Fazl ᶜAllami. *The Aᶜin Akbari*. Translated by H. Bloch-mann. Calcutta, 1927.

Bernier, F. *Travels in the Mughal Empire (1656–1668)*. Edited by A. Constable. London, 1891.

Best, Thomas. *Voyage (1612–14)*. London, 1934.

Della Valle, Pietro. *Travels in India*. Translated by E. Grey. 2 vols. London, 1892.

Du Jarric, P. *Akbar and the Jesuits*. Translated by C. H. Payne. London, 1926.

Elliot, H. M., and Dowson, John. *The History of India as Told by Its Own Historians*. 8 vols. London, 1867–77.

Ferishta. *Gulshan-i-Ibrahimi*. Translated by J. Briggs. London, 1829.

Floris, Peter. *Voyage to the East Indies (1611–15)*. Edited by W. H. Moreland. London, 1934.

Foster, W. *Early Travels in India*. New Delhi, 1968.

Guerreiro, F. *Jahangir and the Jesuits*. Translated by C. H. Payne. London, 1930.

Hawkins, William. *The Voyages*. London, 1878.

Husain, Y. *Selected Documents of Shah Jahan's Reign*. Hyderabad, 1950.

Jahangir. *The Tuzuk-i-Jahangiri; or Memoirs of Jahangir*. Translated by A. Rogers and edited by H. Beveridge. (2 vols. in 1). London, 1909–14.

Khan, S. N. *Maasir-ul Umara*. Translated by H. Beveridge. 3 vols. Calcutta, 1911–14.

Manrique, S. *Travels*. Oxford, 1927.

Manucci, N. *Storia do Mogor*. Edited by W. Irvine. 4 vols. Calcutta, 1966.

Marshall, D. N. *Mughals in India: a Bibliographical Survey*. Bombay, 1967.

Mundy, P. *Travels in Europe and Asia, 1608–1667*. Edited by Sir R. C. Temple. Cambridge, 1907–36.

Pelsaert, F. *Remonstrantie*. Translated by W. H. Moreland. Cam-bridge, 1925.

———. *A Contemporary Dutch Chronicle of Mughal India*. Trans-lated by B. Narain and S. R. Sharma. Calcutta, 1957.

Prasad, Ram Chandra. *Early English Travellers in India*. Delhi, 1965.

Roe, T. *The Embassy of Sir Thomas Roe to India 1615–1619*. Edited by W. Foster. London, 1899.

Tavernier, J. B. *Travels in India*. Edited by W. Crooke. 2 vols. Oxford, 1925.

Terry, E. *A Voyage to East India*. London, 1777.

Historical: Secondary Sources

Abdul, A. "A History of the Reign of Shah Jahan." *Journal of Indian History* 6 (1928): 235–57; 7 (1928): 124–47 and 327–48; 9 (1930): 132–72 and 279–305; 11 (1932): 83–113 and 356–65; 12 (1933): 47–78.

Abdur, R. S. "Ottoman and Mughal Relations During the 17th Century." *Journal of the Punjab University Historical Society*, vol. 14 (June 1962), pp. 67–78.

Ahmad, N. L. "Some Aspects of Life and Culture in Mughal India during the Shah Jahan Period." *Jammu and Kashmir University Review* 6 (1963): 35–62.

Alvi, M. A., and Rahman, A. *Jahangir the Naturalist*. Delhi, 1968.

Amar, V. B. "Shah Jahan's Rebellion and Abdur Rahim Khan Khanan." *Journal of Indian History, Golden Jubilee*, 1973, pp. 438–55.

Anand, Mulk Raj. "Shah Jahan—Architect or Lover." *Marg* 22 no. 3 (1969): 3–33.

Ansari, M. A. "Amusements and Games of the Great Mughals." *Islamic Culture*, vol. 35 no. 1, 1961.

———. "Court Ceremonies of the Great Mughals." *Islamic Culture* 35 no. 3 (1961): 183–97.

———. "Dress of the Great Mughals." *Islamic Culture* 31 no. 1 (1957): 255–67.

———. "Some Aspects of Social Life at the Court of the Great Mughals." *Islamic Culture* 36 no. 3 (1962): 182–95.

Aslam, M. "Jahangir and Hadrat Shaikh Ahmad Sirhindi." *Journal of the Asiatic Society of Pakistan* 10 (1965): 135–47.

Aziz, Ahmad. *Studies in Islamic Culture in the Indian Environment*. Oxford, 1964.

Beveridge, H. "Sultan Khusrau." *Journal of the Royal Asiatic Society*, 1907, pp. 597–609.

Camps, A. "Franciscan Missions to the Mogul Court." *Neue Zeitschrift für Missionswissenschaft*, vol. 15, 1959.

Carroll, David. *The Taj Mahal—India under the Moguls*. New York, 1972.

Caunter, R. *Nur Jahan and Jahangir*. Calcutta, 1950.

Chaghtai, M. A. "Emperor Jahangir's Interviews with Gosain Jadrup and His Portraits." *Islamic Culture* 36 no. 2 (1962): 119–28.

Charpentier, J. "A Note from the Memoirs of Jahangir." *Journal of the Royal Asiatic Society*, 1924, pp. 440–42.

Chopra, P. N. *Society and Culture during the Mughal Age*. Agra, 1963.

Chowdhuri, J. N. "Mumtaz Mahall." *Islamic Culture* 11 no. 3 (1937): 373–81.

Commissariat, M. S. "The Emperor Jahangir's Second Visit to Ahmadabad (April–September 1618)." *Journal of the Bombay Historical Society* 1 (1928): 139–52.

Dasgupta, J. A. *India in the 17th Century as Depicted by European Travellers*. Calcutta, 1916.

Ferrier, R. W. "The Trade between India and the Persian Gulf and the East India Company in the 17th Century." *Bengal Past and Present* 89 (1970): 181–96.

Gascoigne, Bamber. *The Great Moghuls*. London, 1971.

Ghauri, I. F. *War of Succession between the Sons of Shah Jahan*. Lahore, 1974.

Goetz, Hermann. *Bilderatlas zur Kulturgeschichte Indiens in der Grossmogulzeit*. Berlin, 1930.

Gopal, S. "Gujarati Shipping in the 17th Century." *Indian Eco-nomic and Social History Review* 8 (1971): 31–39.

Goswamy, B. N. *The Mughals and the Jogis of Jakhbar: Some Madad-i-Maᶜsh and Other Documents*. Simla, 1967.

Halim, A. "Music and Musicians of the Court of Shah Jahan." *Islamic Culture* 19 no. 1 (1945): 354–60.

Hambly, Gavin, and Swaan, Wim. *Cities of Mughul India*. New York, 1968.

Hambye, E. R. "The Mogul Court, the Portuguese and the

Jesuits." *Journal of Indian History, Golden Jubilee,* 1973, pp. 457–62.

Hansen, W. *The Peacock Throne.* New York, 1972.

Hasan, I. *The Central Structure of the Mughal Empire.* Karachi, 1967.

Hasrat, B. J. *Dara Shikoh: Life and Works.* Santiniketan, 1953.

———. "The Diwan and Quatrains of Dara Shikoh." *Islamic Culture* 18 (1944): 145–66.

———. "The Mingling of the Two Oceans: Hinduism and Islam." *Visvabharti Quarterly* n.s. 15 (1949–1950): 60–74.

Heras, H. "Jahangir and the Portuguese." *Proceedings of the Indian Historical Records Commission* 9 (1926): 18–28.

Hosain, M. H. "Contemporary Historians during the Reign of Shah Jahan." *Islamic Culture* 15 (1941): 64–79.

Hosten, H. "The Jesuits at Agra in 1635–1637." *Journal and Proceedings of the Asiatic Society of Bengal* ser. III, 4 (1938): 479–501.

———. "List of Jesuit Missionaries in Mogor 1580–1803." *Journal of the Asiatic Society of Bengal* n.s. 6 no. 10, 1910.

Hurat, M. C. "Les Entretiens de Lahore entre le Prince Imperial Dara Shikoh et l'Ascète Hindou Baba Lal Das." *Journal Asiatique* 209 (1926): 285–334.

Husain, A. "The Family of Shaikh Salim Chisti during the Reign of Jahangir." *Medieval India* 2 (1972): 61–69.

Islam, R. *Indo-Persian Relations.* Tehran, 1970.

Jalaluddin. "Sultan Selim as a Rebel King." *Islamic Culture* 47 (1973): 121–25.

Khan, B. R. "Royal Dishes and Drinks under Akbar and Jahangir." *Pakistan Historical Society* 17 (1969): 145–60.

Lach, Donald. *Asia in the Making of Europe.* Chicago, 1970.

Maclagan, E. D. *The Jesuits and the Great Mogul.* London, 1932.

Moinul Haq, S. *Prince Aurangzib: A Study.* Karachi, 1962.

Moreland, W. H. *India at the Death of Akbar.* Delhi, 1962.

Muᶜin-ud-Din. *Dara Shikuh: The Magnificent Prince.* Lahore, 1969.

Nath, R. "Augustin Bordeaux and His Relations with the Mughal Court, 1612–1632." *Quarterly Review of Historical Studies* 8 (1968–69): 157–64.

Prasad, Beni. *History of Jahangir.* London, 1922.

———. "The Accession of Shah Jahan." *Journal of Indian History* 2 (1922): 1–19.

Qanungo, K. R. *Dara Shikuh.* Calcutta, 1952.

———. "Some Sidelights on the Character and Court Life of Shah Jahan." *Journal of Indian History* 8 (1929): 45–52.

Quamaruddin, M. "A Study of the Character and Personality of Murad Baksh." *Indo-Iranica* 24 (1971): 64–76.

Rahim, Abdur. "Mughal Relations with Persia and Central Asia." *Islamic Culture,* vols. 8 and 9, 1934–35.

Refai, Gulammohammed. "Aurangzib and Dara Shukoh: Conflict of Ideologies." In *Essays in Indian History in Honour of Cuthbert Collin Davies,* edited by D. Williams and E. D. Potts. London, 1973.

Rizvi, S. A. A. "The Mughal Elite in the 16th and 17th Century." *Abr-Narain* XI (1971): 69–104.

Saksena, Banarsi Prasad. *History of Shah Jahan of Delhi.* Allahabad, 1932.

Sarkar, A. K. "Itimad ud Daula: A Sketch of His Life and Career." *Quarterly Review of Historical Studies* 10 (1971): 154–64.

Sarkar, Jadunath. "A Little Known Chapter in Indo-Iranian Diplomacy in Mid-17th Century." *Indo-Iranica* 25 (1972): 51–56.

———. *Mughal Administration.* Calcutta, 1952.

Sarkar, J. N. *Studies in Mughal India.* Calcutta, 1919.

———. *Moghul Government and Administration.* Bombay, 1951.

Sharma, Ram. *The Religious Policy of the Mughal Emperors.* Bombay, 1962.

Smith, V. A. "Joannes de Laet on India and Shah Jahan." *Indian Antiquities* 43 (1914): 239–44.

Smith, W. C. "Lower Class Risings in the Mughal Empire." *Islamic Culture,* vol. 20, 1946.

———. "The Mughal Empire and the Middle Class." *Islamic Culture* 18 (1944): 349–63.

Standish, J. S. "Persian Influences in Mughal India." *Islamic Quarterly* 12 (1968): 160–73.

Taraporevala, V. D. B. *Mughal Bibliography.* Bombay, 1962.

Varadarajan, L. "Jahangir the Diarist—An Interpretation Based on the Tuzuk-i Jahangiri." *Journal of Indian History, Golden Jubilee,* 1973, pp. 403–13.

Varma, R. C. *Foreign Policy of the Great Mughals.* Agra, 1967.

Yasin, M. "Jahangir in Kashmir, an Account of Accounts." *University Review (Jammu and Kashmir University)* 10 (1968): 41–44.

Art Historical Sources

Agrawala, V. S. *Indian Miniatures.* New Delhi, 1961.

Ahmad, N. L. "A Mogul Miniature in the British Museum." *Proceedings of the 2nd Indian Historical Congress,* 1938, pp. 346–54.

Ahmad, T. "Nadiruᶜl-Asr Mansur." *Indo-Iranica* 25 (1972): 51–55.

Ahmed, Nazir. "The Mughal Artist Farrukh Beg." *Islamic Culture,* vol. 35 no. 2, 1961.

Anand, Mulk Raj. *Album of Indian Paintings.* Delhi, 1973.

———. "Jahangir the Epicurean." *Marg* 11 no. 4 (1958): 26–32.

———, and Goetz, Hermann. *Indische Miniaturen.* Dresden, 1967.

Anonymous. "Shah Jahan's Visit to a Saint." *Rupam* 37 (1929): 62.

———. "Two Mogul Drawings." *Rupam* 15–16 (1923): 106–7.

Archer, W. G. *Indian Miniatures.* New York, 1960.

———. *Indische Miniaturen.* Bern, 1957.

Ardeshir, A. C. "Mughal Miniature Paintings (with illustrations from the collection of Mr. A. C. Ardeshir of Bombay)." *Roopa Lekha* I no. 2 (1940): 19–37.

———. "Mughal Miniature Painting: The School of Jehangir." *Roopa Lekha* II no. 3 (1940): 19–42.

———. "Mughal Miniature Painting: The School of Shah Jahan." *Roopa Lekha* II no. 4 (1940): 23–52.

Arnold, Thomas W. "Indian Painting and Muhammadan Culture." *Journal of the Royal Society of Arts* 69 (1922): 624ff.

———. "The Johnson Collection in the India Office Library." *Rupam* 6 (1921): 10–14.

———, and Grohmann, A. *The Islamic Book.* Paris, 1929.

———, and Wilkinson, J. V. S. *The Library of A. Chester Beatty. A Catalogue of the Indian Miniatures.* 3 vols. London, 1936.

Arts Council of Great Britain. *Indian Paintings and Drawings from Sir William Rothenstein's Collection.* London, 1947.

Auboyer, J. "Un Maître Hollandais du XVIIᵉ Siècle S'inspirant des Miniatures Mogholes." *Revue des Arts Asiatiques* n.s. II vol. IV.

Baquir, M. "Muraqqa Gulshan." *Journal of the Pakistan Historical Society* 5 (1957): 158–61.

Barrett, Douglas. "Review of Richard Ettinghausen, *Paintings of the Sultans and Emperors of India.*" *Lalit Kala* 9 (1961): 68–69.

———, and Gray, Basil. *Painting of India.* Lausanne, 1963.

Beach, Milo C. "An Early European Source in Mughal Painting." *Oriental Art* 22 no. 2 (1976): 180–88.

———. "The Context of Rajput Painting." *Ars Orientalis* X (1975): 11–18.

———. "The Gulshan Album and Its European Sources." *Bulletin of the Museum of Fine Arts, Boston* 332 (1965): 63–91.

————. "The Mughal Painter Kesu Das." *Archives of Asian Art* XXX (1976–77): 34–52.

————. "Painting and the Minor Arts." In *The Arts of India and Nepal: The Nasli and Alice Heeramaneck Collection*, pp. 97–167. Boston, 1966.

Binney, Edwin, 3rd. *Indian Miniature Painting from the Collection of Edwin Binney 3rd*. Portland, Oregon, 1973.

Binyon, Laurence. "Indian Art at Wembley: The Retrospective Exhibition." *Rupam* 21 (1925): 8–11.

————. "The Relation Between Rajput and Mughal Painting." *Rupam* 29 (1927): 4–5.

————, and Arnold, Thomas W. *Court Painters of the Grand Mughals*. Oxford, 1921.

————; Wilkinson, J. V. S.; and Gray, Basil. *Persian Miniature Painting*. London, 1933.

Blochet, Edgar. *Catalogue des Manuscrits Persans de la Bibliothèque Nationale*. Paris, 1905.

————. *Collection de Jean Pozzi—Miniatures Persanes et Indo-Persanes*. Paris, 1929.

————. *Musulman Painting*. London, 1929.

Blunt, W. "Mughal Miniature Painters of Natural History." *Burlington Magazine* 90 (1948): 49–50.

Bogdanon, L. "Indo-Persian and Modern Indian Painting." *Islamic Culture* 1 (1931): 38–52.

Brown, Percy. *Indian Painting under the Mughals*. Oxford, 1924.

————. "Miniature Painting of a Mughal Prince." *Yearbook of the Asiatic Society of Bengal* II (1936): 214–16.

————. "Portrait of a Lady of the Elizabethan Period." *Yearbook of the Asiatic Society of Bengal* II (1936): 196–97.

Bussagli, M. *Indian Miniatures*. London, 1969.

————, and Sivaramamurti, C. *5000 Years of the Art of India*.

Chaghtai, M. A. "Aqa Riza—Ali Riza—Riza-i-Abbasi." *Islamic Culture* 12 (1938): 434–44.

Chandra, Moti. *The Technique of Mughal Painting*. Lucknow, 1949.

Clarke, S. C. *Indian Drawings: Thirty Mogul Paintings of the School of Jahangir and Four Panels of Calligraphy in the Wantage Bequest, Victoria and Albert Museum Portfolios*. London, 1922.

Colnaghi, P. & D., & Co. Ltd. *Persian and Mughal Art*. London, 1976.

Coomaraswamy, A. K. *Catalogue of the Indian Collections in the Museum of Fine Arts, Boston, Vol. VI: Mughal Painting*. Cambridge, Mass., 1930.

————. *Indian Drawings*. London, 1910–12.

————. "Les Miniatures Orientales de la Collection Goloubev au Museum of Fine Arts Boston." *Ars Asiatica*, vol. 13, 1929.

————. "Mughal Painting (Akbar and Jahangir)." *Bulletin of the Museum of Fine Arts Boston* 16 (1928): 2–8.

————. "Mughal Portraiture." *Orientalische Archiv* 3 (1912): 12–15.

————. "Notes on Indian Paintings." *Artibus Asiae* II (1927): 5–11; 132–37; 202–12; and 283–94.

————. "Portrait of Gosain Jadrup." *Journal of the Royal Asiatic Society*, 1919, pp. 389–91.

————. "The Relation of Mughal and Rajput Paintings." *Rupam* 31 (1927): 88–91.

————. "Two Mughal Paintings with Portraits of Ali Mardan Khan." *Yearbook of Oriental Art and Culture* I (1924–25): 33–70.

Das, Asok K. "Bishan Das." *Chhavi—Golden Jubilee Volume*, 1971, pp. 183–91.

————. "Ustad Mansur." *Lalit Kala* 17 (1975): 32–39.

————. "Mughal Royal Hunt in Miniature Paintings." *Indian Museum Bulletin* II no. 1 (1967): 1–5.

————. "A Scene from the Jahangirnama in the Victoria Memorial." *Bulletin of the Victoria Memorial* 11 (1968): 5–9.

Delhi. Museum of Archaeology. *Loan Exhibition of Antiquities: Coronation Durbar 1911*. Delhi, 1912.

Deneck, Marguerite-Marie. *Indian Art*. London, 1967.

Dickinson, Eric. "The Treatment of Nature in Mughal Painting." *Pakistan Quarterly* 1 (1950–51): 40–49.

Dimand, Maurice. "The Emperor Jahangir, Connoisseur of Paintings." *Bulletin of the Metropolitan Museum of Art*, n.s. II, 1944.

————. "An Exhibition of Islamic and Indian Paintings." *Metropolitan Museum of Art Bulletin* XIV (1955): 85–102.

————. *A Handbook of Muhammaden Art*. New York, 1958.

————. *Indian Miniature Painting*. Milan, n.d.

Eastman, A. C. "Four Mughal Emperor Portraits in the City Art Museum of Saint Louis." *Journal of Near Eastern Studies* 15 (1956): 65–92.

Eiter, M. R. "Birds and Animals in Mughal Painting." *Bulletin of the College of Arts, Baghdad University* 1 (1959): 12–18.

————. "The Elephant in the Indian Mughal Painting." *Bulletin of the College of Arts and Sciences, Baghdad* 3 (1958): 81–85.

————. "Some Aspects on Birds and Animals in Mughal Painting." *Deutscher Orientalistentag*, XVII Teil 2 (1968): 673–79.

Erdmann, Kurt. "Eine unbekannte Genealogie des Moghulhauses in Schloss Wilhelmshöhe." *Ostasiatische Zeitschrift* 24 (1938): 12–15.

Ettinghausen, Richard. "The Emperor's Choice." *De Artibus Opuscula XL: Essays in Honor of Erwin Panofsky*. Edited by Millard Meiss. New York, 1961.

————. "Indische Miniaturen der Berliner Museum." *Pantheon* 15 (1935): 167–70.

————. "New Pictorial Evidence of Catholic Missionary Activity in Mughal India." In *Perennitas*. Münster, 1963.

————. *Paintings of the Sultans and Emperors of India*. New Delhi, 1961.

Fondation Custodia—Collection Frits Lugt. *Acquisitions Récentes de Toutes Époques*. Paris, 1974.

Gangoly, A. N. "A Mughal Miniature from the Lahore Museum." *Rupam* 38–39 (1929): 84–86.

Gangoly, O. C. *Critical Catalogue of Miniature Paintings in the Baroda Museum*. Baroda, 1961.

————. "An Historical Miniature of the Jahangir School." *Rupam*, vol. 4, 1920.

————. "An Illustrated Manuscript of the Anvar-i-Suhaili—A New Version." *Rupam* 42–44 (1930): 11–14.

————. "A Rare Moghul Portrait." *Roopa Lekha* 21 no. 2 (1950): 1–5.

Gladstone-Solomon, W. E. *Essays in Mughal Painting*. Oxford, 1932.

————. "Jahangir and His Artists." *Islamic Culture* 3 no. 1 (1929): 38–44.

————. "Masterpieces of Mughal Painting." *Islamic Culture* 4 no. 1 (1930): 144–56.

————. "Mughal Pictures in London: Mr. Y. Dawud's Collection." *Islamic Culture* 12 (1938): 365–67.

————. "Perspective and the Mughals." *Islamic Culture* 5 no. 4 (1931): 582–88.

Gluck, Heinrich, and Diez, Ernst. *Die Kunst des Islam*. Berlin, 1925.

Godard, Yedda. "Un Album des Portraits des Princes Timurides de l'Inde." *Athar-e-Iran* 2 (1937): 179–277.

————. "Les Marges du Murakka Gulshan." *Athar-e-Iran* 1 (1936): 11–33.

Goetz, Hermann. "An Early Mughal Portrait of Sultan Abdullah of Golconda." *Bulletin of the Baroda State Museum* 9 (1952–53): 9–24.

————. *The Art of India*. New York, 1955.

———. "The Early Muraqqas of the Mughal Emperor Jahangir." *East-West* 8 (1957): 157–85.

———. "The Early Muraqqas of the Mughal Emperor Jahangir." *Marg* 11 no. 4 (1958): 33–41.

———. *Geschichte der Indischen Miniaturmalerei.* Berlin, 1934.

———. "Indian Miniatures in German Museums and Private Collections." *Eastern Art* 2 (1930): 143–66.

———. "Indian Painting in the Muslim Period—A Revised Historical Outline." *Journal of the Indian Society of Oriental Art* 15 (1947): 19–41.

———. "Life and Art in the Mughal Period: The Mental Background of Mughal Painting and Its Reflection in Art." *Journal of the University of Bombay* 5 no. 4 (1937): 55–67.

———. "Masterpieces of Mogul Painting—The Album of Emperor Jahangir." *Marg* 6 no. 2 (1953): 39–44.

Gray, Basil. "A Collection of Indian Portraits." *British Museum Quarterly* 10 (1935–36): 162–64.

———. "A Mughal Drawing." *British Museum Quarterly* 13 (1939): 72–73.

———; Codrington, K. de B.; and Irwin, John. *The Arts of India and Pakistan, A Commemorative Catalogue of the Exhibition Held at the Royal Academy of Arts, London, 1947–48.* New York, 1949.

———, and Godard, André. *Iran: Persian Miniatures—Imperial Library.* New York, 1956.

Grek, T. V. "Indian Miniatures in Leningrad Collections." *Proceedings of the XXVI International Congress of Orientalists,* 1964, pp. 637–48.

———. *Indiyskikh Miniatyur XVI–XVII v.v.* Moscow, 1971.

Grube, Ernst. *The Classical Style in Islamic Art.* New York, 1968.

———. *Islamic Paintings from the 11th to the 18th Century—in the Collection of Hans P. Kraus.* New York, n.d.

Hajek, Lubor. *Indian Miniatures of the Mughal School.* Prague, 1960.

Hasan, S. M. "The Mughal Portrait Style." *Dacca University Studies* 10 (1961): 69–77.

Hasan, S. N. "The Mughal School of Zoological Portraiture." *Arts and Letters* 37 (1963): 3–13.

Havell, E. *Indian Sculpture and Painting.* London, 1908.

Hidayat, A. "Shah Jahan." *Marg* 11 no. 4 (1958): 48–49.

Hollis, Howard. "Portrait of a Nobleman." *Bulletin of the Cleveland Museum of Art* 33 (1946): 180–85.

———. "Two Mughal Miniatures." *Bulletin of the Cleveland Museum of Art* 27 (1940): 91–97.

Hosten, H. "European Art at the Mogul Court." *Journal of the United Provinces Historical Society,* 1922, pp. 110–84.

Irwin, John. "A Note on the Two Reproductions." *Marg* 5 no. 4 (1952): 35–36.

Ivanova, A. A.; Ashmushkina, O. F.; Grek, T.; and Gyuzalyana, L. T. *Albom Indiyskikh i Persidskikh Miniatyur XV–XVIII v.v.* Moscow, 1962.

Johnson, B. B. "A Preliminary Study of the Technique of Indian Miniature Painting." In *Aspects of Indian Art,* edited by P. Pal, pp. 139–46. Leiden, 1972.

Kahlenberg, M. H. "A Study of the Development and Use of the Mughal Patka (Sash)." In *Aspects of Indian Art,* edited by P. Pal, pp. 152–60. Leiden, 1972.

Khandalavala, Karl J. *The Development of Style in Indian Painting.* Delhi, 1974.

———. "Five Miniatures in the Collection of Sir Cowasji Jehangir." *Marg* 5 no. 2 (1952): 24–32.

———. "Identification of the Portraits of Malik Ambar." *Lalit Kala* 1 (1955–56): 23–31.

———. *Indian Sculpture and Painting.* Bombay, 1958.

———. "A Mughal Miniature of Prince Khurram Slaying a Lion." *Bulletin of the Baroda State Museum* 10–11 (1953–55): 1–5.

———. "Some Problems in Mughal Painting." *Lalit Kala* 11 (1962): 8–13.

———, and Chandra, Moti. *Collection of Sir Cowasji Jehangir: Miniatures and Sculptures.* Bombay, 1965.

Kheiri, Sattar. *Indische Miniaturen der Islamischen Zeit.* Berlin, n.d.

Krishna, Anand. "A Study of the Akbari Artist—Farrukh Chela." *Chhavi—Golden Jubilee Volume,* 1971, pp. 353–73.

Krishna, K. "Problems of a Portrait of Jahangir in the Musée Guimet." *Chhavi—Golden Jubilee Volume,* 1971, pp. 392–94.

Krishnadasa, R. *Mughal Miniatures.* New Delhi, 1955.

Kühnel, Ernst. "Han Alam und die Diplomatischen Beziehungen zw. Gahangir u. Schah Abbas." *Zeitschrift für Deutschen Morganlandischen Gesellschaft,* vol. 96, 1942.

———. *Indische Miniaturen aus dem Besitz der Staatlichen Museen zu Berlin.* Berlin, n.d.

———. "Die Indische Miniaturen der Slg. Otto Sohn-Rethel." *Pantheon* 8 (1931): 385–89.

———. *Miniaturmalerei im Islamischen Orient.* Berlin, 1923.

———, and Goetz, Hermann. *Indian Book Painting from Jahangir's Album in the State Library, Berlin.* London, 1926.

Kurz, O. "A Volume of Mogul Drawings and Miniatures." *Journal of the Warburg and Courtauld Institutes* 30 (1967): 251–71.

Macaulay, D. "Mughal Art." *Burlington Magazine* 46 (1925): 63–72.

Maclagan, E. D. "Mughal Paintings on Christian Subjects." *Muslim World,* vol. 23, 1933.

Mahfuz-ul-Haq, M. "Dara Shikoh and the Fine Arts of Painting and Calligraphy." *Muslim Review,* vol. II no. 3, 1928.

Marteau, G., and Vever, Henri. *Miniatures Persanes.* 2 vols. Paris, 1932.

Martin, F. R. *The Miniature Paintings and Painters of Persia, India, and Turkey.* London, 1912.

Mehta, N. C. "A New Picture by Bishan Das." *Rupam* 24 (1925): 98–101.

———. "'Red Lilies,' a Newly Discovered Mansur." *Rupam* 19–20 (1924): 117–19.

———. "Notes on Indian Painting." *Journal of Indian History* 7 (1928): 9–11.

———. *Studies in Indian Painting.* Bombay, 1928.

Meredith-Owens, G. M. "The British Museum Manuscript of the Akbarnameh." *Burlington Magazine* 109 (1967): 94.

New Delhi, National Museum. *Manuscripts from Indian Collections,* New Delhi, 1964.

Pinder-Wilson, R. H. "Three Illustrated Manuscripts of the Mughal Period." *Ars Orientalis* II (1957): 413–22.

———; Smart, Ellen; and Barrett, Douglas. *Paintings from the Muslim Courts of India.* Exhibition catalogue, British Museum, London, 1976.

Pozzi, Jean. *Miniatures Indiennes au Temps des Grands Moghols.* Paris, 1950.

Quamruddin, Mohammed. "A Brief Survey of Mughal Painting." *Indo-Iranica* 10 no. 3 (1957): 13–23.

Randhawa, M. S., and Galbraith, J. K. *Indian Painting.* Boston, 1968.

Rawson, Philip. *Indian Painting.* New York, 1961.

Robinson, B. W.; Grube, E.; Meredith-Owens, G. M.; and Skelton, R. W. *Islamic Painting and the Arts of the Book.* Edited by B. W. Robinson. London, 1976.

———. "Shah Abbas and the Mughal Ambassador Khan Alam. The Pictorial Record." *Burlington Magazine* 114 (1972): 58–63.

Sahay, C. M. N. "Indian Miniature Painting with Illustrations from the Collection of the National Museum in New Delhi." *Arts of Asia* 4 no. 4 (1974): 25–41.

Sain, K. "A Note on Five Rare Old Paintings of the Mughal

School." *Journal of the Punjab Historical Society* 9 (1923): 161–71.

Sarre, F., and Martin, F. R. *Die Ausstellung von Meisterwerken Muhammedanischer Kunst in München, 1910.* Munich, 1912.

Schroeder, Eric. *Persian Miniatures in the Fogg Art Museum.* Cambridge, Mass., 1942.

———. "The Troubled Image, an Essay upon Mughal Painting." In *Art and Thought.* Edited by K. B. Iyer. London, 1947.

Schulz, Ph. W. *Die Persische-Islamische Miniaturmalerei.* Leipzig, 1914.

Shere, S. A. "A *Wasli* of Prince Khurram." *Journal of the Bihar and Orissa Research Society* 29 (1943): 171–83.

Singh, Chandramani. "European Themes in Early Mughal Miniatures." *Chhavi—Golden Jubilee Volume,* 1971, pp. 401–10.

Skelton, R. W. "A Decorative Motif in Mughal Art." In *Aspects of Indian Art,* edited by P. Pal, pp. 147–52. Leiden, 1972.

———. "The Mughal Artist Farrokh Beg." *Ars Orientalis* 2 (1957): 393–411.

———. "Review: Richard Ettinghausen, *Paintings of the Sultans and Emperors of India.*" *Oriental Art,* n.s. 8 no. 1 (1962): 34–35.

———. "Two Mughal Lion Hunts." *Victoria and Albert Museum Yearbook* I (1969): 33–48.

Smith, Vincent A. *A History of Fine Art in India and Ceylon.* Oxford, 1911.

———. "Painting and Engraving at Agra and Delhi in 1666." *Indian Antiquities* 43 (1914): 124.

Soustiel, J. *Miniatures Orientales de l'Inde.* Paris, 1973.

———, and David, M. *Miniatures de l'Inde.* Paris, 1974.

Staude, W. "Abdus Samad, der Akbar-Maler und des Millionenzimmer in Schönbrunn." *Belvedere* X no. 5 (1931): 155–60.

———. "Muskine." *Revue des Arts Asiatiques* V (1928): 169–82.

Stchoukine, Ivan. "Un Bustan de Saᶜdi Illustré par des Artistes Moghols." *Revue des Arts Asiatiques* XI (1937): 68–74.

———. *Les Miniatures Indiennes de l'Epoque des Grands Moghols au Musée du Louvre.* Paris, 1929.

———. *La Peinture Indienne à l'Epoque des Grands Moghols.* Paris, 1929.

———. "Portraits Moghols Parts I–IV." *Revue des Arts Asiatiques* VI (1930): 212–41; VII (1931): 163–76 and 233–43; IX (1935): 190–208.

———. "Quelques Images de Jahangir dans un Divan de Hafiz." *Gazette des Beaux-Arts* VI (1931): 160–67.

Strzygowski, Josef. "The Indian Room of the Empress Maria Theresa." *Rupam* 15–16 (1923): 59–66.

———, and Goetz, H. *Die Indische Miniaturen im Schlosse Schönbrunn.* Vienna, 1923.

———; Kramrisch, S.; and Wellesz, E. *Asiatische Miniaturmalerei.* Klagenfurt, 1933.

Van Berge, M.; Gahlin, Sven; and Van Hasselt, Carlos. "Some Mughal Miniatures in a Private Collection in Paris." In *Liber Amicorum Karel G. Boon.* Amsterdam, 1974.

Weibel, A. C. "Young Man Contemplating a Flower, Signed Aqa Riza." *Bulletin of the Detroit Institute of Arts* 24 (1964): 15.

Welch, Stuart C. *The Art of Mughal India.* New York, 1963.

———. "Early Mughal Miniature Paintings from Two Private Collections." *Ars Orientalis* III (1959): 133–46.

———. *A Flower from Every Meadow.* New York, 1973.

———. *Imperial Mughal Painting.* New York, 1977.

———. *Indian Drawings and Painted Sketches.* New York, 1976.

———. "Miniatures from a Manuscript of the Diwan i-Hafiz." *Marg* 11 no. 3 (1958): 56–62.

———. "Mughal and Deccani Miniature Paintings from a Private Collection." *Ars Orientalis* V (1963): 221–34.

———, and Beach, M. C. *Gods, Thrones, and Peacocks.* New York, 1965.

Wellesz, Emmy. *Akbar's Religious Thought as Reflected in Mughal Painting.* London, 1952.

———. "Mughal Paintings at Burlington House." *Burlington Magazine* 90 (1948): 44–48.

Wilkinson, J. V. S. "An Indian Manuscript of the Golestan of the Shah Jahan Period." *Ars Orientalis* II (1957): 423–25.

———. *The Lights of Canopus.* London, 1929.

———. *Mughal Painting.* London, 1948.

———. "Portrait of Shah Daulat." *Journal of the Royal Asiatic Society,* 1950, p. 1ff.

———, and Gray, Basil. "Indian Paintings in a Persian Museum." *Burlington Magazine* 66 (1935): 168–71.

INDEX

The index includes proper names of individuals (although the Mughal emperors are omitted), and the titles of manuscripts or albums discussed. References are to page number, unless printed in bold type, when they indicate catalogue or illustration number.

THE GRAND MOGUL

was designed by Klaus Gemming of New Haven, Connecticut.
It was set in Monotype Bembo, a typeface designed about 1495
for the great Venetian printer-publisher Aldus Manutius
by Francesco Griffo, one of the most accomplished
engravers and goldsmiths of the fifteenth century.
The book was printed by The Meriden Gravure Company
of Meriden, Connecticut, on Lustro Offset Enamel dull coated paper,
made by the S.D.Warren Paper Company of Boston, Massachusetts,
and bound by Mueller Trade Bindery Corp. of Middletown, Connecticut.
The map was drawn by Enrico Arno of Sea Cliff, New York.

CLARK ART INSTITUTE